DIFFERENTIATED READING INSTRUCTION IN GRADES 4 & 5

Differentiated Reading Instruction in Grades 4 & 5

Strategies and Resources

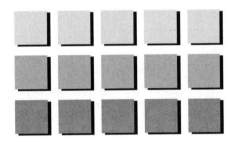

Sharon Walpole
Michael C. McKenna
Zoi A. Philippakos

THE GUILFORD PRESS
New York   London

© 2011 The Guilford Press
A Division of Guilford Publications, Inc.
72 Spring Street, New York, NY 10012
www.guilford.com

Printed in the United States of America

This book is printed on acid-free paper.

Last digit is print number: 9   8   7   6   5   4   3   2   1

Library of Congress Cataloging-in-Publication Data

Walpole, Sharon.
  Differentiated reading instruction in grades 4 and 5 : strategies and resources / Sharon Walpole, Michael C. McKenna, Zoi A. Philippakos.
      p. cm.
  Includes bibliographical references and index.
  ISBN 978-1-60918-216-8 (pbk.)
  1. Reading (Elementary)   2. Individualized instruction.   I. McKenna, Michael C.   II. Philippakos, Zoi A.   III.   Title.
  LB1573.W33 2011
  372.4—dc22
                                                                                          2011008756

To all of the fourth- and fifth-grade teachers
who were left behind during the
Reading Excellence Act and Reading First initiatives

We hope that this book is useful to you.

About the Authors

Sharon Walpole, PhD, is Associate Professor of Education at the University of Delaware, where she teaches graduate courses and conducts research in the area of literacy. She is coauthor (with Michael C. McKenna) of four previous books: *The Literacy Coach's Handbook, Differentiated Reading Instruction, How to Plan Differentiated Reading Instruction,* and *The Literacy Coaching Challenge.* Dr. Walpole's extensive experience both as a literacy coach and as a professional developer working directly with coaches in a number of states has informed her insights into school reform. Her research has been sponsored by the Center for the Improvement of Early Reading Achievement, and her investigations led her to earn an Early Career Achievement Award from the National Reading Conference (now the Literacy Research Association). She has worked with Reading First teachers and coaches in eight states.

Michael C. McKenna, PhD, is Thomas G. Jewell Professor of Reading at the University of Virginia. He has authored, coauthored, or edited 21 books and more than 100 articles, chapters, and technical reports on a range of literacy topics. Four of his previous books were coauthored with Sharon Walpole. Some of his other books include *Assessment for Reading Instruction, Help for Struggling Readers, Teaching through Text,* and *Issues and Trends in Literacy Education.* Dr. McKenna's research has been sponsored by the National Reading Research Center and by the Center for the Improvement of Early Reading Achievement. He was a member of the National Reading First Expert Review Panel and has worked with Reading First teachers in eight states.

Zoi A. Philippakos, MEd, is a doctoral student in Literacy Education at the University of Delaware. She has her master's degree in Reading and has worked as an elementary school teacher and literacy coach. Her interests include reading and writing instruction for students in the elementary grades. Ms. Philippakos provides professional development to teachers about effective reading and writing strategies. She is a cochair and cofounder of the Writing Study Group at the Literacy Research Association (LRA) and a cochair of the Graduate Students as Researchers Study Group also hosted at the LRA. She has published a study with Charles A. MacArthur about writing strategy instruction in the journal *Exceptional Children* and also piloted many of the instructional strategies included in this book.

Preface

Teachers in grades 4 and 5 have been the unfortunate stepchildren of the national emphasis on early intervention. Their needs have been largely ignored by authors and policymakers alike, and they have been left to fend for themselves in finding ways to meet the unique challenges their students present. This book is intended to help remedy this problem. In it we offer practical suggestions for how to provide small-group instruction that meets the needs of upper elementary students.

This book differs in several important ways from our previous books on differentiation, which have focused on the primary grades. In this book, there are fewer and simpler assessments. There is only a limited focus on word recognition. There are many suggestions for fostering reading in content subjects. And there are concrete ideas for motivating students to read.

On the other hand, our basic approach to differentiating small-group instruction remains. We use simple, informal assessments to determine groupings. Each group has a dual focus: (1) word recognition and fluency, (2) fluency and comprehension, and (3) vocabulary and comprehension. Our goal is for children in the first and second of these groups to progress over time to the third, where building word knowledge and comprehension proficiency is an unending challenge. Our most basic group in the primary grades—phonemic awareness and word recognition—is not part of our approach to differentiating in grades 4 and 5. We believe that children who enter the upper elementary grades with severely limited decoding ability are better served through intensive interventions provided by specialists. We are also committed to the idea that all students—not just those who struggle—deserve differentiated attention to their instructional needs. Our most advanced group (vocabulary and comprehension) is designed to serve these students.

Our goal has been to build the right amount of foundational knowledge you will need to differentiate—and no more! We have resisted the temptation to explore in detail topics that are not directly useful to teachers in grades 4 and 5, although we provide many suggestions for further reading.

The first four chapters set the stage for differentiation in the upper grades. In Chapter 1, we introduce our approach in the context of tiered instruction. In Chapter 2, we summarize research findings that have particular relevance for teaching children in the upper elementary grades. Chapter 3 discusses how differentiation must function in the larger context of scheduling, selecting materials, and planning relative to the new Common Core Standards, which we predict will soon affect every classroom in America. Chapter 4 describes the assessments needed to make the approach work. These are surprisingly few in number and are easy to give and interpret.

The next four chapters discuss the dimensions of reading development on which differentiation must focus. Chapter 5 presents ways of building word recognition proficiency beyond the basic level. Chapter 6 examines the idea of oral reading fluency and offers evidence-based methods of providing targeted practice during small-group time. Chapter 7 offers ways to build students' knowledge of word meanings, perhaps a teacher's greatest challenge in preparing students for middle school. Chapter 8 describes how comprehension proficiency can be fostered both in small groups, using authentic texts, as well as during content area instruction.

The last two chapters add discussions unique to the upper elementary grades. In Chapter 9, we present a broad variety of ways to spark an interest in reading during a crucial period when attitudes frequently worsen. Chapter 10 brings the book to closure through a consideration of how our approach can be implemented. Decisions concerning curriculum, assessment, and management are the critical spurs to bringing about the change that is needed.

The book concludes with extensive Appendices of reproducible materials designed to ensure that an effort to differentiate reading instruction gets off to a good start. These resources begin with Tier I planning templates followed by an informal decoding inventory created specifically for grades 4 and 5 and a set of multisyllabic decoding lessons that dovetail with the results of this assessment. A number of comprehension supports follow, including reminders for reciprocal teaching, QARs, and book clubs, plus a set of text structure graphic organizers. The bulk of the Appendices—Appendices H to J—is devoted to an extensive array of model lessons for each of our three groups. These are fully developed lesson plans that are ready for implementation. They make it possible to try our approach without a large investment of planning time.

We heartily invite you to consider differentiating in the manner we describe and with the materials we have prepared. We believe that you will be quickly persuaded by the simplicity of the approach, by the blend of research and common sense, by the practical nature of an approach in tune with the realities of classroom teaching, and, most of all, by the response of your students as they learn and grow as readers.

Contents

Chapter 1

Differentiation and Tiered Instruction

Our work in schools has taught us that meaningful, sustainable differentiation in reading instruction is intimately tied to the real-life demands of classrooms and schools. Those demands include the content and structure of the grade-level curriculum; the needs of students for increased time devoted to math, science, and social studies each year; and the reality that we must engage all students in their learning by providing meaningful instruction and meaningful reading and writing practice. For those reasons, we designed an approach to differentiation that includes all students each day in brief, targeted instruction at one of four levels, each including two areas of literacy achievement: (1) phonemic awareness and word recognition, (2) word recognition and fluency, (3) fluency and comprehension, or (4) vocabulary and comprehension. We designed our instruction to make it possible for an individual teacher to plan and provide it to a mixed-ability group, typical of an elementary classroom. This design phase was the result of collaboration among a large group of administrators, teachers, and literacy coaches who were willing to pilot our lessons and then integrate them into a model of comprehensive literacy instruction.

In order for you to understand what we propose here, extending our model from K–3 into the upper elementary grades, we review some of the basics of that K–3 model, position it within the general models of tiered instruction and response to intervention, and again propose differentiation for all students—this time to include students in the upper elementary grades.

THE K–3 DIFFERENTIATION MODEL

To understand our K–3 differentiation model, you will need some understanding of the setting for which it was originally designed: the fast-paced, high-stakes reform setting that was Reading First. Reading First was a federal program that provided resources for curriculum, assessment, and professional development to kindergarten through third-grade classrooms in struggling schools. Schools had to commit to implementing new core reading programs aligned with findings from reading research. Figure 1.1 presents the five core components of reading development highlighted in all Reading First work.

Schools also had to commit to extended time for reading instruction in uninterrupted blocks. They had to commit to new assessment systems, providing valid and reliable data about reading achievement for all children at least three times each year. Unfortunately, this data analysis indicated that although some students' beginning skills were consistent with the expectations of the grade-level program design, other students' skills were not: The grade-level instruction would either be too easy or, in many cases, too difficult for them. For students with more serious needs, schools provided intensive interventions in addition to the reading instruction they received in the classroom.

The model of differentiated instruction that we designed (Walpole & McKenna, 2007, 2009) was influenced by this Reading First setting. We worked extensively with literacy coaches and principals to understand the challenges in and the potential for increasing early grades' reading achievement in the more basic skills of phonemic awareness, decoding, and fluency. At the same time, however, we knew that basic skills instruction without attention to vocabulary and comprehension would not yield long-term literacy success. In the end, our model made several structural assumptions, and they are pictured in Figure 1.2.

Phonemic Awareness	The ability to notice and manipulate the sound structure of words.	An individual with strong phonemic awareness can take orally presented words and segment them into speech sounds or take speech sounds presented orally and blend them into words.
Decoding	The ability to use letter-sound knowledge to pronounce unknown words.	An individual with strong decoding skills can read new words presented in lists or in context.
Fluency	The ability to read text accurately, with adequate rate and with appropriate prosody.	An individual with strong reading fluency can read text orally, attending to phrasing and punctuation, and at a rate that sounds like regular speech.
Vocabulary	The knowledge of the meanings of individual words and of the connections between words.	An individual's vocabulary knowledge increases across the entire life span, but children with strong vocabularies derive new word meanings from reading and from listening.
Comprehension	The ability to construct meaning consistent with an author's intention.	An individual's comprehension is a complex interaction among the demands of the text, the individual's prior knowledge, and the individual's reading purpose. Individuals with strong comprehension can engage in strategic behaviors when they need to.

FIGURE 1.1. Core components of reading development.

Children's Literature Read-Aloud Grade-Level Core Instruction		
Middle Group	Reading Practice	Reading Practice
Reading Practice	Lowest Group	Reading Practice
Reading Practice	Reading Practice	Highest Group

FIGURE 1.2. Assumptions about time.

We assumed that most teachers would group children within the classroom (as opposed to across classrooms). We assumed that grade-level teams would work together (and with the support of their literacy coach) to decide exactly how to use the core program for grade-level instruction. We also assumed that we could add a read-aloud from children's literature to that grade-level time, providing an opportunity to build vocabulary knowledge and model comprehension strategies for all. After grade-level instruction and the read-aloud, we assumed that most teachers could divide their students by literacy achievement into three groups. They could meet with each of the three groups every day while the others either worked together in literacy centers or engaged in meaningful individual reading practice. In Figure 1.2, the teacher's work is highlighted in the shaded blocks. As the teacher works with each group, the other groups are engaged in reading practice. Another way to think about this type of rotation is that the teacher functions as a "center," with all groups rotating to the teacher for one of the three blocks of time devoted to the combination of differentiated instruction and reading practice.

The within-class grouping model also allowed us to create a flexible differentiation model. We wanted teachers to use data to design their differentiation groups and lesson plans and to evaluate the extent to which their plans were producing gains. For this reason, and because schools typically operate on 6-, 9-, or 12-week marking periods, we designed our model in 3-week units. Every 3 weeks, then, a classroom teacher could change the focus of an intact group or move some children from one group to another. Groupings and instructional focus were only temporary for students; as their skills changed, they could move to more complex work during the differentiation time.

OUR STAIRWAY TO PROFICIENCY

Although attention to time for grade-level instruction, a children's literature read-aloud, and a grouping and rotation plan are essential components of our differentiation model, the real meat of it is the instructional focus. Applying a developmental standard—the idea that students progress as readers in a predictable manner—we assumed that early reading proficiencies could not be "skipped" in favor of grade-level ones. That is, a student with no letter-sound knowledge cannot simply begin to decode single-syllable words; a student with weak oral reading fluency cannot simply engage in independent comprehension of grade-level texts. As a result, we assumed that we had to use simple assessments to reveal those literacy skills that children had mastered, and that our differentiated instruction had to target the next most complex set of skills for each group. Because our model was coupled with grade-level instruction and a read-aloud, it could be entirely skills based; there was no need for it to provide a balanced literacy diet. Rather, it provides a very concentrated dose of skills instruction. Figure 1.3 provides a simple set of choices for instructional focus that we have come to call the stairway to proficiency.

We use the stairway to remind teachers that their students are taking one step at a time, and that movement up a step is a strong sign that differentiation is working. In fact, our goal is that teachers' skills instruction is so effective that more and more students reach the top step—vocabulary and comprehension—every 3 weeks. If a student is continuing to achieve at least benchmark scores in assessments of oral reading fluency, then we know that the grade-level instruction and read-aloud are sufficient in the area of basic skills. Those students, then, can continue to build their vocabulary and apply comprehension strategies to even more complex texts. They use their differentiation time to extend the curriculum. Our differentiation model, then, is not merely a remediation model. It is also a system for extending literacy learning for students with the strongest skills.

Our K–3 differentiation model is more than just the broad conceptual focus of the stairway. Each step needed to be elaborated with specific expectations about how to move forward. For each stair step, we have used our understanding of reading development to predict a sequence of skills areas that are likely to create a logjam for some readers. Figure 1.4 presents the jams that we have anticipated and for which we have already created model 3-week lesson plans.

We have planned for three types of students in the phonemic awareness and word recognition group. The first group, the basic alphabet knowledge group, comprises emergent readers who need to learn their letter names and sounds and build their basic phonemic segmentation skills for initial sounds. It also provides support for basic print concepts if they are needed. The letter-sounds group knows nearly all letter sounds in isolation but needs to learn to blend those sounds together to decode words. The letter-patterns group can decode words using letter sounds but does so very slowly and needs to take advantage of short-vowel patterns. In all three cases, the phonemic awareness and word recognition lessons target only letters, words, and pictures in isolation. The groups needing to build very basic skills in phonemic awareness and word recognition do only that.

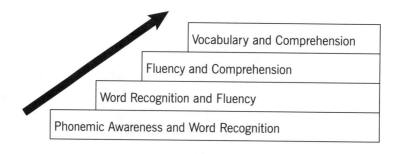

FIGURE 1.3. Stairway to proficiency.

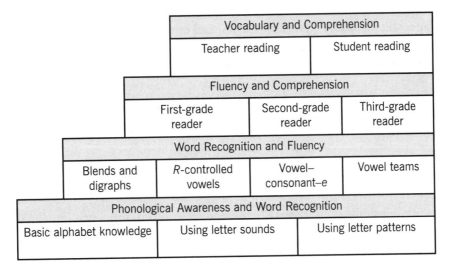

FIGURE 1.4. Potential logjams in reading development.

Once students can recognize short-vowel words fairly reliably, they are ready to work in the word recognition and fluency group. For this group, we have matched specific types of phonics instruction with specific phonetic elements. The blends and digraphs and the *r*-controlled vowels lessons use synthetic sounding and blending phonics. The vowel–consonant–*e* lessons use compare-and-contrast phonics to introduce the idea that, in most single-syllable words short-vowel sounds are typically represented by single letters, and long-vowel sounds are marked by the use of two vowels. Finally, the vowel team lessons use decoding by analogy phonics strategies to help students see that they can use patterns in known words to recognize unknown ones. In all cases, lessons for this group move from a targeted dose of phonics instruction, with a new set of words each day, to an application sequence of whisper, partner, and choral reading in a new decodable text chosen to build students' skills for decoding in context. In addition, all lessons include instruction in a small set of high-frequency words that are unknown by at least one member of the group.

Students who can read single-syllable words with vowel teams have acquired their basic decoding skills and no longer need the support of any decodable text. In fact, decodable text would likely hold them back. For those students, we have designed fluency and comprehension lessons with a very simple structure. Students read a variety of texts (including natural-language chapter books), in a structured sequence of choral or echo reading and then partner or whisper rereading. Then they engage in a short comprehension discussion targeting important inferences. They continue with this concentrated dose of repeated reading and comprehension, with increasingly more complex texts, until their reading rates indicate that they can read grade-level text at rates associated with adequate comprehension.

Those children with strong reading rates do not need the support of instruction in word recognition in isolation, decodable text, or repeated oral reading during their differentiation time. Rather, they need vocabulary instruction and opportunities to extend their use of text structures and comprehension strategies to understand more and more texts. They read narratives, information texts, and even web-based texts. The measure of the differentiation model in a given classroom is the increase in the number of children in this group over time; if differentiation on the lower stair steps is effective, students move to extending and applying rather than shoring up their skills. Although not our original intent, if this differentiation model is fully implemented at a grade level, the school's program is consistent with the basic demands of response to intervention.

DIFFERENTIATION AND RESPONSE TO INTERVENTION

When we were designing our differentiation model, we were influenced by the demands of the Reading First legislation. We knew that teachers had to use new core reading programs in similar ways across classrooms, we knew that they had to have long and protected blocks of time for grade-level work, and we knew that they had to collect data to evaluate student achievement. Our differentiation model was designed to leverage these facts such that regular classroom teachers would find a small-group, data-driven model reasonable to implement every day for all students. Little did we know, but we were actually creating a viable model of tiered instruction. In fact, coaches, administrators, and teachers who work in schools with full implementation of our model will likely find absolutely no differences between it and response-to-intervention (RTI) models.

One reason that we did not know that we were actually designing an RTI model is that RTI came into the national educational policy scene at about the same time that we were designing our model, and it is influenced by some of the very same research that influenced us. RTI is an approach to integrating regular and special education such that formal special education designations are really a last resort. Rather than identifying a child for special education because of a discrepancy between his or her ability and achievement, an RTI approach systematically rules out the possibility that increasingly intensive instruction can increase a student's achievement and eventually eliminate reading (or math or behavior) problems. The goals of RTI, then, are twofold: to reduce the number of students classified as special education who simply need targeted instruction and to replace the discrepancy model for special education services.

There are two general RTI models: the problem-solving model and the standard treatment protocol model (McCardle, Chhabra, & Kapinus, 2008). In the problem-solving model, teachers meet with an intervention team to design specific, measurable "solutions" to individual student problems. Teachers then implement their solutions and track their rate of success. The standard treatment protocol model opts for a set of procedures that can be used across classrooms, with all teachers actually engaging in the same set of interventions in response to data on student achievement. Our differentiation model is consistent with the standard treatment protocol for RTI. It supports a system of tiered instruction and is far easier to implement on a schoolwide basis than the problem-solving model.

Tiered instruction in reading is a plan that increases in specificity and intensity when data are revealing achievement concerns. It is a hallmark of the standard treatment protocol for RTI because it plans for students to receive gradually more intensive instruction if data indicate that they are not "responding" to the intensity of the instruction that they are getting. Brown-Chidsey, Bronaugh, and McGraw (2009) provide a very readable description of the rationale for tiered instruction in the standard treatment protocol. They begin by equating intervention in RTI with instruction. All students need effective, grade-level core instruction (Tier 1) in the model. For students whose needs are not met, more intensive instruction (Tier 2) is the next step. That instruction is provided in a smaller group setting. Once that Tier 2 instruction has been implemented for a reasonable amount of time, a more intensive intervention (Tier 3) is called for; it is provided in an even smaller group and for more time each day. Those students who do not respond to a high-quality tiered system (as evidenced in a system of progress monitoring) are likely to need special education, where some of their skill deficits will be accommodated rather than remediated. As schools work through their own RTI implementations, we will be able to reflect on the extent to which these systems realize their goals (Kovaleski & Black, 2010).

A pyramid is usually used to represent a tiered instruction system (see Figure 1.5). In this RTI structure, the breadth of each level of the pyramid represents the number of students who will need the instruction. The widest level is Tier 1 because all students are included. Only some students (those with below-grade-level performance) are included in the narrower layer of Tier 2. Even fewer require the third layer in the pyramid: intensive intervention.

This standard treatment protocol, with tiered instruction, was embedded in our differentiation model for K–3 and will be included in our extension to grades 4 and 5. Tier 1 instruction, consisting of grade-level core instruction plus an interactive read-aloud, planned consistently across classrooms and using high-quality materials and research-based procedures, is a basic feature. Our differentiation lessons, provided by the classroom teacher during the reading block, comprise Tier 2. And we acknowledge that some students will need even more, recognizing that intensive interventions must be available outside of regular classroom instruction.

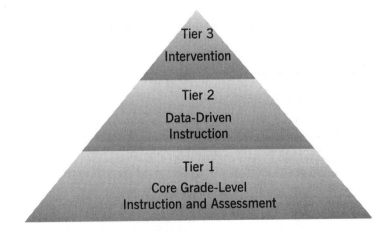

FIGURE 1.5. Tiered instruction pyramid: Differentiation for some.

DIFFERENTIATION FOR UPPER ELEMENTARY STUDENTS

There are two important ways that our model is different from the standard treatment protocol with the tiered instruction pyramid. First, we propose a system where differentiation is provided for all (see Figure 1.6). We argue that Tier 1 (grade-level) and Tier 2 (differentiated) instruction can and should be provided for all students every day, and that we should plan for a small number of students to receive intensive intervention, outside of classroom instruction, using very specialized curriculum materials. In doing so, we acknowledge that this means that we do not expect struggling students to "catch up" with the highest achieving students in the class. Rather, we expect all students to meet or exceed grade-level standards. We take this stance because the alternative suggests that schools should narrow the achievement gap between actual students rather than between struggling students and state standards.

There is another important difference between our differentiation model and the standard treatment protocol. We use our understanding of reading development and of the structure of grade-level curriculum materials to influence our thinking about what reading problems can be addressed in temporary, Tier 2 differentiation lessons and what reading problems must be considered Tier 3 problems. The standard treatment protocol is actually silent on this issue, leaving the decision on how to plan tiered instruction up to states, districts, and schools. We argue for a model that we believe is effective for students and reasonable for teachers. Figure 1.7 presents our thinking.

Our K–3 model for Tier 2 differentiated instruction argues that all four of our differentiation groups (phonemic awareness and word recognition, word recognition and fluency, fluency and comprehension, and vocabulary and comprehension) are reasonable to expect and to address during classroom reading instruction in kindergarten and first grade. At these grades, we do not expect to move immediately to intensive intervention. In second and third grades, though, if students do not have the basic alphabet knowledge and phonemic awareness that would be developed through our phonemic awareness and word recognition lessons, those needs would have to be served in very intense programs outside of the regular classroom. In other words, because of the age of the children and the distance between their skills deficits and the demands of the grade-level curriculum, they would need intensive intervention outside of regular instruction.

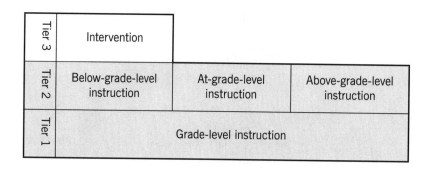

FIGURE 1.6. Differentiation for all.

Grade	Tier 2		Tier 3	
4/5		WR/F		WR/F
	F/C	V/C	F/C	
2/3		WR/F	PA/WR	WR/F
	F/C	V/C		
K/1	PA/WR	WR/F		
	F/C	V/C		

FIGURE 1.7. Reasonable classroom-based tiered instruction. C, comprehension; F, fluency; PA, phonemic awareness; V, vocabulary; WR, word recognition.

Once children are in fourth and fifth grades, phonemic awareness and word recognition instruction in isolation would not even be appropriate in Tier 3; phonemic awareness would have to be part of word recognition and fluency work rather than an end in itself. In the chapters that follow, you will see that we also have a very different set of lessons planned for fourth- and fifth-grade students who struggle with word recognition. Those who are receiving Tier 2 differentiation in this area are students who can read single-syllable words, even with vowel teams. In our lessons, we will build their capacity to attack multisyllabic words. Those few students who still need help reading one-syllable words will have to have intensive, Tier 3 interventions.

LOOKING AHEAD

A tiered instruction model for fourth and fifth grades must be grounded in good science and good sense. It will demand collaboration, and it will rely on assessments and progress monitoring. It will place heavy demands on teachers at first, but these demands will decrease over time as teachers become comfortable with the focus and management required for targeted skills work. In the chapters that follow, we walk you through the design of such a system and give you the tools you need to get started.

Chapter 2

Research on
Upper Elementary Readers

During the past few years, we (like many schoolwide researchers) have focused most of our attention on reading research and instruction for kindergarten through third-grade readers. In order to formulate our stance on the needs of upper elementary readers, we turned to our research colleagues to review recent findings. In this chapter, we describe characteristics of readers in the fourth and fifth grades; in the chapters that follow, we show how you can use these characteristics to direct the design of instruction to maximize student growth during these early adolescent years.

STAGES OF READING DEVELOPMENT

Jeanne Chall (1996), in her seminal book *Stages of Reading Development*, proposes that readers pass through identifiable stages as they acquire reading skills. Stage theorists hold that, during each stage, behaviors are qualitatively different. In the case of reading stages, Chall argues that what is different is the primary focus of the reader. Chall's stages are represented in Figure 2.1. As is evident, she argues that readers move from "pretend" reading to a focus on using letter sounds, to decoding words, to a focus on developing fluency, to a focus on comprehension.

    Chall's proposal is particularly important for us to consider because Stage 3, Comprehension of a Single Viewpoint, should be the stage at which students in the upper elementary grades are normally functioning. Much has been made of the break between Stage 2 and Stage 3, which some have termed the transition from "learning to read" to "reading to learn." Fourth grade is often students' first real experience with the content area textbooks that will dominate much of their subsequent adolescent literacy experience. Fourth grade is also the first time students are tested with the National Assessment of Educational Progress (NAEP), and the results are sobering. Only 67% of fourth grad-

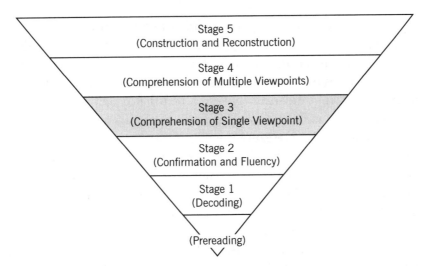

FIGURE 2.1. Chall's stages of reading development.

ers performed above the basic level in 2009; only 33% performed above the proficient level. *Thirty-three percent of fourth-grade students were below the basic level.* NAEP does not test at the early grades, but conventional wisdom (which may well come from the combination of Chall's stage theories, the somewhat problematic learning to read/ reading to learn dichotomy, and the NAEP scores) leads many to speculate that a sizable number of children whose performance appeared to be adequate through third grade experience a dip in fourth grade. This trend has been called the fourth-grade slump and is particularly steep for students living in poverty.

THE FOURTH-GRADE SLUMP

An influential study of the phenomenon of decreasing achievement beginning in the fourth grade (Chall, Jacobs, & Baldwin, 1990) tracked three cohorts of low-income students using measures of word recognition, spelling, word meaning, word analysis, oral reading, and reading comprehension. The data showed that student performance at second and third grades was adequate, but that at fourth grade knowledge of word meanings declined and then at seventh grade word recognition, spelling, and comprehension followed suit. The fourth-grade slump, then, may begin with vocabulary knowledge, with wide-reaching negative effects.

It is probably fair to say that there are nontrivial differences in the reading tasks that children face in the early primary grades compared with those in the upper elementary grades. One difference may be the shift to information texts. Narratives with strong story grammars dominate the reading selections in first grade (Duke, 2000). Jeong, Gaffney, and Choi (2010) examined text use in second-, third-, and fourth-grade classrooms. As in Duke's study, they found very low use of information text at all, even in the fourth-grade classrooms. Perhaps even upper elementary teachers do not necessarily ratchet up their students' text experiences adequately. Information text has different demands—even physical ones—as there are subheadings, headings, graphs, italicized words, and text in nontraditional form (e.g., in columns, in pictures, in captions). Also, the text may have embedded text structures that will require the use of different strategies for information retrieval. For example, the students may read a text that combines compare–contrast, enumeration, and description in its overall structure, and students used to a diet of fiction may not be accustomed to these organizational patterns.

A second reason for the fourth-grade slump may be the increasing demands of reading vocabulary outside of normal speaking and listening vocabulary. In short, reading selections begin to contain a higher percentage of lower frequency words. The words become more abstract and complicated, and some students may not have been exposed to them. This trend is evident in their poor vocabulary performance at fourth grade and in their comprehension beginning at sixth grade. It may be that opportunities for wide reading make it possible for more advantaged students to develop larger vocabularies that they can leverage as the demands of texts increase.

Yet a third reason for the slump may be that attitudes toward reading are declining for some students, especially those at risk. Researchers tested the relationship between reading fluency and reading attitude in fourth grade and reading achievement measured on a state standardized test in fifth grade. Both were significant predictors, with attitude toward recreational reading in fourth grade accounting for the most variance in fifth-grade comprehension (Martínez, Aricak, & Jewell, 2008). Students who develop poor attitudes toward recreational reading will surely read less, missing the chance for incidental vocabulary acquisition that eventually manifests in poor reading comprehension.

Surely there are ways that teachers can work together to prevent these trends. Sanacore and Palumbo (2009) suggest actions to take in light of the fourth-grade slump: (1) increase access to expository discourse throughout the primary grades; (2) engage children in more actual information text reading by reading aloud to them and then providing them access to high-quality classroom library materials for independent reading; (3) teach meaning vocabulary directly; and (4) foster engagement and participation. In addition, simply providing texts for summer reading between third and fourth grades can have a positive effect (Kim, 2006). These same recommendations may also apply to those fourth- and fifth-grade teachers whose students already suffer the fourth-grade slump.

THE POTENTIAL OF HIGH-QUALITY TIER 1 INSTRUCTION

The fact that researchers have produced evidence of a slump and that NAEP scores are at unacceptable levels does not mean that the situation is hopeless. It does mean that upper elementary teachers must be resourceful in their use of textbooks. A recent case study in a fifth-grade classroom highlights a circumstance that many upper elementary teachers might face (Wilfong, 2009). This science teacher had only one set of textbooks to use with her four sections of fifth-grade science, so she was limited in her ability to engage students in wide reading or in reading outside of class. She decided to explore the use of small-group reading structures, adapting the traditional format of book clubs to a science textbook. The discussion director formulated questions that students would use to discuss big ideas; the summarizer prepared a 1- to 2-minute summary; the vocabulary enricher found interesting or unfamiliar words and their definitions; and the webmaster prepared a graphic organizer to represent the relationship of ideas. Both the teacher and her students responded positively to this interactive, discussion-oriented approach to textbook reading. You will see that we use similar structures in our approach to literature circles, which we describe in Chapter 9.

Creative approaches to core reading programs (literature textbooks) are also possible. McKeown, Beck, and Blake (2009) used core reading selections for fifth graders when they compared a strategies approach, a content approach, and typical core instruction. The strategies approach included direct instruction of the comprehension strategies of summarizing, predicting, drawing inferences, generating questions, and comprehension monitoring; the content approach included guided discussion of the content of the week's text following general queries, such as "What is going on here?" All three approaches yielded adequate comprehension, but the content approach was slightly more effective. An interesting component of all three conditions was that the teacher read the text aloud, interspersing questions and engaging the class in discussion of text content without the burden of students reading the text themselves. The authors suggest that findings from this preliminary study be interpreted to encourage teachers to teach comprehension strategies quickly and then to use them flexibly as students discuss text content. This stance informs our suggestions about why and how to use read-alouds to teach comprehension. Chapters 7 and 8 focus significant attention on read alouds.

The importance of vocabulary for upper elementary students cannot be overestimated. Vocabulary and comprehension are intimately related. Students with deeper vocabulary knowledge have an easier time comprehending, and this comprehension also deepens vocabulary knowledge in a reciprocal manner (Stanovich, 1986). Researchers argue both for wide reading as a route to vocabulary building and for direct instruction in word meanings, and these routes can be used across content areas (Baumann, Ware, & Edwards, 2007). The content of direct instruction in vocabulary in the upper elementary grades has to include morphology (the meaning structure of words). It can also include metacognitive training that helps readers to become more conscious of their own word learning and more strategic in their actions when they come across a word they do not know (Lubliner & Smetana, 2005). Fourth and fifth graders' comprehension is related to their understanding of morphology both for native English speakers and for Spanish-speaking English language learners (Carlo, August, & McLaughlin, 2004; Kieffer & Lesaux, 2007). These researchers recommend that we attend to four principles when designing instruction that builds students' understanding of morphology: (1) teach students morphology in the context of their vocabulary and word learning; (2) teach students to examine morphology as a cognitive strategy; (3) build morphological knowledge both explicitly and in context; and (4) use Spanish cognates when appropriate. You will see that we have incorporated the first three principles into both our whole-group and small-group instruction; we focus on these issues in Chapter 5.

THE POTENTIAL OF TARGETED DIFFERENTIATED INSTRUCTION

Researchers continue to document the fact that although entry-level skills matter, instruction also matters. In other words, a focus on word recognition benefits children with weak word recognition skills; a focus on comprehension benefits children with strong word recognition skills. In a recent study, researchers extended this analysis to the fifth grade. They found that fifth graders with weaker achievement benefited more from more time spent in direct reading instruction. We can assume, then, that even fifth-grade students can continue to improve their reading performance if teachers differentiate (Sonnenschein, Stapleton, & Benson, 2010). This is why we are arguing that upper elementary teachers must continue to use achievement data to make decisions about the focus of their small-group instruction. We describe our approach to assessment later in Chapter 4.

A Focus on Comprehension

Providing access to content area texts at different levels may also be important. Concept-Oriented Reading Instruction (CORI) targets fluency, reading comprehension, content knowledge, and motivation within the domain of science. A test of CORI in fourth grade (Wigfield et al., 2008) documented its effectiveness in building comprehension, strategy use, and engagement. A test of CORI for fifth graders (Guthrie et al., 2009) indicated that it was effective in building comprehension, content knowledge, and word recognition skills, for both high- and low-achieving readers. All students read texts that dealt with ecological communities. However, low-achieving readers read texts that were easier than the ones read by their higher-achieving peers. Because all of the texts were related in content, all students developed their content area expertise. Choosing information texts with rich content, connected to the curriculum, may be especially important to upper elementary literacy development.

What students do with text also matters. Clark (2009) analyzed postreading discussions of short stories among small groups of high-achieving fifth-grade students. She documented a host of strategic behaviors, but also found that they were not used with equal frequency. Her coding scheme, reproduced in Figure 2.2, provides a window into the potential richness of peer-led discussions of literature in the upper elementary grades. You will see that we encourage these strategies as ways to facilitate the growth of even the highest achieving readers.

A Focus on Fluency

Is fluency still important at the upper elementary grades? Rasinski, Rikli, and Johnston (2009) tested the relationship between fluency and comprehension at grades 3, 5, and 7 to examine the extent to which fluency exerted an influence on comprehension beyond the primary grades. Results indicated that fluency (measured to include both rate and prosody) was still related to silent reading comprehension beyond the ages at which Chall's stage model might predict. Students gained in fluency from grades 3 to 5, but then seemed to regress at grade 7. For these reasons, we continue to include fluency in our upper elementary model.

Strategic Behavior	Definition
Comparing–Contrasting	Drawing a comparison or distinction between a story character, idea, or event and something else.
Contextualizing	Situating story elements in time, space, or culture.
Stating a confusion	Communicating a point about which the reader is uncertain.
Questioning	Posing a question.
Searching for meaning	Engaging in theme-related inquiry into, or hypothesizing about, the underlying meaning of the story or reasons for events.
Using prior knowledge	Relating information from one's fund of knowledge in support of the group's understanding.
Evaluating	Sharing an assessment, opinion, or conjecture about a story, character, event, or idea.
Interpreting	Taking information from the text and assigning it meaning.
Inserting self into text	Imagining one's participation in the story.
Noting author's craft	Directly or indirectly referencing the manner in which the author constructed the text in support of the group's understanding.
Engaging in retrospection	Relating one's thoughts as they occurred during reading.
Summarizing	Reviewing two or more events or ideas.

FIGURE 2.2. Comprehension strategies evident in the discussions of high-achieving fifth graders. Based on Clark (2009).

If fluency is still developing in fourth and fifth grades, fluency interventions will be important. Repeated reading protocols, a mainstay of fluency interventions, have been applied recently for struggling fourth- and fifth-grade students. Surprisingly, students participating in repeated reading built their vocabulary word reading, and comprehension but not their fluency. The authors (Vadasy & Sanders, 2008) speculated that the students actually needed a word recognition treatment rather than a fluency treatment, a distinction that we address in the chapters that follow and one that we believe is a hallmark of the need for intensive intervention.

THE NEED FOR CONTINUED INTENSIVE INTERVENTIONS

Who struggles in fourth grade? Researchers have investigated the achievement profiles of students who struggle in the fourth grade by looking back at their word reading achievement over time (Lipka, Lesaux, & Siegel, 2006). About one-third of students were simply poor readers—They began school at risk for reading difficulties, and their areas of risk were never resolved. Another one-third were borderline readers: Across time, assessments indicated that they were sometimes within the normal range and sometimes struggling. The final one-third, late-emerging struggling readers, appeared to achieve within the normal range until fourth grade. These students seemed to have been able to achieve normal word reading through the third grade even though they had weak phonological skills, perhaps by relying on their memory for words without really understanding the underlying phonological (sound) or orthographic (spelling) structures. They are truly experiencing a fourth-grade slump, one that requires intensive intervention in word recognition perhaps in addition to an enhanced vocabulary.

Not all struggling upper elementary readers need the same intensive interventions, however. Researchers investigated the achievement profiles of a group of fourth-grade students who had failed their state-mandated test. Results revealed six different types of struggling readers, with different relative strengths and weaknesses (Valencia & Buly, 2004). These profiles are represented in Figure 2.3. Although we stop short of recommending specific Tier 3 interventions, we argue that they must actually be chosen for their match to the specific needs of individuals who are struggling. As Figure 2.3 demonstrates, these individuals exhibit a variety of patterns.

With the growing population of second-language students in American classrooms, understanding their literacy development is especially important. Crosson and Lesaux (2010) investigated the relationship between fluency and comprehension for fifth-grade English language learners. They found that text-level fluency was related to comprehension, but it did not explain the full picture, and it did not have the same predictive power that fluency measures typically have for English speakers. Strong oral reading fluency can be misleading for English language learners. In fact, among these students, it was only for those with very good listening comprehension that text-level fluency was a good predictor of reading comprehension. For fifth-grade English language learners, then, both experience reading connected text *and* consistent attention to the development of listening comprehension are important. That is one of the reasons why we are so adamant that upper elementary instruction contain interactive read-alouds, and that we continue to rely on aspects of the cognitive model of reading assessment (McKenna & Stahl, 2009), discussed in Chapter 4.

As we look at recent research conducted with upper elementary students, we are convinced that high-quality, high-level vocabulary and comprehension instruction is necessary for all students. We also know that some students will need targeted help in fluency and in word recognition. Before we propose a planning and instruction procedure that addresses these needs, we provide an overall structure for program design that brings the pieces of the instructional puzzle together.

Profile	%	Word Identification	Meaning	Fluency
Automatic Word Callers	18	Strong	Somewhat weak	Strong
Struggling Word Callers	15	Somewhat weak	Somewhat weak	Strong
Word Stumblers	17	Somewhat weak	Somewhat strong	Somewhat weak
Slow Comprehenders	24	Somewhat strong	Strong	Somewhat weak
Slow Word Callers	17	Somewhat strong	Somewhat weak	Somewhat weak
Disabled Readers	9	Weak	Weak	Weak

FIGURE 2.3. Profiles of struggling fourth-grade readers. Based on Valencia and Buly (2004).

Chapter 3

Designing an Upper Elementary Reading Program

We hope that many of you are reading this book along with the rest of your school-based team. We spend much of our time with teams, helping districts and schools make the transition from collections of individual classrooms to interdependent, collaborative units, with a sense of collective responsibility for students' school experiences. The most exciting aspect of tiered instruction as it is embedded in RTI initiatives is that it compels schools to consider this type of systems thinking. In this chapter, we introduce concepts that we have learned in the course of our problem-solving work with school-based teams. We have the luxury of working across schools, districts, and states, so we share ideas that we have seen in our travels. We consider some of the nuts and bolts of planning: thinking though instructional time, grouping strategies, the introduction of the Common Core Standards, and strategies for reviewing curriculum materials. You will see that we think of a reading program as a thoughtful use of all available resources, including time and people, rather than a set of materials that are purchased. This series of program design tasks is best undertaken in the spring or summer to prepare for school opening in the fall, because each of them will require thought and teamwork.

INSTRUCTIONAL TIME

As you build an upper elementary reading program, think about the instructional time that you have and how you want to use it. For schools involved in recent federally funded reading initiatives (e.g., through the Reading Excellence Act or Reading First), one issue was a given from the start: All classrooms at grades K–3 had to have protected, extended blocks of time for reading instruction. Depending on the district and school, this was a more or less shocking requirement. Schools with less institutionalized respect for the concept of extended instructional time still plan with the schedules of their specialists (e.g., physical education teachers, speech language pathologists, art and music teachers) driving the train. Such schools are likely to interrupt instruction with announcements and noninstructional activities. Make no mistake about it: If you are to implement a truly differentiated curriculum in the fourth and fifth grades, you need to make time for reading instruction. As you will see in the remaining chapters of this book, that does not mean that you will have to give up science and social studies; in fact, if you take our recommendations to heart, you will actually increase time devoted to science and social studies content by integrating more of it into your English language arts (ELA) time.

The National Center for Educational Statistics (Perie, Baker, & Bobbitt, 2007) tracks time spent in core academic subjects. A recent report lamented that time allocations are increasing for ELA and math and decreasing for other areas. Figure 3.1 summarizes the most recent findings. This might be true for your school. If so, you can probably make better use of the time that you have. One way to do this is to extend the instructional time per session and to have fewer sessions per week. This is especially important as students get older. For example, rather than having science and social studies every day for 35 minutes, each subject could be addressed three times per week for an hour, and one of those hours could be used to complete a writing assignment in each area!

With the advent of RTI, there will come additional pressure on this already-pressured schedule. States are beginning to impose mandatory extra instructional time for students who need Tier 2 and Tier 3 instruction. What we have seen most frequently is the provision of "RTI time" for Tier 2 as an addition to ELA time. We see this as a costly solution to a new mandate, at least from the perspective of student learning. If Tier 2 must be scheduled for 30 minutes three times per week, where will those minutes be found? Will they take the place of science and social studies instruction, where upper elementary students are building essential content and concept knowledge? This need not be the case. Instead of sacrificing content area instruction, we urge you to consider that Tier 2 and Tier 3 instruction can be part of regular ELA time. It is simply a question of retasking that time.

	Minutes per Week	Minutes per Day
English Language Arts	503	100
Math	323	65
Social Studies	178	35
Science	178	35
Art and Music	110	22
Physical Education	105	21
Lunch	142	28
Recess	133	27

FIGURE 3.1. Average time spent in different subjects and activities in elementary schools.

Figure 3.2 provides a potential schedule for ELA time, given the average 100 minutes daily for instruction. We are taking 90 of these minutes each day for Tier 1 and Tier 2 reading instruction, leaving 50 extra minutes each week for writing instruction (which we think you should link to your science or social studies time). In the upper elementary grades, it is difficult to improve students' writing skills unless you give them something compelling to write about.

Remember in Chapter 1 that we argued our approach to differentiation guides us to provide it for everyone. In Figure 3.2, students performing well below grade level (at the 4th and 5th grades, these are students still struggling with single-syllable word recognition) have Tier 1 instruction for 45 minutes and then Tier 3 instruction for 45 minutes—outside of their classroom and with a specialized curriculum. All other students have 45 minutes of Tier 1 instruction and then 45 minutes of Tier 2: one block of instruction with their teacher, one block of follow-up practice, and one block for working through a written response.

At first blush, there are likely to be two aspects of this proposal that are difficult to swallow. First, if you are accustomed to using a core reading program, you may be unable to envision accomplishing your grade-level instruction in such a short amount of time. This is probably because you are accustomed to using workbooks and leveled readers as part of that instruction. Beginning in Chapter 5, we provide you with support for rethinking this approach by considering the core selection as the meat of the instruction and providing meaningful alternatives to workbook pages. This change will save both time and money.

The second difficulty with our proposal might lie in our suggestion that Tier 3 students have only grade-level instruction with their classroom teacher and then move outside the classroom for the remainder of the ELA block. We make this suggestion with great concern for both the teacher and the students. Students requiring this type and amount of support for basic skills are not candidates for differentiation, in our view. They require (and deserve) intensive intervention, which will likely take the form of care-

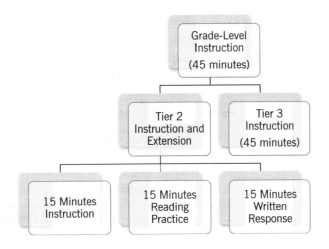

FIGURE 3.2. Time in tiered reading instruction.

fully sequenced commercial curriculum materials. They have already moved beyond the scope of Tier II. They need more than 15 minutes each day, and they may need the services of a special educator or a reading specialist. For them, we are replacing 15 minutes of classroom-based differentiated instruction, 15 minutes of reading practice, and 15 minutes of independent response writing with 45 minutes of very targeted instruction. Their numbers will be small; thus, classes can block their schedules so that Tier 3 students from more than one classroom can move to Tier 3 instruction together. If you have a larger number of intervention staff members, of course, you could also bring them into the classroom to provide this Tier 3 time. The point that we make is that the classroom teacher is unlikely to have the time or resources needed to accelerate the learning of those students performing far below grade level, especially if that teacher's goal is to serve all students every day.

To make the best use of limited resources, consider a staggered schedule. What if you have four sections of each grade level in your school? If fourth grade begins its reading block at 9:00 and fifth grade begins at 10:00, for example, you can likely use the same specialist to serve all Tier 3 students in eight classrooms. Remember that the number of students whom we predict will need this instruction is very small. Figure 3.3 shows what we mean.

If you think about time in this way, you will be set up for tiered instruction. The trick is to fill that time with effective teaching.

GROUPING STRATEGIES

As you build an upper elementary reading program, think about grouping and be purposeful about your decisions. Although we have presented our favorite approach to grouping embedded in the rotation in Figure 1.2, it is not the only one. Our favorite approach is to begin with a set of classrooms heterogeneous by achievement. Many schools accomplish this as a part of regular business by forming classrooms based on student achievement data. They review this data and ensure that each classroom has close to the same number of low-achieving, average-achieving, and high-achieving students. Then, for different times in the instructional day and for different purposes, instruction is provided to groups heterogeneous by achievement and to groups homogeneous by achievement. We believe that both groupings are necessary during an instructional day.

	Fourth-Grade Classroom Teachers	Tier 3 Specialist	Fifth-Grade Classroom Teachers
9:00	Grade-Level Instruction		Math Instruction
9:45	Tier 2 Instruction	Fourth-Grade Tier 3	Grade-Level Instruction
10:30	Math Instruction	Fifth-Grade Tier 3	Tier 2 Instruction

FIGURE 3.3. Staggered reading blocks.

We recommend that schools provide grade-level reading instruction, including both a high-quality read-aloud and a structured shared reading of a core selection, to grade-level groups heterogeneous by achievement. Both segments of that instruction are highly scaffolded by the teacher, making them at least partially accessible to all students. For the highest achieving students, the likelihood that they will build vocabulary knowledge is always a bonus for the read-aloud—and that is why we are so insistent that it be a read-aloud of challenging language and content. For those students whose achievement is closely matched to the level anticipated by the core program authors, the shared reading segment may be just right to build their fluency and to provide the level of challenge and support they need to coordinate their comprehension processes. For those students whose skills are well below those anticipated by the core authors, scaffolding by the teacher, through a skillful, interactive read-aloud and a well-supported shared reading of the week's selection, provides access to grade-level vocabulary and concept knowledge, support for the application of comprehension strategies, and the opportunity to improve sight-word vocabulary. In short, all students are served, but they are not served the same meal.

After this period of heterogeneous grade-level instruction, we move to a segment in which students are grouped homogeneously by achievement. Those who remain in the classroom for Tier 2 instruction are grouped *within* the classroom; those who move out for Tier 3 instruction are grouped *between* classrooms. That means that they join other students with similar achievement profiles so that they can work together with one teacher. We often return to the metaphor of a diet as we think about student achievement and grouping strategies. We do this because we want to provide them with the diet most likely to keep them healthy. We understand that some teachers will disagree with this stance. They are likely to fear that grouping students by achievement is stigmatizing (Moody, Vaughn, & Schumm, 1997). Research indicates, though, that instruction that does not group students by achievement is particularly problematic for the lowest achieving students; they tend to make almost no progress (Schumm, Moody, & Vaughn, 2000). Grouping students by achievement for at least some part of the day, even across grade levels, has long been associated with higher rates of growth (Slavin, 1987). When grouping is accompanied by differences in instructional strategies and materials, as we are proposing in this volume, achievement effects are highest (Lou et al., 1996).

An alternative to the basic within-class grouping format that we have described previously is the use of between-class grouping during Tier 2 time. Many schools are currently using this strategy. Basically, they use a whole-class, grade-level approach to Tier I, and then they move children into homogeneous groups for Tier II. If four teachers teach at the same grade level, then, one would have the highest achieving students (and the largest group), another would have high-average students, a third would have low-average students, and a fourth would have below-grade-level students. This plan may be attractive to many teachers because they are only personally responsible for their grade-level instruction and for instruction for one group. They may view planning for multiple groups as too daunting a task. However, there are two basic costs that come with this approach: (1) Teachers do not provide instruction for a number of their own students and (2) the group sizes will be much larger.

An upper elementary reading program cannot be silent on the issue of grouping. We urge you to weigh your options, choose based on what you predict will be best for students, and then use your professional development resources to make that option work for teachers as well.

COMMON CORE STANDARDS

As you are working on an upper elementary reading program design, your thinking must be influenced by the standards for ELA in your state. At the very least, standards drive the design of state assessments, and state assessments have consequences for children, for teachers, and for schools. Standards also help us to ensure that our reading programs are vertically articulated, that what we teach in one year is actually a logical precursor to the goals for the next year. As we bring this book to press, there is a very new trend in the area of standards. Rather than keeping the writing of standards within the purview of each state's department of education, strong political forces have pressured states to consider instead a set of common standards now and potentially a set of common assessments later. This presents a sea change; even as we write this chapter, we know that at least half of the 50 states have adopted the new common standards and are at this time engaging in careful comparisons (sometimes called cross-walks) to see how the new standards are different from the previous ones, which up until now have provided infrastructure for teaching and testing. According to a recent comparison of these new standards with previous ones, the vast majority of states will find the new standards more rigorous than those used previously (Carmichael, Martino, Porter-Magee, & Wilson, 2010), and this fact will require that they reconsider their approaches to reading instruction. We know this will be a challenge, but we believe that it also presents an opportunity.

The National Governors Association and the Council of Chief State School Officers jointly released the Common Core Standards in June 2010. There are some interesting design issues that we review here because we believe they set the stage for the design of reading programs in the upper elementary grades. First, the initial ELA standards are K–5 because the designers of the document assumed (as we do) that most K–5 instruction addresses all subject areas within one classroom. After that, beginning in grade 6, there are standards for ELA and then standards for literacy in content areas—an attempt to communicate the need for cross-curricular attention to the building of skills and content knowledge. There are 10 standards that run across the K–5 grade levels. These are reproduced in Figure 3.4.

Another interesting feature of the standards is the degree to which they recommend specific and rigorous texts and text characteristics at each grade level. You will see that we have used the standards throughout this book to guide our text and content selection. In the area of basic reading skills, the standards address word recognition and fluency content for K–5 as foundational skills. The concept that these skills are actually foundational for higher order standards is consistent with our thinking about appropriate Tier 2 and Tier 3 targets for the upper elementary grades. As you are building your program, read the standards that apply to your state and district carefully, looking not for how

Key Ideas and Details	
1	Read closely to determine what the text says explicitly and to make logical inferences from it; cite specific textual evidence when writing or speaking to support conclusions drawn from the text.
2	Determine central ideas or themes of a text and analyze their development; summarize the key supporting details and ideas.
3	Analyze how and why individuals, events, and ideas develop and interact over the course of a text.

Craft and Structure	
4	Interpret words and phrases as they are used in a text, including determining technical, connotative, and figurative meanings, and analyze how specific word choices shape meaning or tone.
5	Analyze the structure of texts, including how specific sentences, paragraphs, and larger portions of the text (e.g., a section, chapter, scene, or stanza) relate to each other and the whole.
6	Assess how point of view or purpose shapes the content and style of a text.

Integration of Knowledge and Ideas	
7	Integrate and evaluate content presented in diverse media and formats, including visually and quantitatively, as well as in words.
8	Delineate and evaluate the argument and specific claims in a text, including the validity of the reasoning as well as the relevance and sufficiency of the evidence.
9	Analyze how two or more texts address similar themes or topics in order to build knowledge or to compare the approaches the authors take.

Range of Reading and Level of Text Complexity	
10	Read and comprehend complex literary and informational texts independently and proficiently.

FIGURE 3.4. College and career readiness anchor standards for reading.

they reinforce what you are already doing but for how they can influence you to set even higher goals for yourself and for your students.

EVALUATING INSTRUCTIONAL MATERIALS

Many people would argue that the place to start in designing a reading program is with the instructional materials themselves. We surely disagree. Without a notion of the amount of time you have, how you will group, and what your goals are, it makes no sense to select materials. Reading programs do not come in boxes. Reading programs are more complex and organic than that. However, once you know what you want to do and what resources you have to spend, it makes sense to examine the extent to which commercial materials can make your job easier. Usually, they can. Commercial core reading programs tend to sequence skills and strategies within meaningful themes. At the upper elementary grades, they also tend to integrate narratives with information texts on similar subjects. In 2007, the Florida Center for Reading Research (*www.fcrr.org*) released a helpful tool called *Guidelines for Reviewing a Reading Program.* It is essentially a process for critical analysis of the extent to which a specific core reading program contains design elements derived from reading research. We have no quarrel with the research that was used to derive the elements, and we see the process as serving two important goals: (1) It provides teachers with an opportunity for applied professional development, and (2) it yields a critical evaluation of a particular reading program—either to help you use it better by supplementing weak areas or to choose the best quality program for future adoption. The guide itself is organized to highlight essential elements of reading instruction at the time when they are appropriate. This means, for example, that the guide does not ask you to look for beginning decoding instruction in a fourth-grade program. We have reformatted only the items appropriate for reviewing fourth- and fifth-grade content as a checklist in Figure 3.5. Note that all of the items apply to both grade levels.

The process for reviewing a core reading program involves a team in a careful content analysis. Basically, given the teachers' editions and the program scope and sequence, teachers work together to evaluate the extent that these items are included. That procedure develops a deep understanding of the program's design, and it also highlights areas where teachers will have to work together to strengthen the program. The trick is to go through the process with your own colleagues, even after a district adoption team has made a decision. If you are not working through these items with your core program and your teammates, you will not reap the benefits of a deepened understanding.

It may seem odd for a book about differentiating instruction to give such thorough attention to realizing the potential of a core program. Although we believe that core programs can be very helpful and we suspect they will already be available to you, we also want to emphasize that core programs are *never* enough. They tend to use abbreviated versions of longer works and simply do not have enough text (either by volume or by difficulty level) to ensure a healthy reading diet for all students. They neither review sufficiently for students who are experiencing difficulties nor sufficiently challenge students who are not. This is the focus of the chapters that follow.

Word Recognition Instruction	
This includes learning letter names, sounds, patterns, and specific words as well as decoding strategies to apply to unknown words.	
Are assessments included to measure and monitor progress in phonics?	
Are symbol to sound (decoding) and sound to symbol (spelling) taught explicitly?	
Is spelling taught during word learning so students can make the connection to how sounds map onto print?	
Does instruction progress from simple to more complex concepts (e.g., CVC words before CCCVCC words and single-syllable words before multisyllabic words)?	
Are there frequent and cumulative reviews of previously taught concepts and words?	
Is there an emphasis on fluency practice for each phonics component (e.g., sound identification, CVC blending, word recognition, multisyllabic words, and text reading)?	
Are students taught the strategy of chunking when trying to decode multisyllabic words?	
Does the program provide teacher modeling of a think-aloud strategy to aid in multisyllabic word analysis?	
Are students taught the strategy to read multisyllabic words by using prefixes, suffixes, and known word parts?	
Is instruction explicit in the use of syllable types (e.g., open, closed, vowel–consonant–*e*, vowel combinations, *r*-controlled, and consonant-*le*)?	
Is a section of the program devoted to advanced phonics skills (structural analysis)?	
Are advanced phonics skills taught explicitly, first in isolation and then in words and connected texts?	
Does the program include spelling strategies (e.g., word sorts, categorization activities, word-building activities, and word analogies)?	
Is instruction in the meanings of roots and affixes explicit and are there activities for students to analyze the relationship of spelling to meaning of complex words?	
Are word parts that occur with high frequency (e.g., un-, re-, in-, and -ful) taught rather than those that occur only in a few words?	
Are there activities for distinguishing and interpreting words with multiple meanings?	
Once advanced phonics strategies have been mastered, are they immediately applied to reading and interpreting familiar and unfamiliar connected texts?	
Are words used in advanced phonics activities also found in the student texts?	

(cont.)

FIGURE 3.5. Items to look for in reviewing an upper elementary core reading program from *fcrr.org*.

Fluency Instruction	
Fluency is the ability to accomplish any task without much cognitive attention. It can be applied to any portion of the reading process, but most often refers to the ability to read orally with adequate rate, accuracy, and prosody.	
Are assessments included to measure and monitor progress in fluency?	
Does the program address all dimensions of fluency (speed, accuracy, and prosody)?	
Does the program encourage the teacher to model speed, accuracy, and prosody?	
Does fluency practice involve the teacher providing feedback to students?	
Is fluency instruction integrated into each day's lesson?	
Is the decoding strategy taught so that it becomes automatic?	
Are irregular words taught to be recognized automatically?	
Is there an emphasis on reading multisyllabic words fluently?	
Are research-based fluency strategies included (e.g., timed readings, peer reading, and repeated readings)?	
Is fluency practice introduced after students are proficient at reading words accurately (e.g., in lists, sentences, and passages)?	
Does fluency practice involve decodable texts (texts that include phonic elements and word types students have previously been taught)?	
Are both narrative and expository texts provided for students to read aloud?	
Are teacher prompts included to encourage students to read aloud in order to determine skill application and accuracy?	
After error correction, are students asked to reread the word, word list, or sentence correctly and then to reread it from the beginning?	
Are students given ample practice opportunities to use text at their independent or instructional level to help build fluency?	
Is the number of texts at each level sufficient to provide adequate practice opportunities?	
Does the program clearly show the teacher how to determine independent, instructional, and frustrational reading levels for individual students?	
Is there a guide to help teachers calculate fluency rate?	
Do students have opportunities to time themselves and graph the results after rereading the same text?	

Vocabulary	
Vocabulary instruction develops students' knowledge of individual word meanings.	
Is there an emphasis on listening and speaking vocabulary?	
Is there an emphasis on reading and writing vocabulary?	

(cont.)

FIGURE 3.5. *(cont.)*

Are students exposed to diverse vocabulary through listening to or reading narrative and expository texts?	
Does the program include frequent use of teacher read-alouds using higher level books with explanation and instruction of key vocabulary?	
Does the program include a variety of texts that allow students ample opportunities to engage in wide reading at their independent levels?	
Does vocabulary instruction occur before, during, and after reading?	
Are a limited number of words selected for robust, explicit vocabulary instruction?	
Are important, useful, and difficult words taught?	
Does the instructional routine for vocabulary include: • introducing the word? • presenting a student-friendly explanation? • clarifying the word with examples? • checking students' understanding?	
Are ample opportunities provided to engage in oral vocabulary activities that: • repeat exposure to words in rich and multiple contexts? • use everyday language to explain word meanings? • connect word meanings to prior knowledge?	
Are students given multiple opportunities to use new words in reading sentences, paragraphs, or longer texts?	
Is extended instruction provided in multiple contexts to promote word awareness using word banks, vocabulary logs, writing, semantic maps, concept definition mapping, and word classification?	
Are the processes involved in using a strategy taught over time to ensure understanding and correct application?	
Are meanings of prefixes, roots, and suffixes taught before connecting them to words?	
Is a strategy to determine word meanings based on meanings of prefixes, roots, and suffixes taught?	
Are various aspects of word study included (either under vocabulary or word recognition) such as: • concepts of word meaning? • multiple meanings? • synonyms? • antonyms? • homonyms? • figurative meanings? • morphemic analysis? • etymologies?	
Is dictionary use explicitly taught using grade-appropriate dictionaries?	
Is the use of context to gain the meaning of an unfamiliar word kept to a minimum?	

(cont.)

FIGURE 3.5. *(cont.)*

Comprehension	
Comprehension instruction develops students' abilities to gain meaning from text. It involves both extraction and construction.	
Is learning to determine which strategy to use and why (metacognition) part of instruction?	
When a strategy is taught, is it applied frequently so students understand its usefulness?	
Are students asked to apply previously learned strategies to new texts?	
Is appropriate text provided to practice applying strategies?	
Does the program instruction enable students to establish and adjust purposes for reading (e.g., reading to understand, to interpret, to inform, to enjoy, and to solve problems)?	
Does the program provide instruction and support for the use of multiple coordinated comprehension strategies?	
Are guided and supported cooperative learning groups suggested as an instructional technique?	
Does instruction begin with the use of short passages?	
Does instruction emphasize that students have a conceptual understanding of beginning, middle, and end?	
Does the program provide prompts for the teacher to guide the students through texts using think-alouds?	
Are there ample opportunities for students to listen to narrative and expository text?	
Is instruction in narrative and expository text structures explicit?	
Are there ample opportunities to read narrative and expository texts on independent and instructional levels?	
Are there instructional routines for comprehension strategies for before, during, and after reading (e.g., setting a purpose, prediction, story grammar, main idea, summarization, graphic organizers, and answering and generating questions)?	
Is the main idea strategy taught systematically (e.g., using pictures, then individual sentences, then paragraphs, etc.)?	
Once students have grasped the main idea, are more complex texts used in which the main idea is not explicit?	
Are elements of story grammar (e.g., setting, characters, important events) taught and used for retelling a story?	
Does instruction focus on discussing story grammar and comparing stories?	
Are students taught to use graphic organizers to illustrate interrelationships among concepts in text (e.g., story maps, Venn diagrams, and semantic maps)?	
Are the conventions of expository text (e.g., chapter headings, charts, and graphs) taught?	
Are explicit strategies to interpret information from charts, graphs, tables, and diagrams taught?	
After instruction, is there systematic review of: • literal comprehension? • retelling? • main idea? • summarization?	
Does the program provide instruction for students to become self-directed in comprehension strategies (e.g., rereading, paraphrasing, making explicit connections from text to prior knowledge, underlining and note taking, and visualizing relationships and events in the text?	

FIGURE 3.5. *(cont.)*

Chapter 4

Choosing and Using Assessments

We suspect that many classroom teachers view the idea of reading assessment as a complex and slightly mysterious process, one that involves giving an assortment of tests and applying daunting inferential strategies to arrive at diagnostic conclusions. Although there is some truth to this perception with regard to a small number of challenging cases, we wish to allay any fears you may be harboring about the assessment required to make small-group instruction successful in a classroom. This perception may also stem from the fact that many teachers are forced to give assessments that are not actually used to make decisions or that actually produce conflicting information. The fact is, only a few informal assessments are needed to form groups and to gauge the growth of students.

TYPES AND PURPOSES OF ASSESSMENTS

Assessment serves a critical role in differentiated reading instruction. It guides the process first by grouping students with similar needs, then by helping to plan instruction, and finally by gauging the extent of student learning. A distinction is sometimes made between assessment *for* instruction and assessment *of* instruction. When we assess for instruction, we use the information we gather to target our teaching toward student needs. Assessment of instruction is conducted to determine whether our efforts have been successful. In our approach to differentiated instruction, both kinds of assessment are important. The fact that assessment has multiple purposes has led to more than one type of assessment, and we begin with an overview of the four basic types.

Screening measures provide an indication of achievement in a particular area. Screenings are common in word recognition, fluency, vocabulary, and comprehension. They are sometimes administered individually and sometimes to an entire classroom at once. These measures are limited in what they can tell us. Identifying a problem area is a good first step, but it does not suggest specific actions we might take to address the problem. To accomplish that aim, we administer *diagnostic measures*. These are follow-up tests that break down the area into teachable skills and strategies. For example, if a screening measure of word recognition indicated that a student was performing below expectations in general, a follow-up inventory of specific decoding skills would provide the information needed to identify and address the specific deficit. Screening and diagnostic measures work in tandem to provide the information teachers require in order to meet the needs of their students. Our approach to differentiation in small groups for upper elementary students makes only limited use of diagnostic assessments. Their principal role is in planning Tier 3 intensive interventions for students who are performing well below grade level.

Progress monitoring measures are administered periodically to provide the teacher with feedback as to whether instruction is having the desired effect. The information they provide can be useful in adjusting approaches to instruction in order to improve learning. They answer the perennial educational question *Are they learning what I am teaching?* These measures are frequently the same as those used for screening. This is one example of how the same measure can serve different purposes. Sometimes, though, they are assessments related much more directly to the content of the instruction.

Finally, *outcome measures* help educators judge the effectiveness of instruction on a broader scale. They typically combine the results for many students to measure the achievement of classrooms, schools, districts, and the nation. They include (but are not limited to) the high-stakes tests that so often concern teachers and administrators because of the pressures they create, the time they require to administer, and the public's preoccupation with them. On the other hand, outcome measures serve an important purpose by providing stakeholders with the information they require. Because outcome assessments come near the end of the school year, it is too late to use them to plan instruction, but the results can shed light on how effective the instruction has been and possibly suggest modifications for the next year. Our concern is that teachers make the best use of outcome measures—and that use is very limited. At best, they provide tentative screening information for the upcoming year, although it is frequently too dated to be of much use. Outcome measures do not provide information that is specific enough to guide instructional planning. Moreover, their use for progress monitoring would be cumbersome and inappropriate. What is troubling is that teachers in grades 4 and higher rely mainly on outcome measures (Torgesen & Miller, 2009). It is important to avoid this pitfall by becoming aware of the variety of available assessments and how to use them in concert.

ORGANIZING FOR ASSESSMENT

The thought of assembling a battery of useful assessments and then coordinating their use may seem daunting. There are so many types of assessments and so many possibilities for using them. As you will see, however, accomplishing this aim is not difficult. We begin with a few simple guidelines about reading assessment for small-group instruction.

■ *Aim for the fewest assessments to answer the questions that are important.* We don't assess for the sake of assessing. An assessment system that is "lean and mean" is far preferable to one that generates a great deal of data that no one will use. Because administering assessments takes time, a minimalist system helps to ensure that the time left for instruction will be adequate.

■ *Assessments must be coordinated to account for the important aspects of reading.* Identifying a single area of need and directing all our resources toward meeting that need may not be enough to ensure that students become proficient. Too often, students are experiencing multiple problem areas, and it is crucial for teachers to arrive at conclusions concerning a particular student's status in word recognition, fluency, vocabulary, and comprehension.

■ *All students must be screened.* The fact that students in the upper elementary grades are performing at benchmark levels does not mean that no assessments are needed (Torgesen & Miller, 2009). "Students must acquire many additional reading skills after third grade in order to be proficient readers in high school" (p. 10). This fact requires that we assess even students who are not presently struggling in order to ensure that they continue to make progress.

■ *Formative assessments are the key to successfully using data to guide instruction.* Formative assessments are informal measures that help teachers plan and adjust their instruction. There are three types of formative assessments: (1) those embedded in ongoing classroom instruction, (2) periodic benchmark assessments, and (3) screening and diagnostic assessments (Torgesen & Miller, 2009). All three have a place in our model of differentiated instruction. In curriculum-based measurement, a distinction is made between general outcome assessments, which are good for temporarily classifying students and for gauging their progress from time to time, and skills-based and mastery measures, which are useful for determining whether specific instructional objectives have been attained (Hosp, Hosp, & Howell, 2006). This distinction is very similar to the difference between screening and diagnostic assessments. The former are used to classify and monitor; the latter are short term in nature and help us plan instruction from cycle to cycle.

We turn now to assessments useful in gathering information about the major dimensions of reading. In order to plan appropriate instruction, we will need information in four areas. As you will see, however, the assessment burden is light.

Assessing Fluency

Oral reading fluency is the ability to read aloud grade-level text at an appropriate rate and with a high level of accuracy and natural intonation. This definition contains the three dimensions of fluency that are important to assess: rate, accuracy, and prosody. Most screening in the area of fluency targets the first two of these, and it is common to use a combined metric consisting of words correct per minute (WCPM). Consensus benchmarks for each grade have been established and are presented in Figure 6.2. A brief sample of oral reading, typically 1 minute, can provide a quick indicator of whether a particular student is performing below benchmark. Rasinski's (2003) spring benchmark for grade 4 is 118 WCPM and for grade 5, 128 WCPM. This is a modest increase, but it reflects the fact that the texts students encounter in grade 5 are somewhat more challenging than those in grade 4. It also reflects the fact that oral reading rate begins to plateau in the upper elementary grades. This is a natural phenomenon, for students are approaching the rate of natural speech and they should never be expected to read faster than that aloud.

We consider fluency to be a pivotal proficiency in students' reading development. This is because students who are dysfluent devote too much attention to word recognition and too little to comprehension. Fluency is, therefore, a prerequisite of comprehension, although it by no means guarantees that comprehension will be adequate. We assess fluency to identify it (or rule it out) as a cause for concern and as a target of instruction. For those students who fall below the fluency benchmark, it is tempting to assume that they are best served by evidence-based instructional approaches for building fluency. However, this is only the case when a full range of word recognition skills has been acquired. Deficits in skill acquisition are one cause of dysfluency, and it is important to determine whether these deficits exist. If they don't, fluency work is indeed appropriate. If they are present, addressing fluency alone is not likely to result in improved proficiency.

Assessing Word Recognition

When students reach the upper elementary grades, they have received instruction on a full array of decoding skills. They will also have encountered many unfamiliar words in text, and they have attempted to apply their skills in decoding those words. By fourth grade, students should possess the skills needed to decode many multisyllabic words. Their ability to do so is grounded in more basic skills. Namely, they should be able to decode most single-syllable words, and they should be able to recognize many words on sight without having to decode them consciously. A full diagnostic workup on children who are still struggling with these foundational skills would be time consuming to say the least. It would also require considerable expertise. We are not suggesting that fourth- and fifth-grade teachers conduct such detailed assessments. Far from it. When problems in word recognition appear to be causing dysfluency, we recommend only a brief decoding inventory. We have included such an inventory in Appendix B. Its components are listed in Figure 4.1. We have structured this assessment so that it begins with the more basic application of decoding skills in monosyllabic words, followed by their application in multisyllabic words. However, we recommend that the most efficient way to administer this inventory for fourth- and fifth-grade students is to start with Part 2. This practice may seem puzzling, but it saves time and avoids unnecessary testing. Only students who struggle with multisyllabic decoding are given Part 1.

The assessment strategy is simple. If a student does poorly on Part 2, provide instruction that includes work with multisyllabic words. If this instruction does not produce results, a focus on more basic skills is required. Administering Part 1 of the inventory

Part I: Single-Syllable Decoding
• Short Vowels • Consonant Blends and Digraphs • *R*-Controlled Vowel Patterns • Vowel–Consonant–*e* • Vowel Teams
Part II: Multisyllabic Decoding
• Compound Words • Closed Syllables • Open Syllables • VC-e Syllables • *R*-Controlled Syllables • Vowel Team Syllables • *Cle* Syllables

FIGURE 4.1. Components of the Informal Decoding Inventory.

can help verify this need and identify specific instructional targets. However, we do not believe that Tier 2 instruction in these basic skills is realistic in fourth and fifth grades. Tier 3 intervention is called for, not small-group instruction in the classroom. This advice should come as good news. It simplifies matters for the fourth- and fifth-grade teacher and makes an assessment-driven approach practical and easy to manage. Commercial intervention programs in the area of decoding typically include their own assessments. Once informal assessments have indicated the need for such a program, these built-in assessments should be used to guide instruction (Torgesen & Miller, 2009).

Assessing Vocabulary

Although no one disputes the importance of vocabulary knowledge in reading, the problem of assessing that knowledge has proved difficult to solve. The National Reading Panel (National Institute of Child Health and Human Development, 2000) identified vocabulary assessment as an especially troublesome area. There are relatively dependable screening tests available, to be sure, but they are time consuming and provide little information helpful in planning differentiated reading instruction. Diagnostic tests of vocabulary, in contrast, are nonexistent. This is because a diagnostic test delineates an area into the specific skills a student may lack. In the case of vocabulary, these skills are the equivalent of individual word meanings. That is, every new word is a "skill." Because there is no agreed-upon vocabulary curriculum for each grade, we cannot simply assess a student to determine which words need to be taught. Even if there were such a curriculum, it would contain too many words to make diagnostic assessment feasible.

In our approach to differentiated instruction, however, there is a place for vocabulary assessment. It is limited to those words actually taught in the context of small-group lessons. Further, it is limited to postassessments conducted at the end of a cycle of instruction. We do not preassess students' knowledge of the words they will encounter during a cycle. The reason is that multiple exposures to a word are needed for an individual to internalize a deep representation of its meanings. In the same small group, some students may be altogether unfamiliar with the word while others have had several exposures but not enough to fully grasp it. Consequently, all students will benefit from attention to the word, and preassessment would serve no purpose.

Assessing Comprehension

Comprehension is unquestionably the most important dimension of reading—the bottom line—and yet assessing comprehension is difficult. However, screening measures, such as the comprehension subtest of a group achievement test, can be useful in determining how a student is performing relative to grade-level expectations. Like vocabulary, there are no diagnostic tests of comprehension, but the reason is different. Attempts to delineate comprehension into specific skills and strategies have proved fruitless because assessments of these skills are highly correlated (McKenna & Stahl, 2009). A student who scores high on one skill is likely to score high on others, for example. The best way to diagnose a comprehension problem is to examine the various factors that might contribute to that problem. These include difficulties with word recognition, limited vocabulary and background knowledge, lack of familiarity with various text and sentence structures, and the failure to apply comprehension strategies for specific purposes. We are not suggesting that assessments in each of these areas are needed to implement differentiated reading instruction, but comprehension assessment is nevertheless a part of our approach to differentiated instruction.

   Let's begin by considering the two reasons to assess comprehension. One is to determine a student's overall level of proficiency; the other is to gauge the student's understanding of a particular text. These are very different goals and both are important. Consequently, in our approach, two kinds of comprehension assessments are needed. The first is a screening measure designed to provide an overall level, usually translated into grade-level terms or Lexiles, a newer metric used to rank students' ability on a scale ranging from beginning reading (a scale score of 200) well into advanced ranges (see *www.lexile.com*). Both grade-level metrics and Lexile scores can be used to compare students and texts. Figure 4.2 demonstrates how a teacher might judge the suitability of a particu-

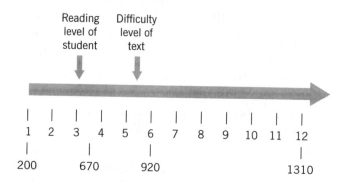

FIGURE 4.2. Using grade levels or Lexiles to judge the match between students and texts.

lar book for use with a particular student or with a small group of students. In this case, the text will be very challenging.

We offer two caveats with respect to determining an overall level of proficiency in this matter. The first is that these metrics create the illusion of precision. In reality, they are merely estimates that must be weighed, together with teacher judgment. The second is that a precise match between a student and a text is not possible; getting reasonably close is good enough. And in some ways a precise match may not always be desirable. Inspecting this example might prompt one to think that this hypothetical text is too difficult. Keep in mind, however, that in small-group instruction the teacher is in a position to provide considerable support so that challenging texts are sometimes appropriate. From the standpoint of assessment, the important thing is to become aware of the fact that the same metric can be used to gauge the match between students and materials.

The second comprehension assessment useful in small-group differentiated instruction is the day-to-day informal information a teacher derives while interacting with students. This information might come from asking questions, thinking about the questions students generate, or judging the quality of written work. If these examples seem imprecise, so be it. Comprehension of a particular text is difficult to reduce to a number or set of numbers even under the best of conditions, and certainly not in the give-and-take of small-group instruction. What is important is for teachers to judge whether comprehension is adequate. If it isn't, adjusting the level of support or switching to an easier text may be required.

Given the imprecision inherent in comprehension measurement, we do not expect a teacher to chart gains in comprehension over the course of a year, and certainly not over a matter of 3 weeks. The tools available for this purpose are simply not very good. Other than informally monitoring students' assessment of each text they read, nothing more is needed. We focus instead on using assessments to address the underlying factors that impair comprehension and providing a rich diet of texts, high in vocabulary, text structures, and other nutrients.

Assessing the Affective Dimensions of Reading

Affect is a dimension of reading development that is frequently overlooked. It involves how well students like to read, what they like to read, and what they think of themselves as readers. Given the well-documented downward trajectory of reading attitudes and habits, we believe that these factors have a place among the assessments classroom teachers use to improve their understanding of how their students function as readers. We confess that simply documenting that a student harbors a negative attitude or has come to view him- or herself as a poor reader is not of very much help in planning instruction. Other than selecting books that are engaging and accessible, we typically do not make the affective side of reading a primary target. We argue, however, that affect should instead be an indirect target. By supplying an abundance of interesting texts, by facilitating students as they engage those texts, and by working to build the skills and strategies needed to comprehend them, attitudes can improve.

The chief usefulness of assessing affect lies in gauging changes over the course of a school year, not in planning instruction for a group. We suggest that three assessments are sufficient: an interest inventory, an attitude survey, and a self-perception survey. These are group assessments, given at the beginning and end of the year.

An interest inventory is simply a list of topics that might be of interest to students. It could be generated using a checklist format, allowing students to easily identify those topics about which they might be interested in reading. Some teachers prefer to use graduated responses so that students can indicate their degree of interest. For example, students might be asked to give each topic a "grade." Interest inventories are of two kinds: general and content specific. A general inventory lists a range of topics and types of fiction. A content inventory lists aspects of a subject area that students might like. A science inventory, for example, might include subtopics of likely appeal (e.g., poisonous snakes, strange phenomena, black holes). Content inventories have utility beyond small-group instruction. The results can be useful in recommending books to students in connection with content area instruction. An example of a general interest inventory is presented in Figure 4.3. Note that it contains a few blanks. The reason is that an interest inventory is essentially a ballot, and every ballot should have a place for write-in candidates. Although you are welcome to duplicate the inventory in Figure 4.3, it is a good idea to create your own so that you can modify it as needed. For example, you may find that some topics are rarely checked or that topics you overlooked are frequent write-ins. You can edit your inventory accordingly. Finally, you must be able to deliver the goods. It is pointless to include topics for which you have no texts to recommend or to use for small-group work.

A reading attitude survey asks students to respond to statements or questions that are matters of personal judgment and opinion. Questions such as "How do you feel about reading on a rainy Saturday?" are quickly rated on a Likert or pictorial scale. Summing the results provides an overall indicator of whether a student's attitude is positive, negative, or indifferent. A free attitude survey long popular in the upper elementary grades is the Elementary Reading Attitude Survey (ERAS), a pictorial instrument based on the cartoon character Garfield (McKenna & Kear, 1990; McKenna, Kear, & Ellsworth, 1995). It is group administered and easy to score and interpret. It contains two subscales: one measuring attitude toward academic reading and another assessing attitude toward recreational reading. The ERAS has excellent psychometric properties and has been used as the basis of numerous research studies. It may be downloaded free at *www.professorgarfield.org*.

An assessment of self-perception is designed to provide teachers with an idea of how students view themselves as readers. A free instrument specifically designed for grades 4–6 is the Reader Self-Perception Survey (RSPS; Henk & Melnick, 1995). The RSPS assesses four dimensions: (1) progress (how the student views his or her progress in becoming a more proficient reader), (2) observational comparison (how the student compares his or her proficiency with that of peers), (3) social feedback (input the student has received from peers and family about his or her reading), and (4) physiological states (internal feelings that the student experiences during reading, such as comfort or frustration). Like the ERAS, the RSPS is nationally normed, group administered, and easy to interpret.

Name _____

Which topics do you like the most? Pretend you're a teacher and give each one of these a grade. Give it an A if you really like it, a B if you like it pretty well, a C if it's just OK, a D if you don't like it, and an F if you can't stand it! If I've missed some topics you really like, please write them on the lines at the bottom of the page.

_____ sports		_____ monsters
_____ animals		_____ horses
_____ magic		_____ detectives
_____ jokes		_____ love
_____ exploring the unknown		_____ famous scientists
_____ sharks		_____ ghosts
_____ camping		_____ other countries
_____ UFOs		_____ dogs
_____ spiders		_____ comic books
_____ the jungle		_____ the ocean
_____ drawing, painting		_____ music
_____ riddles		_____ science fiction
_____ friendship		_____ cats
_____ snakes		_____ families
_____ the wilderness		_____ the desert
_____ fishing		_____ computers
_____ manga		_____ video games

What other topics do you really like? Write them here:

_____

_____

_____

_____

_____

_____

FIGURE 4.3. Example of a general interest inventory.

A COORDINATED PLAN FOR ASSESSMENT

Now that we have explored the characteristics of various assessment instruments likely to be useful in guiding small-group reading instruction, it is time to take stock of what we need and bring the components together in an instructional tool kit. In our books focusing on differentiation in the primary grades, such a tool kit included inventories of basic phonics skills and phonological awareness. These will not be needed in grades 4 and 5. A far simpler tool kit will meet our needs. Its contents are listed in Figure 4.4. The left-hand column lists the types of assessments you will need; the right-hand column indicates specific assessments that would be suitable (with room to write in specific instruments that might be available).

Using Assessments Systematically

These tools are enough to accomplish the principal goals of our differentiation model: (1) place students into appropriate small groups, (2) plan instruction that targets the needs that group members share, and (3) gauge the impact of that instruction on student progress.

Forming small groups requires systematic use of a few basic assessments from our tool kit. Placement of students into groups is not a precise process. It involves estimation and compromise, but its benefits are considerable. It is useful to think of struggling readers beyond grade 3 as falling in either of two broad categories (Torgesen & Miller, 2009). One includes students who are reasonably fluent but who lack the vocabulary, background knowledge, and comprehension strategies to understand grade-level text. The other includes students who are not fluent and who lack the more fundamental decoding skills needed to become fluent. Fluency screening can help teachers in grades 4 and 5 quickly decide which category is the better fit for a given student. Students who fall in the second category (usually far fewer in number than the first) require additional informal assessment at the word level. Figure 4.5 represents how fluency screening can drive this process.

Assessments You Need	Assessments You Have or Can Get
Oral reading fluency screening test	
Comprehension screening measure	
Inventory of decoding skills	Informal Decoding Inventory (Appendix B)
Reading interest inventory	Figure 4.3 or a modification
Attitude toward reading	ERAS
Self-perception as a reader	RSPS

FIGURE 4.4. Assessment tool kit for small-group differentiated reading instruction.

The point of giving formative assessments is to follow them with the kind of effective, targeted instruction that the assessments indicate (Torgesen & Miller, 2009). Once groups are populated, such instruction is determined by the focus of the group. As Figure 4.5 illustrates, there are only three types of groups, each with a dual focus: (1) vocabulary and comprehension, (2) fluency and comprehension, and (3) multisyllabic word recognition and fluency. There is an intended overlap of four areas in these three groups. In the next four chapters, we discuss instruction in each of these four areas.

For now, it is important to note how few assessments are needed to form the groups. Let's consider four students in Ms. Jefferson's fourth-grade class as examples to make the process clear. Tammy, Hector, Lakesha, and Bill have all been given an oral reading fluency screening measure. Only Tammy has scored at benchmark on this test. Ms. Jefferson will place her in the vocabulary and comprehension group. We have noted before that students like Tammy, who do not now exhibit specific difficulties, tend to be overlooked when the time comes to provide instruction targeted to their needs. Placing her in the highest of our small groups is a step toward correcting this situation.

Her three classmates are below benchmark in fluency and present with different instructional challenges. Ms. Jefferson administers Part 2 of the Informal Decoding Inventory to all three. You will recall that Part 2 targets the decoding of multisyllabic words. Hector scores above the criterion of 80%. His performance on this measure sug-

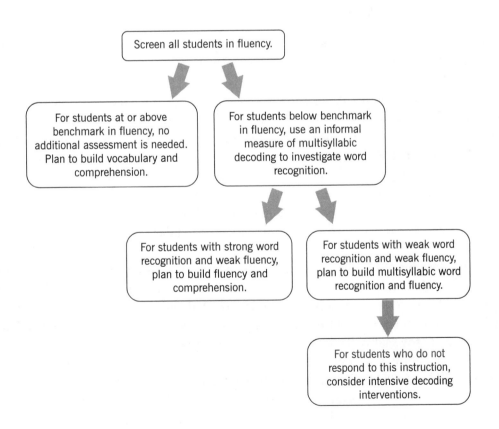

FIGURE 4.5. Using assessments to determine group placement.

gests that he possesses considerable decoding skill and that providing him with oppor-tunities to enhance his fluency will be beneficial. Ms. Jefferson places him in the fluency and comprehension group.

Lakesha and Bill do not fare as well on Part 2 of the Inventory. Their scores are well below the 80% criterion. At this point, Ms. Jefferson does not take the time to adminis-ter Part 1, which targets their ability to decode one-syllable words. Instead, she places both students in the word recognition and fluency group. After teaching a 3-week cycle, she is in a better position to appraise their progress in decoding. Each lesson contains a segment on multisyllabic decoding, and Ms. Jefferson concludes the entire cycle by read-ministering those parts of the inventory on which Lakesha and Bill did poorly. The results indicate that Lakesha has made some progress during the 3-week interval, although gaps remain. Bill, however, has displayed little growth. Bill is a candidate for Tier 3 interven-tion in decoding, although Ms. Jefferson may decide first to try another 3-week cycle in the word recognition and fluency group. If he eventually receives Tier 3 instruction, it may be delivered as part of a commercial program that contains its own assessments, or it may be planned by a specialist, who could begin by administering Part 1 of the Informal Decoding Inventory. In either case, Bill's needs are not likely to be met by his continued participation in the word recognition and fluency group.

Using Assessments from Cycle to Cycle

Formative assessments are most useful when they are given periodically, after regular intervals. In our approach to differentiated instruction, we recommend 3-week cycles. This length of time not only fits conveniently into marking periods, but it also guaran-tees that teachers will regularly take stock of student progress and adjust their instruc-tion accordingly. Our experiences suggest that 3-week intervals are optimal for gauging progress. They are not so frequent that time is devoted to unnecessary assessment, nor so lengthy that ineffective instruction is allowed to go on too long. However, if your school requires more frequent assessments, try to make our system fit with them rather than spending additional time. The formative assessment system we recommend has these characteristics: (1) it couples screening and diagnostic assessments in ways that directly inform instructional planning and (2) it provides for regular cycles of progress monitor-ing.

After forming the groups, a teacher will embark on a 3-week instructional plan for each group. Each day will bring informal assessment information during the allotted 15 minutes. Making a few notes about how individual students are responding to instruction will be useful. In the case of Ms. Jefferson, attending to how well Lakesha and Bill are responding to the multisyllabic decoding portion of the lesson will be useful in making a decision about the best course to pursue at the end of the 3-week cycle. The last day of the cycle is devoted entirely to assessments that target the work the students have under-taken during the past 3 weeks. The teacher is then in a position to judge which group will best serve each student's needs during the next cycle. These cycles continue throughout the year, and assessments are used to determine group membership in a truly flexible

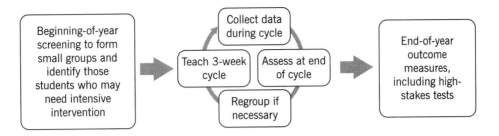

FIGURE 4.6. A year-long plan for using assessments.

way. Remember that there is no room in this approach for stable groupings that offer little opportunity for upward mobility. Gone are the days of the Eagles, the Bluebirds, and the Buzzards!

Figure 4.6 illustrates this continuing process, beginning with initial screening and proceeding from cycle to cycle through the year, ending in outcome measures, including high-stakes assessments. We note that this year-long model, which is an adaptation of the one proposed by Torgesen and Miller (2009), occasionally includes a midyear screening assessment.

Maintaining Records of Assessment

We have deliberately created a Tier 2 instructional system in which assessment plays an important but limited role. Despite its limited nature, however, the information acquired for individual students is surprisingly extensive when we consider it across the course of the school year. This information allows us to track students and to gauge their progress at a glance. One might argue that as long as the general blueprint laid out in Figure 4.6 is followed, there is no pressing need to keep records over time. We disagree and can suggest three persuasive reasons for doing so. First, the decision a teacher must make at the end of each cycle, although based largely on the student's performance during that cycle, can also be affected by the longer history of small-group work. Second, this history will be useful as evidence of the need for Tier 3 intervention. The decision to provide such instruction will probably be reached not by the classroom teacher alone but in conjunction with a specialist or team, who will benefit from examining the student's history. Finally, maintaining records over time can play a role as part of a larger RTI plan. For example, if Tier 3 instruction for Bill proves ineffective, the next step is to consider the appropriateness of special education services. The team that convenes to consider this option should include his classroom teacher, who can provide useful input as to his history of small-group differentiated instruction.

There are clearly many ways to record data for individual students. Some teachers prefer to keep portfolios on each student. We do not quarrel with this practice, although we find it time consuming. Our focus here is on a simple system for maintaining records for an entire class over the course of a year. Our motto is: Simpler is better.

Name	Reading Level	Fluency Screen	Decoding Part II	1st 3 weeks	2nd 3 weeks	3rd 3 weeks	4th 3 weeks	5th 3 weeks	6th 3 weeks

FIGURE 4.7. Class assessment form.

Name	Reading Level	Fluency Screen	Decoding Part II	1st 3 weeks	2nd 3 weeks	3rd 3 weeks	4th 3 weeks	5th 3 weeks	6th 3 weeks
Tammy	890L	Above Benchmark		V&C	V&C	V&C			
Hector	770L	Below Benchmark	90%	F&C	F&C	V&C			
Lakesha	750L	Below Benchmark	70%	W&F	W&F	F&C			
Bill	640L	Below Benchmark	40%	W&F	W&F	Tier III			

FIGURE 4.8. Examples of student data.

Figure 4.7 provides a reproducible template for record keeping for the first half of the year. It captures the essential components of the system we have described.

Updating this form is a simple matter. As examples, we present in Figure 4.8 information for the four students in Ms. Jefferson's class. Note that once the beginning-of-year data are entered, Ms. Jefferson continues by noting only which group a student is a member of during each cycle. A change in group implies that the data she has collected justify such a change. In maintaining a long-range chart of this sort, there is no need to record the specific assessment results for each cycle.

These examples illustrate the very different trajectories that are possible over time. Tammy has maintained her position in the vocabulary and comprehension group by responding well to the instruction and by showing no signs that her fluency is slipping. After spending 6 weeks in the fluency and comprehension group, Hector's fluency has improved and Ms. Jefferson moves him into the vocabulary and comprehension group. This is an example of the "upward mobility" we strive for in this approach to differentiated instruction. Lakesha began the year by scoring below the 80% criterion on Part 2 of the Informal Decoding Inventory. You will recall that at the end of the first 3-week cycle, Ms. Jefferson readministered those portions of the inventory on which Lakesha did poorly. As Figure 4.8 indicates, there was still work to be done in multisyllabic decoding, and Ms. Jefferson decided to keep Lakesha in the word recognition and fluency group for the second cycle. We can infer from the chart that her decoding then improved to the point that her needs were best served by moving her into the fluency and comprehension group—another instance of upward mobility. Bill's case is more difficult, however. His score on Part 2 of the inventory was very weak, and Ms. Jefferson placed him the word recognition and fluency group, hoping that this environment would lead to improvements. After 3 weeks, she was disappointed but decided to try one more cycle in this group. As the chart indicates, his performance remained weak, and Ms. Jefferson arranged for him to receive Tier 3 intensive intervention. Her hope is that the intervention will be effective and that he can resume small-group instruction within her classroom.

A FINAL WORD

Choosing and using assessments as part of a differentiated instruction plan is not difficult. Those required are few in number and easy to administer. They lead to straightforward group placement, and they provide the information needed to regroup appropriately. They also facilitate a simple long-term record-keeping system that allows a teacher to track the progress of students over time and make decisions about the kind of instruction that will best meet their needs.

Chapter 5

Building Word Recognition

In this chapter, we present a tiered instructional model for developing fourth- and fifth-grade students' word recognition. In order to introduce the model, we first present some foundational knowledge about the structure of words. For Tier 1 instruction, we argue that direct instruction in the sound, spelling, and meaning of a small set of words before students read can both improve their comprehension and build their understanding of the way that words work. We also argue that, for some students, more strategic and concentrated work on recognizing long words can be a reasonable segment of their Tier 2 instruction; we provide readers with a sequence of words to get started, along with a systematic plan for engaging these students in analyzing words. Finally, we also argue that upper elementary students who are still struggling with basic word recognition skills for single-syllable words must have access to Tier 3 intensive interventions.

FOUNDATIONAL KNOWLEDGE
ABOUT WORD RECOGNITION DEVELOPMENT

We imagine that most fourth- and fifth-grade teachers will be relieved to know that they do not have to teach basic word recognition skills; in fact, they really will need to do little at the level of the individual sound. When we meet new words, as skilled readers, we actually do not sound them out one sound at a time. Rather, we automatically look for ways to avoid that laborious process, using other words with similar structures as models or looking for spelling patterns. For example, if the word *morpheme* is new to you, you will process its syllables (*morph* and *eme*) to generate a pronunciation, using chunks around the vowels to fairly automatically divide and conquer the word even as you wonder what it means. (A *morpheme* is a unit of meaning, by the way, just as a phoneme is a unit of sound.) If we then use the word *morphemic*, you will automatically recognize that this word has a suffix (-ic) and that the second syllable (phem) actually experienced an *e*-drop with the addition of that suffix and will still be pronounced with a long -*e* sound. This type of decoding, which we call structural analysis, is the focus of word recognition instruction for upper elementary readers. In order to understand how to teach children to attack long words, we first need to become conscious of how we ourselves, as skilled readers, have learned to recognize most words with relative ease—even long words and even the first time they are encountered in print. Figure 5.1 defines some important words about words that will help us in this quest.

Syllable	A syllable is a unit of pronunciation that is easy to isolate because it contains one and only one vowel sound. The word *word* is a syllable; the word *pronounce* has two syllables (*pro- nounce*).
Morpheme	A morpheme is the smallest unit of meaning in a word. A word contains one or more morphemes. A morpheme can be free (meaning it can stand alone as a word) or bound (meaning it can only be used in combination with other morphemes). Prefixes and suffixes are bound morphemes, but so are Greek and Latin word roots that do not stand alone. For example, *listen* is a free morpheme. It stands alone as a word, and it can be combined with other morphemes to become *listening, listens,* or *listener. Audi* is a bound morpheme meaning *hear*. It cannot stand alone as a word, but it can be used in combination with other morphemes to make *audible* or *auditory*.
Root Word	A root or base word is a free morpheme to which prefixes and suffixes may be added. A root word with prefixes and/or suffixes is a derivative of that root. *Test* is a root word. Derivatives include *pretest, retest,* and *tester.*
Prefix	A prefix is a bound morpheme added to the beginning of a root word to change its meaning. Prefixes sometimes also change the word's part of speech. The prefix *en-* changes both meaning and part of speech when it is added to the root word *slave.* The prefix *pre-* changes the meaning but not part of speech when it is add to the root *view.*
Inflectional Suffix	An inflectional suffix is a bound morpheme added to the end of a root word to indicate plurality, possession, tense, person, or comparison. Inflectional suffixes do not change a word's part of speech. The inflectional suffixes are -*s*, -*es*, -*'s*, -*s'*, -*ed*, -*ing*, -*er*, and -*est*.
Derivational Suffix	A derivational suffix is a bound morpheme added to the end of a root word to change its meaning. Derivational suffixes change a word's part of speech. The derivational suffix -*ly* changes *soft* from an adjective to an adverb.
Compound Word	A compound word is made up of two or more free morphemes (e.g., *cupcake*). In most compounds, the meaning of each word is retained and the meaning of the combination is clear. However, some compounds have obscure histories that do not help young decoders (e.g., *turnpike*). Although linguists often include compounds separated by a space (e.g., *high school*), we are not concerned with these because they present no decoding difficulties.
Contraction	A contraction is formed by replacing one or more letters with an apostrophe. It is possible sometimes to confuse contractions with possessives (e.g., *Tom's* could mean belonging to Tom or it could be the contracted form of *Tom is*). Context resolves such ambiguities, which are surprisingly frequent. The contraction *she'd* could mean *she had* or *she would* depending on the sentence context.

FIGURE 5.1. Words about words.

Thinking about how words are built can be helpful in breaking them apart in order to read and understand them. The word *speech*, for example, is a free morpheme, or base word, because it is a meaningful unit that can stand alone. Because *speech* is a noun, we can create the word variants *speeches* (adding an inflected ending to indicate plurality) or *speech's* (adding an inflected ending to indicate possession). We can also derive a very different word—*speechless*—by adding a derivational suffix. This new word is an adjective. If we add another derivational suffix, we can retain the new meaning but change the word back to a noun: *speechlessness*. The root word *teach* offers additional possibilities. It is a verb, so it can be inflected as *teaching* or *teaches*. It can also be changed into a noun (*teacher*) by adding a derivational suffix. The meaning of the root word can be extended to *coteach* or *preteach* or *reteach* through the addition of common prefixes, or the part of speech can be changed to an adjective (*teachable*) through the addition of a common suffix. Clearly, the generative nature of prefixes and suffixes makes them key building blocks in students' vocabularies. Figures 5.2 and 5.3 provide a list of common prefixes and suffixes, respectively, adapted from Eldredge (2005).

	Meaning	Examples
un-	not, opposite of	*uninterested, uninformed*
dis-	not, reversing of an action	*displease, discredit*
re-	do again	*reapply, reappoint*
en-	to make into, to put into	*entrap, enclose*
co-	together with	*coexist, copilot*
mis-	wrong	*misinterpret, misrepresent*
in-, im-, il-, ir-	not	*incorrect, impolite, illegal, irregular*
anti-	against	*antibiotic, antiwar*
extra-	beyond	*extraordinary, extracurricular*
fore-	in front	*foreground, forewarn*
inter-	between	*interstate, intersect*
intra-	within	*intramural, intravenous*
non-	not	*noncommercial, nonsense*
post-	after	*postseason, postmortem*
pre-	before	*premade, preview*
semi-	half	*semicircle, semiannual*
sub-	under	*submarine, subzero*
super-	above	*supernatural, superscript*

FIGURE 5.2. Common prefixes. Based on Eldredge (2008).

Common Noun Suffixes		
	Meaning	Examples
-al, -ance, -ment, -ation, -sion, -tion	act of	dismissal, continuance, payment, specialization, division, connection
-ation, -ment, ness, -hood, -dom, -ship, -ion, -ice	state of	desperation, contentment, kindness, boyhood, freedom, kinship, corruption, cowardice
-ist,- er, -or, -eer	one who	pianist, server, creditor, engineer
Common Adjective Suffixes		
	Meaning	Examples
-ful, -ish , -y, -ive, -able	full of, having, capable of	regretful, selfish, guilty, instinctive, manageable
-able	capable of	workable

FIGURE 5.3. Common suffixes. Based on Eldredge (2008).

Advanced decoding is not about individual sounds; it is about breaking words into manageable chunks. The easiest chunks to recognize are those that represent meaning—root words and their affixes (prefixes and suffixes)—especially when those root words are unbound. Unbound morphemes, though, are not the only way that long words are built. Words are also built through adding suffixes to bound morphemes and through combinations of syllables that represent sound and not meaning. Bound morphemes are units of meaning, but they do not stand alone as words. The most common are the Greek and Latin roots, some of which are presented in Figures 5.4 and 5.5, respectively.

	Meaning	Examples
ast(er)	star	asteroid, astronomy
auto	self	autobiography, auto
bio	life	biography, biology
chrono	time	chronology, synchronize
geo	earth	geography, geology
graph	write	autograph, calligraphy
path	feel	empathy, pathetic
phil	love	bibliophile, philosopher
phon	sound	phonics, phonograph
photo	light	photograph, photosynthesis
tele	far off	telephone, telegraph

FIGURE 5.4. Common Greek word roots.

	Meaning	Examples
audi	here	*audio, audible*
bene	good	*benefit, benefactor*
dict	say	*dictate, dictionary*
gen	give birth	*generate, genetic*
jur/jus	law	*jury, justice*
luc	light	*lucid, translucent*
omni	all	*omnipotent, omnivore*
port	carry	*transport, portable*
scrib/script	write	*enscribe, transcript*
sens	feel	*sensitive, resent*
terr	earth	*territory, terrestrial*
vid/vis	see	*video, visible*

FIGURE 5.5. Common Latin word roots.

Upper elementary readers may not recognize these roots as units of meaning until they learn basic etymology. Instead, they will have to recognize them as syllables. Syllables are units of pronunciation that are easily isolated because they contain a vowel sound. Remember that more than one vowel letter (and sometimes a vowel plus *y, w,* or *r*) can work together to make one vowel sound. *Hot* has one vowel letter, one vowel sound, and one syllable; *hotel* has two vowel letters, two vowel sounds, and two syllables. *Fountain* has two vowel sounds and two syllables, even though it has four vowel letters.

Syllables (whether they carry meaning or not) can be tricky to decode because vowel letters represent more than one sound. We have to rely on syllable patterns to know which sound to use. Eldredge (2005) reports some interesting facts about words that may help convince you that the spelling system actually uses a relatively limited number of patterns; we define the six most common patterns in Figure 5.6. An analysis of the 3,000 most common single-syllable words in the language revealed that 45% have single vowels with short-vowel sounds, 38% have vowel teams or *r*-controlled vowel sounds, and 16% have vowel–consonant–*e*. A very small percentage (< 2%) are single vowels pronounced with their long sound, as in *he, she,* and *we.* From these building blocks, represented in familiar one-syllable words, a virtually endless number of multisyllabic words can be built. When meaningful morphemes cannot be recognized, knowing the patterns used in most syllables is the key to multisyllabic decoding.

Although this system of using morphemes and syllable types to recognize words will not account for the accurate pronunciation of every word in the English language, it

Syllable Type	Description	Examples
Closed	A single vowel is followed by one or more consonants and is pronounced with a short sound.	*trash* *trac*tor
Open	A single vowel is at the end of a syllable and is pronounced with its long sound.	*she* *re*mote
Vowel–Consonant–e	A final silent *e* marks the long-vowel sound in a syllable.	*time* en*rage*
	OR The final silent *e* is dropped when a vowel suffix is added, but the vowel is still long.	*blam*ing
r-Controlled	A vowel and *r* are linked to make a vowel sound that is neither long nor short.	*shark* *pur*pose
Vowel Team	Two vowels (and sometimes *w* or *y*) work together to represent one sound. It can be long, short, or neither.	*team* con*tain* *boy*ish
Consonant–*le*	A single consonant sound is followed by -*le* (representing the sound /ul/ in an unaccented syllable at the end of a word.	*candle* en*able*

FIGURE 5.6. Six syllable patterns.

works for many words. The basic building blocks of morphemes and syllables provide a foundation on which to build upper elementary word recognition. Instruction, then, will teach students to recognize the units and to use them to attack new words. These skills are necessary so that students can both engage in fluent reading and encounter enough new words to constantly build their meaning vocabularies, a topic to which we turn in Chapter 7. For readers interested in learning more about the structure of words, Figure 5.7 lists some resources we find especially helpful.

Bear, D. R., Invernizzi, M., Templeton, S., & Johnston, F. (2007). *Words their way* (4th ed.). Columbus, OH: Prentice Hall.

Fry, E. B., Kress, J.E., & Fountoukidis, D. L. (2000). *The reading teacher's book of lists* (4th ed.). San Francisco: Jossey-Bass.

Ganske, K. (2000). *Word journeys: Assessment-guided phonics, spelling, and vocabulary instruction*. New York: Guilford Press.

Ganske, K. (2006). *Word sorts and more: Sound, pattern, and meaning explorations K–3*. New York: Guilford Press.

Ganske, K. (2008). *Mindful of words: Spelling and vocabulary explorations 4–8*. New York: Guilford Press.

Johnston, F. R., Invernizzi, M., & Bear, D. R. (2004). *Words their way: Word sorts for syllables and affixes spellers*. Boston: Allyn & Bacon/Pearson.

Templeton, S., Johnston, F. R., Bear, D. R., & Invernizzi, M. (2004). *Words their way: Word sorts for derivational relations spellers*. Boston: Allyn & Bacon.

FIGURE 5.7. Resources about words.

TIER 1 INSTRUCTION IN WORD RECOGNITION

The key to efficient Tier 1 instruction for upper elementary readers is the link between the components of word recognition and the rest of the students' reading diet: fluency, vocabulary, and comprehension. Texts at this level provide multiple opportunities to teach the pronunciation, spelling, and meaning of words directly; they also provide multiple opportunities for students to recognize longer words in context that have not been taught in isolation. The core program texts used in Tier 1 will provide ample opportunity for building word recognition; often, but not always, teachers' editions for those texts will include specific words to use and the teaching language that makes them transparent.

Content

Word recognition instruction at this stage must attend to the important units: multisyllabic words, with their constituent morphemes and syllables. The *Guidelines for Reviewing a Reading Program* (Florida Center for Reading Research, 2007) targets the following structural analysis concepts for fourth- and fifth-grade word recognition: syllable types; prefixes, suffixes, and morphemes; and spelling. It also indicates that the strategy of chunking words should be taught explicitly, and that teachers should engage in think-aloud modeling of how a reader attacks a multisyllabic word.

All students, then, need a working knowledge of the six syllable types. They need to know that single vowels can be pronounced as short or long, or with the schwa sound; they also need to know that vowel teams and *r*-controlled vowels have specific pronunciations. They need to know what a prefix, a suffix, and a root is. To put this knowledge to work, they need to learn some strategies that can help them to break words into chunks. Figure 5.8 presents a series of steps that teachers can use to think aloud as they chunk multisyllabic words. These strategies are related to the specific building blocks (morphemes and syllable types) for each word.

There is one spelling generalization that is also essential for mastery during the upper elementary grades. According to developmental spelling theories, students at this age are most likely working at the syllables and affixes stage. That means that their attention is likely to be drawn to understanding the junctures of syllables, especially to whether consonants should be doubled or not. For example, students will be wondering whether the word *commit* + *ment* will have two *t*s or one. Teaching students to use the doubling principle consistently and with a deep conceptual understanding will help them to understand how longer words work. Application of the doubling principle, which guides spelling changes as suffixes are added to base words, forces students to understand and use concepts of syllable type. Figure 5.9, based on Bear, Invernizzi, Templeton, and Johnston (2008), illustrates the doubling principle.

Instructional Strategies

There are a few robust instructional strategies that teachers can use consistently in Tier 1. The first is thinking aloud, and it applies to both word recognition and spelling. In order

Compounds	Closed–Closed	Open–Closed	Consonant-*le*
breakfast *myself* *snowstorm* *throughout* *folktale* *downpour*	*napkin* *happen* *magnet* *dentist* *plastic* *absent*	*music* *robot* *female* *fever* *human* *basic*	*table* *battle* *handle* *bugle* *cable* *sample*
Divide between words you know	Divide between consonants	Divide between the vowel and the consonant	Divide before the C*le* syllable

Prefix Only	Suffix Only	Both Prefix and Suffix	
misjudge *pretest* *unicycle* *tripod* *nonsense* *extend*	*roughly* *weakness* *plentiful* *lengthy* *cautious* *craziest*	*unhappiness* *mistreatment* *subtraction* *pretreatment* *returning*	
Divide between the prefix and the rest of the word	Divide between the suffix and the rest of the word	Divide between both the prefix and the suffix and the rest of the word	

FIGURE 5.8. Strategies for chunking words.

Base Word Patterns	Adding a vowel suffix	Examples
CVVC, CVCC *leak, dump*	Add the suffix with no change to the base.	*leaked, leaking* *dumped, dumping*
CVC *hop*	Double the final consonant and add the suffix.	*hopped, hopping*
CVCe *dine*	Drop the final *e* and add the suffix.	*dined, dining*
Cy *cry*	Add -*ing* with no change; change the *y* to *i* before adding -*ed*.	*crying, cried*
Vy *stay*	Add the suffix with no change to the base.	*stayed, staying*
Two-syllable words with accented last syllable *resent, uncap, derive, rely, enjoy*	Use the pattern in the final syllable to determine your action.	*resented, resenting* *uncapped,* *uncapping* *derived, deriving* *relied, relying* *enjoyed, enjoying*
Two-syllable words with unaccented last syllable *open, focus*	Add the suffix with no change to the base.	*opened, opening* *focused, focusing*

FIGURE 5.9. The doubling principle. Based on Bear et al. (2008).

to teach students to read words, we must teach them how words are spelled. You should think of this type of spelling lesson as conceptual. By that we mean that we are teaching principles of the spelling system, using specific words as examples, rather than a list of spelling words. For example, a teacher writing a vocabulary word on the board can model how to think through that word as he or she is spelling it:

> "I am thinking about how to spell *momentary.* I know that it comes from the word *moment.* I hear two syllables in *moment.* The first one sounds like an open syllable. That means that I can spell it with just the single vowel *o.* The second syllable sounds like a regular closed syllable. Now I have to spell the suffix, and it begins with a vowel. I can see that my base word ends with two consonants, so I can just add the suffix."

> "I am thinking about how to spell the word *combination.* I know that it comes from the root *combine,* so I will start there. I'm going to spell the schwa sound in the second syllable with an *i* to keep it consistent with the root. Now I'll think about the suffix. It starts with a vowel, so I'll drop the silent *e* from the root, and then add the suffix. I know that the suffix can have two different spellings: *-sion* and *-tion.* I have to decide which one looks right."

After consistent modeling, the teacher can move to guided practice, asking individual students to think aloud while they spell words. The best time to do this, of course, is when students are actually writing. A teacher can use an existing spelling error as a teachable moment, directing a student to look back at the word, pronounce it, and think it through. Using consistent language (e.g., "Try thinking about the syllable type," "Try thinking about the spelling pattern," "Try thinking about the root") ensures that students will get multiple opportunities to apply a small set of ideas.

On the first reading of a new story, a teacher can think aloud the decoding of new multisyllabic words in much the same way.

> "Put your finger on the third word in the first paragraph (*assertion*). I want to show you how to think through that word. I haven't seen that word before, so I have to divide it. I see a suffix, so I'll split that off first. Now I see a double consonant in the base, so I'll split between them. That gives me *as-ser-tion.* Closed, *r*-controlled, suffix. It must be … *assertion.* Now I see that the base word was actually *assert* with the suffix *-ion,* not *-tion.*"

One additional strategy that teachers can use is to take each of the focus words from the week's reading and take a moment to create a list of derivations. This is a very brief activity, and it begins to create a sense of word consciousness. Here's how this might work:

"Our first word today is *submit*. Say the word. It's a verb. One meaning of *submit* is to hand over. For example, 'You submit your writing pieces to me.' Let's look at how this word works. I see two single vowels, so I know that it has two syllables. I also see two consonants between the vowels, and they are not blends or a digraph, so I'll divide between them. Now I have two closed syllables. Easy to read, easy to spell. Since it's a verb, let's see what it looks like in other forms. For *submitting* or *submitted*, I'll have to double the final consonant because the final syllable is closed and I want to keep that short vowel sound. If I want to create a noun form, I can add a suffix. A paper you submit is your submission. Look at how that spelling changes. You can add a prefix to either the noun or the verb form. You can resubmit and you will have a resubmission. So our first word today is *submit*, and it means to hand over."

Instructional Planning

Planning Tier 1 instruction for upper elementary students involves a decision about how to use the core program materials. One way to view core programs at these grade levels is to see them as a sequence of reading selections that provide opportunities to develop and apply word recognition, spelling, fluency, vocabulary, and comprehension strategies. Core program teachers' manuals provide choices, suggestions, and language for teachers to use as they guide students through these selections, but those choices can be overwhelming. We think that a simple, repetitive frame is preferable. We will populate that frame gradually, both here and throughout the next three chapters. You will see that, in effect, we are arguing that many core programs' wide choices actually make instruction across classrooms at the same grade level very different; we also think that some of those choices move teachers and students away from the essential reading proficiencies that should be the heart of the instruction. Also, because we are advocating for a single classroom teacher to accomplish both Tier 1 and Tier 2 instruction in reading for a heterogeneous group of students, including all students in Tier 2, we have to be careful about how we use time. For this reason, we argue that teachers can increase their focus during Tier 1 instruction and also reduce the time that they need to do it.

There are two planning templates, each assuming that there are 45 minutes for Tier 1 instruction; if there is more time, the schedule can be adjusted proportionally. We are also assuming that there is a weekly selection around which core instruction is built. The first template, presented in Figure 5.10, is used until the teacher has finished reading the entire core selection once. The only real word recognition planning required here is the selection of a list of words from the core selection whose meanings and spelling patterns can be taught and thinking through the language that one can use to make the spellings of those words transparent to the students. In many cases, the teacher's manual will already identify a list of words for vocabulary instruction, and we suggest that those words also provide opportunities for teaching more generalized word recognition concepts; teachers can add additional ones as they see opportunities. If the selection is long,

Time	Activity	Description
5 min	Strategy Introduction	
15 min	Interactive Read-Aloud	
3 min	Introduce Written Response	
10 min	Vocabulary	The teacher introduces core vocabulary for the week, introducing meanings, thinking aloud about the spellings, and listing derivatives.
12 min	Choral Reading of the Story	

FIGURE 5.10. Tier 1 word recognition introduction planning.

this same plan can be used again the next day with the next segment of the selection. The second planning template is presented in Figure 5.11.

It is evident that we have not reserved much time or attention to word recognition instruction during Tier 1. That is because, developmentally, most students will not need much instruction. That does not mean that this small dose of instruction is necessarily easy for teachers to accomplish. For upper elementary teachers new to thinking aloud about a word's spelling, there are some strategies that may help. Consider first isolating prefixes and suffixes. With what remains, discuss the division of syllables and the syllable types. Establish a consistent shared language about the structure of words, perhaps supported by a classroom chart that defines these word parts. We have provided a sample chart in Figure 5.12. If this is a daily part of instruction, students will come to internalize analysis as a part of learning a new word.

Most students in the upper elementary grade levels will continue to build their word recognition with this fairly simple combination of attention to words in isolation and in the context of the week's text. For others, though, a more targeted daily segment of instructional time for small-group instruction will be necessary. This is Tier 2.

Time	Activity	Description
2 min	Strategy Introduction	
10 min	Interactive Read-Aloud	
10 min	Vocabulary Review	The teacher reviews core vocabulary for the week, including meanings, spellings, and derivatives.
10 min	Partner Reading	
10 min	Whisper Reading	
3 min	Introduce Written Response	

FIGURE 5.11. Tier 1 word recognition additional planning.

	When you are reading a new word, divide into syllables and conquer!	
When you look for syllables, some word parts should stay together.		When you look for syllables, some word parts should be divided.
Blends Digraphs Vowel teams *Cle*		Compound words Prefixes, suffixes, and base words Double consonants
Conquer your word by finding the syllables, saying the syllables, and blending the syllables.		

FIGURE 5.12. Classroom words about words.

TIER 2 INSTRUCTION IN WORD RECOGNITION

Tier 2 instruction in word recognition is appropriate for upper elementary students who do not meet oral reading fluency benchmarks and who struggle with multisyllabic decoding. Teachers identify these students by first testing the entire class in oral reading fluency and then testing those who are below the grade-level benchmark with an informal decoding inventory such as the one that we have reproduced in Appendix B. Upper elementary students who are prime candidates for Tier 2 instruction in word recognition will have mastered single-syllable decoding through long-vowel teams but perform poorly on multisyllabic tasks. For them, the explicit, opportunistic analysis of the selection of words targeted for instruction in the week's selection may not provide enough examples of the same types of words on which to build a more general understanding of how words work. Researchers have demonstrated that direct instruction in syllabification and word recognition builds word attack skills and fluency, even for students identified with reading or learning disabilities (e.g., Diliberto, Beattie, Flowers, & Algozzine, 2009).

Content

For these students, more practice with words with similar structures is necessary. The content, then, for Tier 2 instruction in word recognition is multisyllabic words with similar structures, combining the six syllable types with common prefixes and suffixes, and a set of explicit strategies about how to divide and decode words (Roberts, Torgesen, Boardman, & Scammacca, 2008). Word lists can help generate this content. It is very difficult to think of words with common features without using any references. Figure 5.13 presents a list of words that we have reorganized by their features. In this case, the words

Closed Syllables	Open Syllables	Vowel Team Syllables
ra<u>ll</u>y	<u>ra</u>lly	raid
ram	<u>ra</u>ven	rail
<u>ran</u>som	re<u>cent</u>ly	raw
<u>ras</u>cal	<u>re</u>cess	ray
ra<u>ven</u>	re<u>flect</u>	re<u>a</u>sonable
rea<u>so</u>nable	<u>re</u>freshment	reed
re<u>cent</u>ly	re<u>gard</u>	refug<u>ee</u>
re<u>cess</u>	re<u>gion</u>	re<u>gion</u>
re<u>ckon</u>	re<u>gret</u>	re<u>hearse</u>
re<u>flect</u>	re<u>hearse</u>	re<u>pay</u>
re<u>fresh</u>ment	<u>re</u>ly	res<u>tau</u>rant
re<u>fuge</u>	re<u>mark</u>	re<u>view</u>
re<u>gi</u>ment	<u>re</u>pay	
re<u>gret</u>	rep<u>u</u>tation	
rep<u>u</u>tation	res<u>o</u>lution	
res<u>o</u>lution	re<u>view</u>	
res<u>tau</u>rant	re<u>vo</u>lution	
re<u>vo</u>lution		
rhythm		
ri<u>di</u>culous		
rink		
ri<u>pp</u>le		
ro<u>tten</u>		
ru<u>dd</u>er		
ru<u>gg</u>ed		
rung		
rust		

VCe Syllables	C*le* Syllables	*r*-Controlled Syllables
ref<u>uge</u>	reason<u>able</u>	re<u>gard</u>
rhyme	ri<u>pple</u>	re<u>mark</u>
ridic<u>ul</u>ous	remark<u>able</u>	ro<u>ller</u>
rove		ru<u>dder</u>

Prefixes	Suffixes	
<u>re</u>flect	reason<u>able</u>	
<u>re</u>flection	re<u>cently</u>	
<u>re</u>freshment	re<u>flec</u>tion	
	re<u>fresh</u>ment	
	re<u>gi</u>ment	
	remark<u>able</u>	
	re<u>puta</u>tion	
	re<u>solu</u>tion	
	re<u>volu</u>tion	
	re<u>volu</u>tionary	
	ridic<u>ulous</u>	
	ro<u>ller</u>	
	ro<u>tten</u>	
	ru<u>gged</u>	

FIGURE 5.13. Fifth-grade words sorted by word parts.

come from a fifth-grade list of words frequently taught in core reading programs (Taylor, 1989). They are presented in that text in alphabetical order, but we have reorganized the words beginning with *r* to group them by their possibilities for highlighting word parts.

Any grade-level word lists are good sources of content for word recognition lessons that highlight word parts. Fifth-grade science words beginning with *c* include *calcium, calorie, cell, cerebellum, cerebrum, characteristics, chemical, circulatory, circumference, cloud, cocoon, compass, compound, concave, conduction, connective, consume, consumer, controlled, convection, cornea, corrosive, crater, crystal,* and *cycle.* This short list includes all of the syllable types. Once you embrace the idea that direct teaching of the structure of words will build students' decoding skills, you will see opportunities for identifying word parts everywhere. Researchers also have demonstrated that direct instruction in decoding skills improves students' spelling skills, even for readers with disabilities (Wanzek et al., 2006).

A word to the wise: Do not avoid words that you cannot explain. As you work with longer words, you will see that many times the vowels in unaccented syllables are pronounced with a schwa sound, similar to a short *u*, rather than the short sound that their syllable type would suggest. It is better to address these syllables and to teach students to be flexible. Often, if they actually have the word in their listening vocabulary, pronunciation with the short vowel intact will cue the actual pronunciation of the word with its schwa syllable. For example, if students use their knowledge of syllable types to pronounce *cocoon* as co -coon, context will usually help them arrive at the true pronunciation. There are also syllables that are simply spelled irregularly. You might call these syllables oddballs. For example, if you separated the word *pronunciation* into syllables, you would find *pro-nun-ci-a-tion.* The third syllable looks open, but the vowel represents the long *-e* sound rather than that long *i.* Despite the reality of these oddballs, the number of syllables that conform to the types is much greater than the number that do not.

The second content aspect of Tier 2 decoding lessons is strategies for division. Again, a flexible set of division options is probably more useful than a very complex protocol. In Figure 5.14, we adapt a protocol called DISSECT (Deshler, Ellis, & Lenz, 1979). Students work down through the protocol until they are confident that they have recognized the word.

Instructional Strategies

Tier 2 instructional strategies build on the think-aloud strategy used in Tier 1 instruction but include additional guided practice and every pupil response. We have found optimal engagement when each child has his or her own word list. The model lessons included in Appendix C contain 10 or 12 words for each day's lesson and are organized by their common features. We recommend four simple instructional strategies: (1) marking up the words, (2) identifying syllable types, (3) reading the words with partners, and (4) reading the words chorally.

Generally, finding the correct division is the most challenging part of reading longer words. The first strategy that we have found useful is to have students quickly mark up the words. Students should first circle any prefixes or suffixes they see. Then they

	DISSECT
D	**D**iscover the context.
I	**I**solate the prefix.
S	**S**eparate the suffix.
S	**S**ay the stem.
E	**E**xamine the stem: If it begins with a consonant, underline three letters. If it begins with a vowel, underline two letters. If that doesn't work, redo without the first letter.
C	**C**heck with someone.
T	**T**ry the dictionary.

FIGURE 5.14. DISSECT division rules.

work through the sequence of letters that remain, identifying syllables. Each syllable has to have one vowel sound. Ask the students to place a dot under each single vowel and underline a vowel team. Then they can divide the syllables with a line, ensuring that each syllable has only one vowel sound. Because they are actually marking their words, it is easy to monitor their work by watching what they do. This is a form of every pupil response and provides useful feedback about whether individual students are coming to understand syllable structures or not.

Once students have marked vowels and divided the words, identifying syllable types reinforces the fact that these are repetitive structures rather than simply individual words. To maintain a brisk pace and high engagement, use every pupil response. Simple, repetitive teacher talk is helpful here:

> "You have divided your words. Point to your first syllable. When I say 'Go,' tell me the syllable type. Go. Next syllable. Go."

Students can answer in unison, and when there are errors, you can explain them. That way you will not waste time explaining syllables that all of the students had correct. Here is a sample of the language you can use for error correction. One of the students has just said that the first syllable in *vintner* is open.

> "That first syllable is closed. I saw two single vowels separated by three consonants. I kept the *nt*-blend together and divided between the single consonant and the blend, like this: *vint - ner*. Then the syllable had a single vowel followed by two consonants, so it is closed."

After students have marked words and identified syllables, they can read their words to a partner. We have found it useful for them to read each syllable separately and then to read them together. They can alternate reading words. For a list of open–closed words, then, they would read like this: *re-cent—recent*; *si-lent—silent*, *fo-cus—focus*.

Finally, a simple management system that creates yet another chance for the students to read the words is to have them read chorally with the teacher. They can use the same format as for partner reading (reading each syllable and then blending them to form the word), but this time the teacher's voice ensures that they read them together and that they have read each syllable and word correctly.

Instructional Planning

Generally, explicit instruction in any content area demands a scope and sequence of instruction and instructional tasks that progress in difficulty over time. In the word lists that we have constructed for these students, we have taken the stance that meaning-based divisions are easiest. To teach meaning-based divisions, we first move from compound words to words with high-frequency prefixes and suffixes. Next, we move to combinations of syllable types, again working with the simplest ones first before moving to more complex examples. Figure 5.15 provides a scope and sequence for our lists, and they are provided in full in Appendix C.

If these lessons are not sufficient for your students, the key to planning additional ones is to organize words by their common characteristics, as we did in Figure 5.13. You can use any available sets of words—spelling lists, core program word lists from the previous year, or content area words from an upcoming unit. Simply decide on syllable combinations to target (e.g., closed–closed; closed-*r*-controlled) and sort your words into these combinations. If you can identify particular syllable patterns that are troubling your students, you can be diagnostic about your list design.

The most rigorous evidence that this instruction is working will come from measures of oral reading fluency. Students who have truly built their word recognition skills and strategies should read natural text more quickly and accurately. Along the way, however, you may want to use the nonsense word sections of our informal decoding inventory (Appendix B) to monitor progress in multisyllabic decoding.

CHOOSING TIER 3 PROGRAMS FOR WORD RECOGNITION

We want to emphasize that a truly tiered program for upper elementary readers must have more than a core program and a plan for systematic Tier 2 instruction. Some students' needs in word recognition will not be met in this combination. Two groups of students will require Tier 3 programs: (1) those fourth and fifth graders who have not mastered single-syllable decoding through vowel teams and (2) those fourth and fifth graders who have mastered single-syllable decoding but have not benefited from consistent, high-quality Tier 2 instruction in multisyllabic decoding. Those students require more intensive and systematic instruction, and we argue that that instruction will likely

Week	Content	Patterns
1	Compound Words	
2	Prefixes and Suffixes	*un-, re-, -ful, -ly*
3		*over-, mis-, -ed, -ness,*
4		*pre-, dis-, -able, -er, -ar, -or*
5		*fore-, trans-, -ing, -en*
6		*under-, after-, -some, -ment*
7	Closed Syllables	CVC Syllable Pattern
8	Open and Closed Syllables	CVC and CV Syllable Patterns
9	Closed, Open, and VCe Syllables	CVC, CV, and VCe Syllable Patterns
10	*r*-Controlled Syllables	*(ar, or, or, ir, ur)*
11	Vowel Team Syllables	(e.g., *ai, ea, ou, oy*)
12	Consonant–*le* Syllable	
13	*-ed* and *-ing*	
14	Changing *y* to *i* or No Change	
15	Combinations of Syllable Types in Multisyllabic Words	
16	Accent and the Schwa Sound	
17	Accent in Two- and Three-Syllable Words	
18	Accent in Two- and Three-Syllable Words	

FIGURE 5.15. Scope and sequence for one series of multisyllabic decoding lessons.

require a commercial (or published) program provided outside of regular classroom instruction (Kamil et al., 2008). In many cases, a Tier 3 program will be comprehensive (incorporating more than just word recognition). In the area of word recognition specifically, the program is likely to be significantly more controlled and rules driven than our Tier 2 lessons. Researchers continue to demonstrate that various interventions that target word recognition, or word study, for older struggling readers or for older readers with special education classifications can yield gains (Scammacca et al., 2007).

We stop short of recommending commercial programs because we lack sufficient empirical evidence to recommend one over the other. In addition, as researchers turn attention to the needs of young adolescent students within an RTI framework, improvements in the efficacy of interventions will likely be realized. When we look for evidence about the effectiveness of interventions, we turn to two Internet sources that are currently updated frequently: (1) the Institute of Education Sciences' *What Works Clearinghouse* (*www.ies.ed.gov/ncee/wwc*) and (2) the *Center on Instruction* (*www.centeroninstruction. org*). When you search for evidence on the efficacy of intensive interventions for word recognition for upper elementary students, consider searching both in the early primary (K–3) section and in the adolescent (4–12) section.

Chapter 6

Building Fluency

In this chapter, we describe fluency development for students in fourth and fifth grades and then define fluency instruction for Tier 1 and Tier 2 instructional time. On the basis of the planning template we will continue to use, all fourth and fifth graders will be able to observe fluent reading and be given opportunities to build their own fluency through wide and repeated reading. Those who need additional fluency building will get it as part of their work during Tier 2 time.

Fluency refers to the ability of a reader to read with appropriate rate, accuracy, and prosody, with "appropriate" referencing the reader's age as well as the complexity of the text. A first grader is expected to read one word per second, and the text he or she will process will be relatively short, with simple sentences and content. For fourth and fifth graders, the demands of the text are much different. Students at that age and grade read longer texts with complex sentence structures and more nuanced meanings. It is essential for those students who are still developing fluency to be able to listen to fluent reading of these complex texts and to be given opportunities to practice fluent reading during reading instruction.

Building fluency as a regular part of reading instruction requires a systematic plan for how to use time and resources. To accomplish this, we propose a variety of organizational structures. In the sections that follow, we show how to provide a healthy fluency diet within Tier 1 and Tier 2 instruction. In addition, we provide management suggestions. For students who require even more support, we describe fluency-building curriculum resources for Tier 3.

FOUNDATIONAL KNOWLEDGE ABOUT FLUENCY DEVELOPMENT

Why is fluency so important? The answer is that readers find it difficult to attend to more than one challenging task at the same time. A student who is able to process text with appropriate rate, accuracy, and intonation will be able to allot cognitive energy to meaning making instead of tediously working to decode words. That student's attention will shift from the word level to a more global understanding of text and its features. In this way, fluency is a stepping stone to reading comprehension—the act of extracting and constructing meaning (RAND Reading Study Group, 2002). This act requires cognitive energy, which if allotted to lower level decoding cannot be used for meaning making (Laberge & Samuels, 1974).

Almost all students reading at fourth- and fifth-grade levels will have developed their accuracy and rate; however, prosody, the meaningful chunking of phrases, is a component of fluency that needs further development during this time. Students in fourth and fifth grades reading below grade level may still need to develop their accuracy and rate; they need to be supported with additional instruction at the word level (see Chapter 5). However, text-level fluency is what fuels comprehension, and for this to develop, students need support to read with the type of expression that will enable their meaning-making processes. Oral reading fluency can have a significant effect on comprehension and may be an indicator of overall reading competence (Fuchs, Fuchs, Hosp, & Jenkins, 2001).

Fluency is a composite of reading rate, accuracy, and prosody, and these components are related to one another (see Figure 6.1). For older readers, fluency also requires endurance (Deeney, 2010).

Reading accuracy and *automaticity* refer to readers' ability to recognize or decode a sufficient number of words within a given time. Automaticity is captured through measures of reading rate, or time needed to read, usually reported in words correct per minute (WCPM). For example, if a student reads 90 words within 1 minute and makes 13 mistakes, you will subtract the number of total mistakes and report 77 WCPM. The WCPM goals increase with the reader's grade level. There are specific goals for reading rate at each grade level, and these are derived from research studies. The goals for each grade level are presented in Figure 6.2. As you examine these, note that the text read at each successive benchmark is more difficult than the previous one.

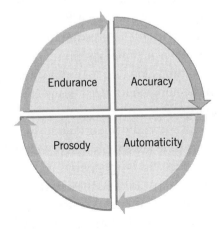

FIGURE 6.1. Components of fluency.

Grade	Fall	Winter	Spring
1	—	—	60 WCPM
2	53	78	94
3	79	93	114
4	99	112	118
5	105	118	128
6	115	132	145
7	147	158	167
8	156	167	171

FIGURE 6.2. WCPM goals by grade. Adapted from Rasinski (2003). Copyright 2003 by Scholastic. Adapted by permission.

Reading accuracy is related to automaticity, but specifically targets readers' ability to pronounce a word correctly within a given context. For example, a student reading the word *record* might say reorder—an obvious error—but might also read with the emphasis or stress on the wrong syllable. *Record* can be a verb ("I need to record the show so that I can watch it later") or a noun ("I keep a record of my choice reading"). Either reading a word incorrectly or reading it without the correct pronunciation for the context constitutes an error in accuracy. Students who read inaccurately will obviously have fewer words *correct* per minute. Note that when we compute WCPM we are combining accuracy and automaticity in a single number.

Prosody is a term borrowed from the study of poetry and refers to readers' expression and ability to read phrases in chunks that represent their meaning. Labored, word-by-word reading or inaccurate phrasing can pose obstacles to comprehension. Prosodic reading sounds like natural speech; readers attend to meaning and conventional punctuation markers in the text, and their voices are unforced. On the basis of a study conducted in 2002, the National Assessment for Educational Progress has developed guidelines for measuring prosody (see Figure 6.3). It is interesting to note that guidelines were developed with fourth-grade students. A nationally representative subsample of 1,779 fourth graders was recorded while reading aloud a fourth-grade passage. Approximately 40% of the students were placed in the nonfluent range because they lacked the expression that could assist meaning making.

Reading endurance may be especially important during the upper elementary years. Texts that students read at this time are simply longer, requiring more time on task and also more thinking; they are likely to be peppered with new words, new uses of old words, and entirely new concepts. In addition, these texts include longer sentences, with more embedded clauses. Reading them fluently, then, requires the willingness and the ability to stick with it, even though it will be difficult at times.

An additional scale for the evaluation of fluent reading was presented by Zutell and Rasinski (1991). The authors provided a rating scale for oral reading fluency in three

Fluent	Level 4	Reads primarily in larger, meaningful phrase groups. Although some regressions, repetitions, and deviations from text may be present, these do not appear to detract from the overall structure of the story. Preservation of the author's syntax is consistent. Some or most of the story is read with expressive interpretation.
	Level 3	Reads primarily in three- or four-word phrase groups. Some small groupings may be present. However, the majority of phrasing seems appropriate and preserves the syntax of the author. Little or no expressive interpretation is present.
Nonfluent	Level 2	Reads primarily in two-word phrases with some three- or four-word groupings. Some word-by-word reading may be present. Word groupings may seem awkward and unrelated to larger context of sentence or passage.
	Level 1	Reads primarily word-by-word. Occasional two-word or three-word phrases may occur—but these are infrequent and/or they do not preserve meaningful syntax.

FIGURE 6.3. NAEP Oral Reading Fluency Scale. From U.S. Department of Education, Institute of Education Sciences, National Center for Education Statistics, National Assessment of Educational Progress (NAEP), 2002 Oral Reading Study (*nces.ed.gov/nationsreportcard/studies/ors/scale.asp*).

dimensions: phrasing, smoothness, and pace. Figure 6.4 provides the components in each section.

Your fluency instruction must be influenced by the goals set by the department of education in your state. Although each state has developed standards to guide instruction, they are all influenced by similar sources. The Common Core Standards that are currently being considered provide a source that cuts across state lines. The Common Core Standards for English language arts and literacy in history/social studies and science suggests that fluency development should begin at the kindergarten level. Goals for each grade level build on the previous ones. In the case of fluency, early attention to sound-level fluency yields to word-level fluency and then to fluency at the text level. That progression for fluency development is represented in Figure 6.5.

It makes sense to review the Common Core Standards beginning at grade 3 to better understand what is expected in the upper elementary grades. Figure 6.6 summarizes the Common Core Standards suggestions in the area of fluency.

By the end of grade 3, students achieving grade-level standards should be able to read text fluently and expressively. They can allocate their attention to identifying the genre and the appropriate purpose for processing a specific text. Context can be used to confirm the accurate decoding of words, to select among multiple meanings of words, and to understand sentences, but it will not be used to guess words. This constellation of skills allows readers to apply skills and strategies that will assist in the meaning-making process. Specifically, these skills will help the reader detect when meaning breaks down and to self-correct by using fix-up strategies such as rereading.

On the basis of the standards in grades 4 and 5, students who have achieved fluency should work with informational text and with general literature independently. Gradually, the goal is for students to become comfortable with a variety of text structures and for their reading to be done not for practice but rather for gaining new understandings.

	Use the following scales to rate reader fluency on the three dimensions of phrasing, smoothness, and pace.
	A. Phrasing
1.	Monotonic with little sense of phrase boundaries, frequent word-by-word reading.
2.	Frequent two- and three-word phrases giving the impression of choppy reading; improper stress and intonation that fails to mark ends of sentences and clauses.
3.	Mixture of run-ons, mid-sentence pauses for breath, and possibly some choppiness; reasonable stress/intonation.
4.	Generally, well-phrased, mostly in clause and sentence units, with adequate attention to expression.
	B. Smoothness
1.	Frequent extended pauses, hesitations, false starts, sound-outs, repetitions, and/or multiple attempts.
2.	Several "rough spots" in text where extended pauses, hesitations, etc. are more frequent and disruptive.
3.	Occasional breaks in smoothness caused by difficulties with specific words and/or structures.
4.	Generally smooth reading with some breaks, but word and structure difficulties are resolved quickly, usually through self-correction.
	C. Pace (during sections of minimal disruption)
1.	Slow and laborious.
2.	Moderately slow.
3.	Uneven mixture of fast and slow reading.
4.	Consistently conversational.

FIGURE 6.4. Multidimensional Fluency Scale. Based on Zutell and Rasinski (1991).

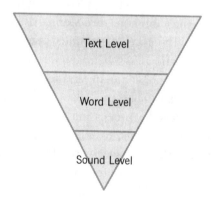

FIGURE 6.5. The development of fluency over time.

General Goal	Evidence
Grade 3	
The students achieve accuracy and fluency.	Read on-level text with purpose and understanding. Read on-level text orally with accuracy, appropriate rate, and expression.
The students develop fluent reading to support comprehension.	Use context to aid word recognition and comprehension by self-correcting when necessary. Apply additional strategies such as rereading to confirm word recognition and comprehension.
Grade 4	
The students achieve proficient reading.	Independent, proficient, and fluent reading of on-level informational text.
Grade 5	
The students achieve proficient reading.	Independent, proficient, and fluent reading of on-level literature.
The students are reading challenging texts with support.	Read with scaffolding texts designed for grades 6–8.

FIGURE 6.6. Fluency Standards from the Common Core.

In short, as students advance to the upper elementary grades, text demands increase *and* students are required to read more independently. The emphasis on informational texts will mean that content and structure are less familiar. The standards identify a goal that students are able to read both informational and narrative texts with accuracy, prosody, and comprehension; what they don't tell us is how to plan instruction that will yield that level of reading competence.

The reality is that students in the upper elementary grades must learn to process texts that are linguistically more challenging and less connected with their everyday experiences. Their fluency must become broader and more flexible. For students who do not continue to build fluency during this time, comprehension will surely not improve (Jacobs, Baldwin, & Chall, 1990).

Selecting books for fluency development and instruction need not be a challenging or time-consuming task. As you build your own skills and resources for book selection, connect yourself with those whose business is books: your school library media specialist and the librarians at your local public library, for example. They will have insights about what students are choosing to read, and you can leverage that interest. You also have to consider the level of difficulty that individual books pose for readers. The Lexile Framework for Reading: Matching Readers with Texts website (*www.lexile.com*) provides access to a quantitative system for leveling books. For example, a text on the site will be described with a number followed by the letter *L*. The number that is generated for a book is an indicator of the text's difficulty. Text difficulty is calculated based on sentence length and word frequency. For example, the book *The Watsons Go to Birmingham—1963*, by

Christopher Paul Curtis, has a Lexile of 1000. Based on the Lexile map for translating Lexile scores into grade-level approximations (also available on the site), this would be a text appropriate for many seventh-grade readers. Remember, though, that the system cannot evaluate text content. A book may be within the appropriate range of difficulty, but its content may not be appropriate for your students. Therefore, we urge you to read the books prior to making your choices.

The Lexile website can also generate book lists based on a Lexile range you provide. This method can assist you in selecting books for your classroom library and for your small-group instruction. Remember that students who are building fluency and improving their rate, accuracy, and prosody should be provided with many opportunities to read and reread different texts. This fluency practice has the potential to improve their comprehension because they will be processing text as it was intended. Reading with appropriate intonation and phrasing supports the extraction and construction of meaning, which is our ultimate reading goal. In the next sections, we discuss how you can support reading fluency during Tier 1 and Tier 2 instruction.

TIER 1 INSTRUCTION IN FLUENCY

Tier 1 instruction in fluency will be provided to all of the students in your classroom. During Tier 1 instruction you will work in all areas of reading: word recognition, fluency, vocabulary, and comprehension. Fluency instruction will focus on the four components of fluency: rate, accuracy, prosody, and endurance. In this section, we describe the content, instructional strategies, and instructional planning required to support fluency.

Content

It may be odd to think about the content of fluency instruction. The content, actually, is the increasingly complex texts that students read accurately, automatically, and with appropriate phrasing and endurance. Because the texts that students must read in the upper elementary grades include both narratives and a wide variety of informational text structures, your Tier 1 instruction must include modeling of fluent reading in these genres as well as ample opportunities for student practice, both with your support and independently. The *Guidelines for Reviewing a Reading Program* (Florida Center for Reading Research, 2007) target daily practice in reading fluency with the inclusion of reading strategies that encourage the students to reread when comprehension demands it. Further, they suggest that students be exposed to both narrative and expository texts and be prompted to reread after error corrections, a procedure that supports their text-level fluency. Besides opportunities for student rereading, the guidelines also target teacher modeling of fluent reading. The content of fluency instruction for upper elementary students will be addressed through modeling of appropriate phrasing, rate, and accuracy during diverse daily read-alouds and during shared reading of grade-level texts as well as through wide independent reading.

Instructional Strategies

We cannot overemphasize our commitment to a daily read-aloud, which will allow students to hear fluent reading every day. When you read with intonation and process sentences with challenging syntactic structures, you are modeling fluent reading. You will chunk phrases in a way that attends to the author's intended meaning, you will read by changing your pitch based on different conventions and clauses, and you will adjust your speed based on the content and the navigational cues provided by the punctuation. In addition, you will apply word recognition strategies when you read unfamiliar multisyllabic words and model rereading procedures when necessary instead of "zooming" through words and phrases. The incorporation of read-alouds into your instruction is essential for providing a model of "good" reading to your students, who may still need support in fluency (Allington, 1983).

For example, consider reading aloud the following selection from *A History of Western Art*, by Antony Mason:

> The Mycenaeans are named after the ancient city of Mycenae, but there were a number of other similar cities on the Greek mainland, such as Athens, Tiryns, Pylos, and Thebes. Their warlike nature is reflected in the massive stone fortifications that they built to protect their palaces. Their art is similar to that of the Minoans, but is rather stiffer and more formal, and tends to focus on more aggressive themes, such as warriors and hunting. (p. 15)

This excerpt from an information text contains multisyllabic words that may be unfamiliar, longer sentences, and challenging syntax. This is the type of text that your students will be expected to read independently as they progress through the middle grades. By reading aloud, you can model syllable division strategies for any words that stump you, rereading for expression at the sentence level and eventually demonstrating appropriate intonation and phrasing. In fact, if you read aloud from a text like this and stumble on words or phrasing, you will be able to talk to your students about this, showing them that all readers actually make word recognition and fluency errors and reread to fix them. Also, reading aloud will allow you to think aloud and model the use of comprehension strategies, a reading goal we examine in Chapter 8.

Read-alouds, although important, are not enough. Fluency develops through reading practice. Repeated oral readings can build students' reading fluency. In our previous work, we have presented instructional strategies for repeated oral reading strategies on a continuum from most to least teacher support (Walpole & McKenna, 2009). That concept can still be applied with upper elementary students. Figure 6.7 presents three modes of student oral reading, presented from most to least supportive, that can provide foundational structures for building fluency.

What you do not see here is round robin oral reading, a system of oral reading with students taking turns reading aloud. Although it may be a method that you have relied upon for managing your group and covering your content, we do not recommend this practice. Round robin reading may give the illusion that it supports students' fluency, but there is no evidence to suggest that it in fact does (Ash, Kuhn, & Walpole, 2009). Stud-

	Strategy	Teacher's Role	Students' Role
More to Less Support	Choral reading	The teacher leads an oral reading, in unison, supporting both word recognition and phrasing.	The students follow the teacher's lead, matching their voices to the teacher's voice as closely as possible.
	Partner reading	The teacher pairs students to read together and monitors and supports the work of the pairs, providing assistance if needed.	Students take turns reading aloud, with the silent partner following in the text and providing prompts if words are miscalled.
	Whisper reading	The teacher sets a purpose to reread to build fluency and comprehension.	Each student reads the text aloud in a quiet voice, such that only the student can hear the reading. All students in the class are reading at the same time, but at individual rates.

FIGURE 6.7. Strategies for repeated oral reading fluency.

ies examining the effects of round robin reading found that it did not have any effects on students' fluency, vocabulary, or comprehension. It has also been found to be less effective than shared reading as a means of increasing accuracy (Eldredge, Reutzel, & Hollingsworth, 1996). Round robin reading may also increase anxiety among students with weak oral reading fluency and direct their attention to reading ahead in order to practice silently so that they will not be embarrassed when their turn comes. It can lead to boredom for students with strong oral reading fluency who must listen to weaker readers. Therefore, whether it is called popcorn reading, popsicle reading, or combat reading, round robin reading is not a method you should use. Round robin reading can be replaced with choral reading, partner reading, and whisper reading procedures. In all cases, these alternative procedures increase the amount of text that all students read. For example, in a class of 20 participating in round robin reading, each child would receive 5% of the time allotted for oral reading. Compare that with partner reading, during which each child would practice for 50% of the same allotted time. The teachers with whom we work find these data impressive, and they have successfully integrated these procedures while maintaining well-managed classrooms.

We suggest two different structures you may use to coordinate your instructional strategies for fluency building during Tier 1 instruction. Either one will facilitate supported repeated reading of your core selection. The first is a structured shared reading of the basal text, systematically incorporating choral, paired, and whisper reading. You will see that this shared reading structure fits easily into our Tier 1 planning template, but that is surely not the only way for you to organize your time. The second one is a paired reading protocol called Peer-Assisted Learning Strategies (PALS). The criteria for selecting a structure can be based on the texts you will use as well as management decisions you will make. We describe the two formats next.

Core reading programs usually provide many suggestions for instruction and activities within an instructional day. However, it may not be clear how to choose what to do

Time	Activity	Description
5 min	Strategy Introduction	
15 min	Interactive Read-Aloud	The teacher chooses an interesting and challenging piece of authentic literature, either narrative or information text, and reads it aloud, modeling fluent oral reading.
3 min	Introduce Written Response	
10 min	Vocabulary	The teacher introduces core vocabulary for the week, introducing meanings, thinking aloud about the spellings, and listing derivatives.
12 min	Choral Reading of the Story	Students and teacher read the selection together. The teacher stops when needed to monitor and develop comprehension. If the story is long, this same procedure is used again the next day—with the rest of the story.

FIGURE 6.8. Tier 1 fluency initial planning.

or how to manage and divide time to maximize learning for upper elementary students. We suggest that, instead of wrestling with time to include all the suggested activities, you follow a repetitive format with a structured model for your daily instruction. Figure 6.8 presents our evolving lesson template, adding the fluency components to the word recognition work we introduced in Chapter 5.

We assume that most core reading programs have one major selection each week. In our model, the teacher and students first read that selection in a choral reading format. The teacher reads at a reasonable rate for the students' age, and the students read along and follow the teacher's voice. This is an opportunity for the teacher to model and support intonation and appropriate reading rate while appropriately chunking words and phrases to represent the meaning they are meant to have within the context. This choral reading format is used until the teacher has read the entire selection once. Depending on the length of the selection, this may require more than 1 day. You will see that in Tier 1 instruction of 45 minutes we have allocated 12 minutes for this. If you want to understand how long and how far in the selection 12 minutes of choral reading can get you, simply read aloud from a core selection and check.

After the completion of the initial choral reading (perhaps Wednesday, Thursday, and Friday of the week), the students reread in partners and then independently. Figure 6.9 presents this slightly altered template. The reasons for this rereading should be made clear to the students. You can explain that rereading supports fluency (accuracy, rate, and prosody) and also builds comprehension. You can also provide a comprehension or response-oriented purpose. For example, with a narrative, you can ask students to reread to consider the actions and feelings of a particular character or to examine the role that direct dialogue plays in the selection. You can ask them to visualize the events or to think about how the text is similar to one that you have previously read. In an information text, you can ask students to focus on finding the main idea or on a cycle or sequence of events.

Time	Activity	Description
2 min	Strategy Introduction	
10 min	Interactive Read-Aloud	The teacher chooses an interesting and challenging piece of authentic literature, either narrative or information text, and reads it aloud, modeling fluent oral reading.
10 min	Vocabulary Review	The teacher reviews core vocabulary for the week, including meanings, spellings, and derivatives.
10 min	Partner Reading	Students reread with a partner and purpose—to improve their expression and their understanding.
10 min	Whisper Reading	Students reread independently for fluency and to complete a purposeful task.
3 min	Introduce Written Response	

FIGURE 6.9. Tier 1 fluency additional planning.

You can ask them to consider questions that they would have for the author. You can ask them to consider the role that the headings play in signaling the content of the text. The possibilities are virtually endless, but the important thing is to set a new purpose with each successive reading.

Another format you may use is drawn from the PALS. This model comes from research by Douglas and Lynn Fuchs and their colleagues (Calhoon, 2005; Fuchs, Fuchs, Mathes, & Simmons, 1997; Simmons, Fuchs, Fuchs, Hodge, & Mathes, 1994). PALS has been shown to support the fluency and comprehension of students at different grade levels and with different levels of skills (McMaster, Fuchs, & Fuchs, 2006). PALS allows the students to work with partners to practice fluency and comprehension during the reading of connected text. The students are paired based on ability, with higher performing students working with lower performing ones. The pairs are assigned by rank-ordering the students based on reading ability (either fluency or comprehension scores) and then splitting the groups in half. Figure 6.10 presents this system. The class depicted has 20 students. The first column represents the top 10 readers in the class and the second column the second half of readers, numbered 11 through number 20 based on skill. Rows represent pairs. The top reader is paired with the reader with the 11th best performance. Therefore, within each pair there is always a higher performing student, but the distance between their performances is controlled. This allows the stronger readers (e.g., Reader A) to model for the weaker readers (e.g., Reader B) as they alternate in reading aloud and discussing the text.

During their reading, the students work on both fluency and comprehension. Figure 6.11 presents the activities that students engage in during PALS. Note that the times are specific and come from the researchers' design. PALS takes 32 minutes, and researchers recommend that it be used every other day.

Reader A	Reader B
1	11
2	12
3	13
4	14
5	15
6	16
7	17
8	18
9	19
10	20

FIGURE 6.10. Planning pairs for PALS.

PALS requires the teacher to teach students their roles and procedures for repeated reading, paragraph shrinking, and prediction relay and to keep time. The students use cue cards to remind them of the steps in each segment of the lesson. In addition, once the procedures are in place, the teacher motivates students by providing points for on-task behavior, for cooperation, and for catching mistakes on score cards. These points can then be exchanged for rewards. We describe each of the PALS procedures in more depth next.

During partner reading, Partner A (the stronger reader) reads aloud for 5 minutes while Partner B plays the role of coach. Then the students switch roles, with Partner B rereading the text that Partner A has modeled, while Partner A takes on the role of coach. Figure 6.12 shows the two mistakes the coach will look for (careless mistakes and hard

Time	Activity	Description
10 min	Partner Reading	The higher performing student (Partner A) reads first for 5 minutes to model for the lower performing student; then the lower performing student rereads that same section of text for the remaining 5 minutes.
2 min	Retelling	Students take turns reviewing what they have read in partner reading. They can use sentence frames and look back in the book: The first thing that happened was … The next thing that happened was. …
10 min	Paragraph Shrinking	The students alternate reading one paragraph and retelling its content in 10 words or less.
10 min	Prediction Relay	The students alternate making a prediction about upcoming content, read half a page, decide whether their prediction was correct, and then use the paragraph-shrinking procedure.

FIGURE 6.11. Template for PALS instruction.

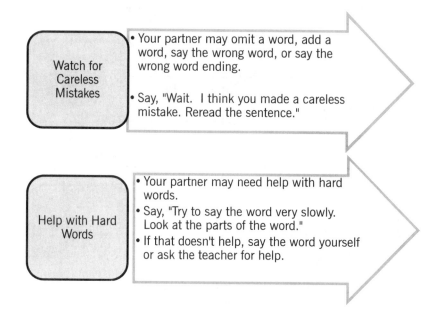

FIGURE 6.12. Cue card for partner reading.

words) and the language the coach should use to help; the figure can be used as a cue card. In all cases, if neither student can identify a word, they should ask for the teacher's support. If students have their hands raised for assistance too often, you know that the text is too challenging, and you could switch to choral reading.

After 10 minutes of partner reading, the pairs engage in 2 minutes of retelling. The purpose of retelling is to support comprehension. Partner A begins by retelling the first event, and then Partner B retells the second. The partners alternate retelling another event or fact until time is called. The questions used to prompt the retelling are meant to keep the partners involved and to support them in sequential recall. Figure 6.13 provides the types of questions asked during retelling.

The next segment of PALS, paragraph shrinking, requires reading additional text, paragraph by paragraph, and identifying the main idea. Again, students take turns as

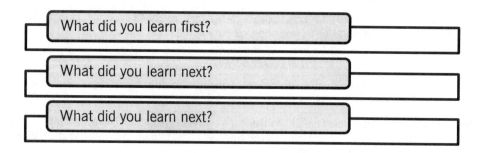

FIGURE 6.13. Cue card for retelling.

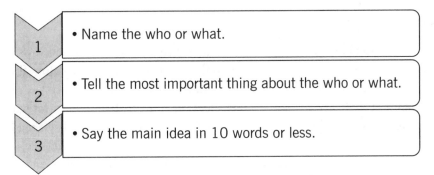

FIGURE 6.14. Cue card for paragraph shrinking.

reader and coach. The coach in this process can monitor the partner's performance and provide feedback. Figure 6.14 presents the three-part procedure. Once the reader has answered the questions and has generated a main idea, the coach counts words in that main idea. If the main idea exceeds 10 words, the coach guides the partner to shrink the main idea.

The next section of the intervention combines prediction with paragraph shrinking, and the procedures are represented in Figure 6.15. The prediction students make is an immediate one: what they think will happen in the next half page. After the students complete the reading of that next section, they check whether their prediction was correct or not and then summarize the information using the paragraph-shrinking procedure again. In all instances the students are both accountable for the task. To learn more about PALS, visit the researchers' website (*www.kc.vanderbilt.edu/pals*).

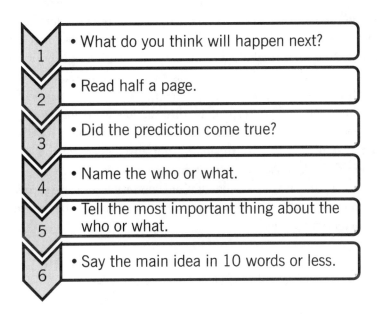

FIGURE 6.15. Cue card for prediction relay.

Instructional Planning

A daily read-aloud and either structured shared reading or use of the PALS procedure within Tier 1 instruction have the potential to support students' reading fluency. Once you have established your classroom procedures, neither one of these systems requires much planning at all, at least not beyond selection of the instructional strategies. The only real planning required for Tier 1 fluency work will be selecting books to read aloud.

For your read-alouds, try to select books that will motivate and engage the students. The texts do not need to be narratives; you can use information texts and model fluent reading and meaning-making strategies. The texts can be connected with the theme of your weekly selection or with your instruction in science and social studies. It would make sense after devoting time on a topic in these content areas to read aloud a book with the same theme. Each grade-level team can choose a different set of engaging read-alouds. We encourage you to consider award-winning books. The Association for Library Service to Children (*www.ala.org/ala/mgrps/divs/alsc/index.cfm*) has classified lists of books by award. This is one resource you may want to consult prior to purchasing books or borrowing them from the library.

The Lexile website (*www.lexile.com*) can also assist you in selecting read-aloud texts in different genres as well as books for use in PALS, if you do not use your core selection. From our experience, teachers are often reluctant to select challenging read-alouds because they think they will be too difficult for their students. However, you need to consider that the read-aloud books are books that the students are not reading on their own. They are exposed to them through your scaffolding and modeling. Therefore, if you are teaching fourth grade, the Lexile range of the books the students would read themselves would be from 645L to 780L. In your read-alouds, though, you should feel free to exceed that range and read books above 780L, since you will be the one reading the longer sentences and rarer words. As long as you have a clear purpose for the book selection and a plan for its use, you should select challenging books and books with interesting and engaging content. Note that read-alouds can serve a variety of purposes. Although our focus here has been on their role in fostering fluency, we revisit read-alouds in Chapter 8 as a method of developing comprehension proficiency.

The procedures we have described in this section were for Tier 1, whole-group instruction. However, some students may need additional support with fluency. This additional support will be provided in small-group instruction during Tier 2 time. The following section describes Tier 2 instruction for students who struggle with fluency. Remember that in our stairway model fluency and comprehension are supported together. In the following section, we only address fluency, but we bring the two together in the lesson plans provided in Appendix I.

TIER 2 INSTRUCTION IN FLUENCY

Tier 2 instruction is designed for students who have poor oral reading fluency but who have achieved proficiency in decoding multisyllabic words. These students are identified by an initial oral reading fluency measure that will place them below benchmark. A cautionary note to always keep in mind is that after you identify students who have weak fluency, you must conduct a further diagnostic measure such as our Informal Decoding Inventory to exclude decoding as the root cause of the fluency problem. It would add to students' frustration if they are in need of word recognition instruction and you support them only in fluency. In the following section, we examine the content, instructional strategies, and planning for Tier 2 small-group instruction to build fluency.

Content

Upper elementary students who need additional support with fluency are able to read multisyllabic words and apply syllabification strategies. They may be accurate in reading words in isolation, but their performance changes when they read from texts. They process text in a manner that may be awkward, without giving words and phrases the intonation and timing they require to reveal the author's intended meaning. In addition, they may not be aware of the different ways that fluent readers read different genres. For example, when good readers read poetry or stories or nonfiction, their prosodic attention to the text differs; they also read at different rates. Students who need support in fluency need additional practice as well as exposure and opportunities to process different genres. The content for students in Tier 2 fluency building is the very same content that was targeted in Tier 1: fluent processing of a very wide range of sentence structures within texts. The difference between Tier 1 and Tier 2 fluency work is only in volume; these students will, in effect, have a double dose of fluency building until they have met their goals. We suggest that you choose an *additional* text to increase the number of words and sentences that students process successfully. In this way, they will do fluency work with their grade-level core selection *and* with a text that you have chosen for Tier 2 every day.

Instructional Strategies

Fluency instruction is very easy to manage. In small-group instruction, we use the same instructional strategies: choral reading followed by partner reading and whisper reading. The teachers' reading and text processing become the blueprint for students' intonation and expression. This time, though, the group will be smaller and the teacher can attend more directly to the students. In addition, the teacher may choose to alternate attention between fluency and comprehension every other day. That is, the teacher may have students reading and rereading one day and then engaging in a comprehension discussion the next.

In the interest of time, students will only read chorally with the teacher. When they reread in partners or whisper read by themselves, it doesn't make sense for them to be sitting with the teacher. Rather, they can do this back at their desks while the teacher works with another group. A small-group fluency session is simple and targeted. You can start by asking:

"Who can remind me us of what we learned in the last chapter? We will read the third chapter of our book together today. I want you to hear your voices while I read with you. Keep your eyes on the page and pay attention to the punctuation marks the author provided to guide our reading."

After a very brief comment on the content of that new chapter, you can end your small-group session for the day. To initiate partner and whisper reading practice, you can say:

"Now that we've seen this chapter once, I want you to reread it with your partner. You should take turns while reading. Remember to follow along with your partner and correct him or her when needed. When you are the reader, you can also ask for your partner's help. When you finish the partner reading, read the section independently in a whisper voice. Remember that rereading can improve your expression, and it will help you to prepare for our discussion during small-group time tomorrow."

Because fourth- and fifth-grade students are capable of independent work and are likely to crave peer interactions, it makes good sense to structure some of their group work to occur after they meet with the teacher. Both partner and whisper reading strategies require virtually no teacher support, so they may be done independently while the teacher is working with another group, addressing the needs of other students. After students complete their rereadings outside of the teacher-led group, they are better able to engage in a meaningful discussion with the support of the teacher. This second meeting brings into focus the importance of the students' independent work and their purpose for rereading both to build fluency and to comprehend the selection.

We have always favored the use of new texts or text segments every day in fluency-building programs, but we are taking a different stance as students reach the upper elementary grades. If you reserve 15 minutes to work with your group, you will be able to complete a choral reading of a substantial new segment of your text and also provide a very brief comment on the text. Students may then reread with a partner and whisper read independently outside of your group for the purpose of improving their prosody and deepening their comprehension. You can leverage that deepened comprehension the next day, when you turn your attention to vocabulary and comprehension, and we provide models for doing that in the chapters that follow.

Because this plan is different from our plans for younger students, we would like to explain our thinking. Although we have always planned for both fluency and comprehension within a brief Tier 2 daily lesson in our K–3 instructional model, we don't think that that will work well in the upper elementary grades. You will find that many texts at those levels (especially interesting ones!) have such complex structures and content that their explanation simply requires more time. That is why we encourage you to alternate between work with fluency and work with comprehension. Figure 6.16 presents the structure for the fluency practice portion of this 2-day lesson. The first reading of the text will allow the students to develop prosody and overall fluency; in addition, they will view the content of the text as a whole and have a representation of the text's overall structure.

Days	Format	Activity	Teacher's role	Student's role
Day 1	With Teacher	Choral reading	Teacher reads the text with intonation and expression, modeling text processing	Students follow the teacher's lead
Day 1	Outside of the Group	Partner reading		Students reread the text with a partner, monitoring and supporting one another's reading
Day 1	Outside of the Group	Whisper reading		Students reread same text segment independently
Day 2	With Teacher	Engage in comprehension discussion	Teacher explains text structure or addresses a comprehension skill/strategy (see Chapter 8)	Students and teacher apply this strategy with teacher support
Day 2	Outside of the Group	Whisper reading		Students reread same text segment independently

FIGURE 6.16. Template for fluency practice.

When they reread the text immediately, with partners and then independently, you will have gradually released responsibility to them to read on their own. Also, this concentrated attention to fluency building will guarantee that those students whose weak fluency was the result of a lack of reading practice will get the practice they need.

Instructional Planning

For upper elementary students who need to build fluency, book selection will be the only real planning task, and this is as important as the delivery of your instruction. We suggest you select high-quality, authentic books for your work with these students. Remember that these texts must be engaging enough *to the students* that they will participate in repeated readings. They also must be difficult enough that fluency builds through repetition but accessible enough that the students are not frustrated. The Lexile website can support you in making this choice with books on, above, and below grade level for different genres, but book selection is never an exact science.

For fourth- and fifth-grade students in the word recognition and fluency group, we suggest that you select books that will be lower than the grade-level Lexile range. These students are not only practicing fluency but are also learning syllabification practices. A book at their grade level may be too frustrating because of the number of longer words and sentences. For students in the fluency and comprehension group, you may select text that will be on grade level. These students will be supported initially through choral reading and subsequently through their own repeated readings. Remember, though, that the only real test of the fit between your readers and the texts you select is to try them. If you have made a poor choice, simply replace the text with a different one. Figure 6.17 provides Lexile ranges to guide your thinking.

	For Word Recognition and Fluency Groups	For Fluency and Comprehension Groups	For Independent Reading in a Classroom Library
Grade 4	600L–725L	645L–780L	450L–900L
Grade 5	645L–780L	730L–845L	600L–1000L

FIGURE 6.17. Lexile ranges for different purposes.

We share model lessons in Appendices H and I, bringing together fluency and comprehension work from Chapter 8 or fluency and word recognition work from Chapter 5. In this chapter, we have described fluency development and instruction and presented models you can use for Tier 1 and Tier 2 instruction. In the next two chapters, we complete our Tier 1 templates to include instructional strategies for comprehension and vocabulary to support upper elementary students. We acknowledge, however, that this combination of Tier 1 and Tier 2 instruction will not be enough for a small number of students whose word recognition and fluency achievement are much farther from grade level. For those students, you will need to find Tier 3 solutions.

CHOOSING TIER 3 PROGRAMS FOR FLUENCY

Even if you provide strong and explicit Tier 1 and Tier 2 instruction, there will be students who will continue to struggle with fluency. In that case, you should first examine whether fluency problems are a reflection of difficulties with lower level skills involving word recognition. We remind you that students will not show improvement if misplaced in a group that cannot support their needs. However, if students are correctly placed in the fluency and comprehension group and make no progress in fluency and comprehension, they will need to receive intensive support outside your classroom by specialized personnel who can address their needs.

As in Chapter 5, we do not provide a list of commercial programs for Tier 3 instruction. Recommendations for interventions for students in the upper elementary grades can be found at the Center on Instruction website (*www.centeroninstruction.org*). These resources can help you identify programs and methods that can support additional needs in fluency and comprehension.

Chapter 7

Building Vocabulary

In this chapter, we present a tiered instructional model for developing fourth- and fifth-grade students' vocabulary. To understand the model, we first present some foundational knowledge about vocabulary instruction and its importance. For Tier 1 instruction, we argue that direct instruction in the meanings of a small set of words before students read can both improve their comprehension of a specific text and lead to incremental improvements in vocabulary knowledge. We also argue that, for students who have achieved grade-level standards in word recognition and fluency, building vocabulary is a reasonable (and important) goal for their Tier 2 instruction. We provide a short list of strategies teachers can use to get started. Finally, we argue that a small number of upper elementary students, especially English language learners, may also require intensive Tier 3 vocabulary instruction.

FOUNDATIONAL KNOWLEDGE
ABOUT VOCABULARY DEVELOPMENT

Because there are so many types of vocabulary—listening, sight, and others—it is important to be clear about the focus of this chapter. Our concern is with children's knowledge of word meanings, regardless of whether they encounter those words in oral or written language. We are interested in both technical words (those that children learn in their study of a particular discipline or content area) and general words (those of broad utility that children might encounter in any text).

The great problem with vocabulary instruction is that there are so many words to teach and so little guidance for choosing them. Some linguists argue that the English language contains more words than any other language, although the true number is unknown. Some experts contend that the number of words in English the language is almost limitless because of rules that allow us to coin new words. English language users follow set rules for coining new words, thus adding greatly to the number of potential words in the language. Consider this sentence:

The mail carrier likes our street because it is dogless.

You had no difficulty determining why the mail carrier likes our street, even though the word *dogless* is not in the dictionary and you were unlikely ever to have encountered it before.

Children learn new words at different rates and in different quantities, depending on aptitude and environment. Large differences in the meaning vocabulary of children have already developed by the time they reach kindergarten. Hart and Risley (1995) estimated that the children of college professors averaged knowing about 5,000 words compared with children whose parents lacked educational and economic advantages. These children possessed vocabularies that averaged about 1,500 words.

Long-term studies allow us to project an ever-widening gap in word knowledge as children pass through school. What are schools doing to narrow this gap and to ensure that all children have the vocabulary they need to succeed in school? According to Andy Biemiller (2004), very little. "Vocabulary levels diverge greatly during the primary years," he observed, "and virtually nothing effective is done about this in schools" (p. 29). He maintains that the greatest gaps occur in the primary years and that the rate of learning is about the same for the highest and lowest achieving children thereafter. The size of vocabulary is not just an abstract statistic. It bears directly on comprehension and consequently on school success. In 1997, Cunningham and Stanovich reported that oral vocabulary at the end of first grade is a significant predictor of comprehension 10 years later. This stark finding indicates the true importance of vocabulary.

Vocabulary knowledge is central to comprehending what we read, to a degree that might surprise you. Let's consider a famous example from a research study (Beck & McKeown, 1994). The following paragraph is from a fifth-grade social studies text. Read it and see if you have any comprehension difficulties.

In 1367, Marain and the settlements ended a seven-year war with the Langurians and Pitoks. As a result of this war, Languria was driven out of East Bacol. Marain would now rule Laman and the other lands that once belonged to Languria. This brought peace to the Bacolean settlements. The settlers no longer had to worry about attacks from Laman. The Bacoleans were happy to be part of Marain in 1367. Yet a dozen years later, these same people would be fighting the Marish for independence, or freedom from United Marain's rule.

As you may have suspected, there's a trick involved. Some of the key terms have been replaced by nonsense words. Even the four digits of the date were scrambled. Now take a look at the original text.

In 1763, Britain and the colonies ended a seven-year war with the French and Indians. As a result of this war, France was driven out of North America. Britain would now rule Canada and the other lands that once belonged to France. This brought peace to the American colonies. The settlers no longer had to worry about attacks from Canada. The Americans were happy to be part of Britain in 1763. Yet a dozen years later, these same people would be fighting the British for independence, or freedom from Great Britain's rule.

No doubt you found this version a little easier. However, the participants in the study were not teachers. They were fifth graders. Surprisingly, the students found both versions equally difficult! This little experiment illustrates how powerful an effect that preteaching important words can have on the comprehension of children with limited prior knowledge.

How do we go about bridging this gap so that students leave the upper elementary grades for middle school with the vocabularies they need to succeed? One way is to teach as many words as possible. Although we strongly endorse this practice and offer suggestions for doing so in this chapter, there are simply too many important words to teach them all explicitly. We must also provide opportunities for children to acquire new word meanings through wide reading. Researchers have documented the fact that word meanings are acquired incidentally, even through just one exposure (Swanborn & de Glopper, 1999). These opportunities also help them deepen their understandings of familiar words. Stanovich (1986) and others have suggested that the relationship between vocabulary knowledge and reading is circular. On the one hand, knowing more words makes you a better reader. On the other hand, being a better reader enables you to read more and to develop a larger vocabulary through reading.

We can think of this relationship in terms of a circle, depicted in Figure 7.1. Having a larger vocabulary makes you a better reader, being a better reader makes it possible for you to read more, and reading more gives you a greater vocabulary. This circular relationship tends to increase the difference in vocabulary size between good and poor readers over time. On the positive side, better readers tend to read more, acquire larger vocabularies, and become even better readers. On the negative side, poorer readers tend to read less, fail to develop large vocabularies, and find reading increasingly difficult as the vocabulary demands of the texts they must read increase (Stahl & Nagy, 2005).

You might be tempted to conclude that wide reading is enough to acquire an ade-

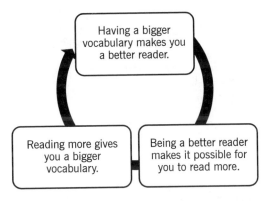

FIGURE 7.1. How reading fosters vocabulary growth and vice versa.

quate vocabulary. We obviously know thousands of words that were never formally taught to us in school. We picked up their meanings through incidental exposures. If this is the case, why bother teaching vocabulary at all? Why not provide children with opportunities to meet new words through reading and conversation? Wouldn't that be enough? Marzano (2004) points out that there are persuasive arguments on both sides. The case for wide reading alone is based on the fact that it is impossible to explicitly teach all the word meanings we need. On the other hand, context is usually too weak to allow a reader to infer word meanings, and many words occur too infrequently to learn through wide reading. However, there is no need to choose between the two approaches, he argues: "There is no obvious reason why direct vocabulary instruction and wide reading cannot work in tandem" (2004, p. 112). And in the case of technical vocabulary (science, math, and social studies terms), direct instruction is desirable.

As we begin to consider instructional approaches, it is vital to note that our knowledge of words is not all or nothing. It is better to think of our understanding of any word as a matter of degree, ranging from no knowledge to a deep appreciation. Imagine an out-of-school context in which you must attempt to learn the meaning of a new word you hear someone else use. Think back to your first encounter with the word *quidditch* in the Harry Potter series. You learned that it was a game, and that was helpful in learning the word. However, this first encounter was only a small step along the path to acquiring the full meaning of the word. In fact, you also had to learn the meanings of *snitch* and *seeker* and *quaffle*. Each encounter with a word helps us narrow a new word's meaning. As you read about the quidditch match, your understanding deepened considerably. Beck, McKeown, and Kucan (2002) suggest a continuum of word knowledge. The ideal is a thorough appreciation of a word's meaning involving "decontextualized" understanding. That is, even without a specific context, the word alone calls to mind an abundance of useful asso-

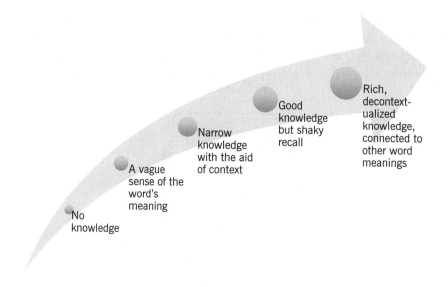

FIGURE 7.2. A continuum of word knowledge.

General Goal	Evidence
Grades 4 and 5	
The students determine word meanings.	Determine or clarify the meaning of unknown or multiple-meaning words through the use of one or more strategies, such as using semantic clues (e.g., definitions, examples, or restatements in text); using syntactic clues (e.g., the word's position or function in the sentence); analyzing the word's sounds, spelling, and meaningful parts; and consulting reference materials, both print and digital. Use a known root word as a clue to the meaning of an unknown word with the same root (e.g., *telegraph, photograph, autograph*).
The students understand word relationships.	Build real-life connections between words and their various uses and meanings. Define relationships between words (e.g., how *ask* is like and unlike *demand*; what items are likely to be *enormous*). Distinguish a word from other words with similar but not identical meanings (synonyms).
The students use words appropriately.	Use grade-appropriate general academic vocabulary and domain-specific words and phrases (in English language arts, history/social studies, and science) taught directly and acquired through reading and responding to texts.

FIGURE 7.3. Vocabulary standards from the Common Core.

ciations. In between the extremes, our knowledge of a particular word may be relatively weak or strong. Figure 7.2 demonstrates this continuum.

As children reach grades 4 and 5, they are expected to continue acquiring a broad vocabulary, both general and technical. They are expected to be able to use their word knowledge appropriately as they read and write. They are also expected to be able to determine the meanings of unfamiliar words by a number of means, such as using context, structural analysis, and reference materials. These characteristics are embodied in the Common Core Standards. Because there are almost no differences between the fourth- and fifth-grade standards, we have combined them in Figure 7.3.

We encourage you to continue building your knowledge of vocabulary instruction. The sources listed in Figure 7.4 are appropriate for individual professional reading or for group study with your colleagues.

Baumann, J. F., & Kame'enui, E. J. (Eds.). (2004). *Vocabulary instruction: Research to practice.* New York: Guilford Press.
Beck, I. L., McKeown, M. G., & Kucan, L. (2008). *Creating robust vocabulary: Frequently asked questions and extended examples.* New York: Guilford Press.
Beck, I. L., McKeown, M. G., & Kucan, L. (2002). *Bringing words to life: Robust vocabulary instruction.* New York: Guilford Press.
Blachowitz, C., & Fisher, P. J. (2009). *Teaching vocabulary in all classrooms* (4th ed.). Upper Saddle River, NJ: Pearson/Merrill/Prentice Hall.
Stahl, S. A., & Nagy, W. E. (2005). *Teaching word meanings.* Mahwah, NJ: Erlbaum.

FIGURE 7.4. Resources for vocabulary instruction.

TIER 1 INSTRUCTION IN VOCABULARY

Without a core program to narrow the scope of vocabulary instruction, teachers would have little to guide them in choosing words and selecting instructional strategies. The core is a safety net that helps ensure that vocabulary is represented in Tier 1 instruction and that its inclusion is somewhat systematic. This does not mean that teachers have no decisions to make during Tier 1 time, but understanding what the core offers is the essential first step.

Content

In sizing up the vocabulary component of your core, you might find it helpful once again to refer to the *Guidelines for Reviewing a Core Reading Program* (Florida Center for Reading Research [FCRR], 2007). Not surprisingly, these guidelines do not include a list of words that all fourth and fifth graders should know. There are simply too many words (and too many opinions) to make that possible. Instead, the guidelines specify only that "important, useful, and difficult words" be taught (p. 15), and they make clear that only a limited number can be singled out for explicit instruction. In addition, vocabulary instruction should be assessed and monitored, and it should provide for cumulative review. It should entail familiar routines that include instruction that occurs before, during, and after a reading selection. It should involve frequent read-alouds and opportunities to read independently. It should also include instruction in word analysis and the use of context to decide among multiple meanings of a word (topics we have addressed in Chapter 5). It is easy to see the overlap between the FCRR guidelines and the Common Core Standards and to see that both derive from our knowledge of how important vocabulary development is for success in the upper elementary grades.

Most core programs provide an abundance of choices concerning activities and emphases. You cannot possibly implement all of the suggestions concerning vocabulary. Instead, you must select wisely, using your knowledge of effective instructional approaches and the needs of your students. This will mean adapting the core and supplementing it with strategies you know to be important.

Instructional Strategies

Tier 1 instruction should begin with a careful examination of what the core provides. Several vocabulary strategies are likely to be found in any core program, and we discuss the most important of them here, together with suggestions for modifications.

■ *Preteach key words to improve comprehension.* At first, this idea seems self-evident. If a teacher ensures word knowledge in advance, comprehension will improve when the students actually read. It is a principle well worth stating, however, because the vocabulary demands of fourth- and fifth-grade materials are considerable. This is a challenge best met through careful preteaching. And, of course, when fourth and fifth graders are expected to read a selection independently, there is no chance to define words as they are encountered, and preteaching is more critical.

■ *Provide more than definitions.* Definitions are only a start. Some teachers fall into the trap of assuming that if a child can match a word to its definition, the word's meaning has been acquired. This reasoning hearkens back to stimulus–response behaviorist notions (and may be represented in a series of vocabulary work sheets in your core program that we believe are neither useful nor necessary for vocabulary building). You say the word, your student recites its definition. We concede that this approach works well with low-level skills, such as learning to recognize high-frequency words or letter sounds or addition facts. Even in the case of learning word meanings it may have some limited initial value, but more is needed. Consider an example from a middle grades vocabulary exercise. Mike McKenna's daughter Katy found this definition of *truncate* in her book: "to cut off." (*Truncate* really means to abbreviate in some manner, especially when using calculators and printers. A decimal fraction might be truncated on the screen of a calculator, for example, because there aren't enough places to represent it on the screen; similarly, a printout could be truncated if the margins aren't set properly.) However, based on the simplistic definition she found, Katy was misled. We know this because of the sentence she wrote to illustrate her understanding of the word: "She truncated the lights."

■ *Combine definitions and contextual examples.* To really understand the meaning of a word, an assortment of contexts is needed, plus multiple exposures over time. Researchers estimate that 12 to 15 encounters with a word are needed to adequately learn its meaning (Stahl & Nagy, 2005). This is a long and winding road, indeed, and it is not traversed in a single day. Fourth- and fifth-grade teachers are, however, in a position to start their students down this road by increasing the number of times they meet important new words in contextual settings. These contexts might come from wide reading, read-alouds, or direct instruction. (Note how the examples we provided for *truncate* might have helped you appreciate its meaning.) Where appropriate, negative examples, demonstrating incorrect usage or misconceptions, can be useful as well. In explaining the meaning of the word *dolphin*, for example, a teacher might point out not only that a dolphin is a mammal but that it is not a fish.

■ *Minimize rote copying of definitions.* Children gain very little from this tedious exercise. It keeps them occupied, however, and probably serves a classroom management function for some teachers. But this is far from an acceptable justification. There are better ways to ensure that children know the meanings of words. Instructional time is in short supply, and it is essential to use it wisely. We strongly advise teachers to reconsider the practice of asking their students to look up definitions and write them down.

■ *Introduce new words in related clusters.* The most effective teaching strategies in the area of vocabulary are based on teaching groups of words that have connections in meaning. They are not based on teaching a list of unrelated words. In content subjects, clustering is natural. Ironically, this fact gives teachers an edge in teaching technical terms. General vocabulary (words not associated with a particular content subject) can be clustered as well. Examples include words that denote moods (*depressed, disaffected, neutral, engaged, ebullient*) or efforts (*lackadaisical, haphazard, concerted*). However, the general vocabulary words you might choose from a particular text are not likely to be related in meaning. This fact makes them harder to teach.

■ *Provide brief, periodic review.* This notion is one of the most reliable principles of learning. It always works. In fact, some psychologists speak of it not as a principle but as a law. Let's examine how it works. Einstein was famous for "thought experiments." These were experiments he lacked the time or resources to actually carry out. He just thought about what would happen if he did conduct them. Let's try one. Imagine that we have two groups of participants and that we teach the same 20 words to each group. We'll teach the 20 words in an hour to the two groups combined. For Group 1, we'll follow up later with a 1-hour, uninterrupted intensive review. Group 2 will also receive an hour of review, but the hour will be divided across time into six 10-minute segments. Through this plan, both groups will get the same amount of review. It will just be scheduled differently. Assuming that no one encounters any of the 20 words again, which group would do better on a test after a delay of 10 years? The answer, of course, is group 2. Its members received distributed practice that resulted in superior retention of word meanings. The difference can be described in terms of massed practice (lengthy, intensive review) versus distributed practice (brief, periodic review). For vocabulary learning, distributed practice requires that you remember the words you have taught, and take advantage of every opportunity to review their meanings and to use them in new contexts.

Instructional Planning

Incorporating these strategies into Tier 1 instruction is a matter of using core suggestions wherever appropriate and making opportunities to apply them whenever the core treatment is light. You will be working within a whole-class schedule that includes components other than vocabulary, and we turn again to the planning templates we introduced in Chapter 5. We have already suggested that part of Tier 1 word recognition instruction will require you to show how the words are built, identifying spelling patterns, syllable types, and any prefixes, roots, or suffixes. We have also recommended that you present derivatives. Our attention now is directed toward the meaning component. We are assuming that a single core selection will be the mainstay of instruction for the week. On Monday, the teacher introduces a few words from the selection, providing student-friendly definitions and sentence contexts. It is important to ensure that the definition you provide does not contain words that are unknown to your students. Begin by looking up the words and then, for words with multiple meanings, locate the definition the students will need when they encounter the word in the selection. Be prepared to edit the definitions so that they are within the grasp of your students. An example may help to underscore this point. A fourth-grade teacher we observed recently wished to preteach the word *disoriented*. She used a definition she found in the dictionary: "bewildered; perplexed; lacking in attention to time or place." We suspect that few of her students found this definition very useful.

Remember that the words have been chosen in advance by the core authors. In the case of a fiction selection, there may be no relationships among the word meanings. For nonfiction, however, the words will be linked conceptually, inviting the teacher to help students think though the connections. There may be opportunities later in the day to briefly revisit the words. In any event, they should be reviewed each day as the students return to the core selection.

Note that the planning templates set aside time for a daily interactive read-aloud. Its purpose is to model fluency and to develop both vocabulary and comprehension. We have developed an eight-step process for planning interactive read-alouds of information trade books. Because of their focus on both vocabulary and comprehension, we introduce the first two steps here and the last six steps in Chapter 8, where our focus is on their use in comprehension instruction.

1. *Size up the book.* The first step in planning a nonfiction read-aloud is to appraise the book carefully. Start by reading the book from beginning to end for content. Self-assess your own understanding and think about your own comprehension. It is vital that you resolve any difficulties you may have encountered so that you have a thorough understanding of the content. Above all, be honest with yourself. What portions of the book are difficult to understand and why? If you yourself have difficulties, you can bet that your students will require support if they are to learn from the book. It may be that the book is simply too difficult for them, even in read-aloud form. This is a judgment that you need to make early so as to not waste time. You alone are in the best position to judge whether there is an appropriate match between the book and your students.

Once you judge the book to be an appropriate choice and have learned the content, read it again, this time attempting to empathize with your students. What knowledge does the author assume they have but that they probably lack? What new technical vocabulary is introduced, and how is it linked to your curricular objectives in science or social studies, as reflected in your state standards? How has the author organized the book? Are there sidebars that represent complex patterns that might present difficult choices about what to read next? What graphics are included, and how useful are they? Are the graphics stand alone or are they referred to in the text? These are critical questions and we address them here and in Chapter 8.

2. *Decide how to preteach the key vocabulary.* Most information trade books focus on a set of technical vocabulary words. Surprisingly, these words are easier to teach than an equal set of unrelated, general vocabulary terms because the teacher can take advantage of the relationships among the words. Two of the author's primary goals are to introduce these words and to tell how they are related.

However, if these are the author's goals, what purpose is served by preteaching? After all, the author has usually done a very good job of presenting all of the words and describing their relationships. Shouldn't that be sufficient? For many children the answer is no. As you will recall, research has clearly shown that preteaching vocabulary improves comprehension, even for books in which the word meanings are clearly presented. There are good reasons why this is the case. First, learning new content from nonfiction text, even when it is read aloud, requires the use of sophisticated strategies. Fourth and fifth grad-ers may have problems applying multiple strategies in concert independently, especially in a book written at a challenging level. Second, we have stressed that multiple exposures to new words are required for adequate understanding of their meanings, and a single read-aloud is hardly enough. Third, by preteaching key words, the teacher can informally assess how much the students know and then modify instruction to make meanings clear and to fill in gaps in prior knowledge. Fourth, the teacher can employ graphics that will help the children understand how the terms are related. Fifth, the teacher can tie the new terms to the science or social studies curriculum and to previous lessons in these subjects. The graphics might be used for this purpose—for example, by adding familiar vocabulary to a semantic map intended primarily to introduce new vocabulary. Finally, the materials the teacher creates for preteaching, such as diagrams on chart paper, can be displayed for later review.

We hope that these reasons have convinced you that preteaching key terms is impor-tant to a nonfiction read-aloud! Let's consider how to plan effectively for this portion of the lesson. To begin with, remember that some of these concepts are likely to be alto-gether new to your students while others may be somewhat familiar. This distinction is not very important. Preteaching is simply a *review* of some words for some students and an *introduction* of the words for others. Next, it is necessary to think about how the vocabulary is related to previous learning. What recent lessons have addressed related topics? Think about ways of reviewing that learning, of bridging backward, to show how the new relates to the known. One method of doing so is to use a diagram that shows how the words are related. Another is to construct a feature analysis chart that contains both familiar and new vocabulary. We discuss these techniques in detail later in this chapter. Try to include ways for the students to contribute to creating this diagram or chart. Doing so will make the process interactive, and by drawing on their prior knowledge you will be able to tell how detailed your instruction needs to be. Finally, decide on a medium (e.g., whiteboard, chart paper on easel) and plan to leave the graphics on display throughout the read-aloud and perhaps afterward for review.

Remember that there is not a single formula to follow in preteaching key terms. You must think carefully about the content of the selection and look for clear ties to previous instruction. A number of well-researched methods are available, and your only difficulty may lie in choosing among them. This is a good problem to have!

Figures 7.5 and 7.6 provide a review of the concepts necessary for planning Tier 1 vocabulary instruction, both for the interactive read-aloud and for the core selection. Remember that we need two templates: one for the "first run" through the story and one for the rest of the week. The read-aloud will be a new text (or a new section of the same text) each day, with new chances to introduce and explain new words. For the core selec-tion, though, you will be reviewing words on the second day.

Reviewing core vocabulary throughout the week is a means of cumulative review. One engaging way to return to the new words is to encourage students to become "word wizards" (Beck, McKeown, & Kucan, 2002). The words are placed in a chart, along with students' names. Whenever a child uses one of the words, a check is placed in the cor-

Time	Activity	Description
5 min	Strategy Introduction	
15 min	Interactive Read-Aloud	The teacher chooses an interesting and challenging piece of authentic literature, either narrative or information text to read aloud. The teacher quickly preteaches any words that are essential to the text's meaning and also provides synonyms or quick explanations of word meaning during reading. The teacher reads the book aloud, modeling fluent reading.
3 min	Introduce Written Response	
10 min	Vocabulary	The teacher introduces core vocabulary for the week, introducing meanings, providing multiple sentence contexts, thinking aloud about the spellings, and listing derivatives.
12 min	Choral Reading of the Story	Students and teacher read the selection together. The teacher stops when needed to monitor and develop comprehension. If the story is long, this same procedure is used again the next day with the rest of the story.

FIGURE 7.5. Tier 1 vocabulary initial planning.

Time	Activity	Description
2 min	Strategy Introduction	
10 min	Interactive Read-Aloud	The teacher chooses an interesting and challenging piece of authentic literature, either narrative or information text to read aloud. The teacher quickly preteaches any words that are essential to the text's meaning and also provides synonyms or quick explanations of word meaning during reading. The teacher reads the book aloud, modeling fluent reading.
10 min	Vocabulary Review	The teacher reviews core vocabulary for the week, including meanings and multiple sentence contexts. Students are invited to provide additional possible examples and to engage in word wizard activities.
10 min	Partner Reading	Students reread with a partner and with purpose: to improve their expression and their understanding.
10 min	Whisper Reading	Students reread independently for fluency and to complete a purposeful task.
3 min	Introduce Written Response	

FIGURE 7.6. Tier 1 vocabulary additional planning.

	altercation	entail	placate	entice
Toby	✓		✓	
Lakesha			✓	
Raul				✓
Sue	✓	✓	✓	
Johnny				
Amber	✓	✓	✓	✓
Russ	✓			✓
Dwayne		✓	✓	✓
Rosa	✓	✓		

FIGURE 7.7. Word Wizard chart.

responding box. The teacher may set any criterion for becoming a word wizard. For example, a student may be required to use each word once, each word twice, and so on. Figure 7.7 provides an example of how such a chart might look. These words come from a fiction selection, and it is plain to see that although they are useful, their meanings are unconnected. One way of forging connections is to ask "silly questions." The questions are "silly" because the words are not often thought of together. Would you placate someone to avoid an altercation? If you wanted to entice someone, what might that entail? Each of these is a silly question that forms a connection between two words that are unrelated. To answer, a student must think about the meanings of both words; doing so provides good practice and additional exposures.

What about instructional approaches useful for teaching the technical terms found in nonfiction? In our discussion of read-alouds, we hinted at several of these strategies. In the next section, we examine three of them in detail. They are incredibly versatile. You will find them useful not only in Tier 2 instruction but also in Tier 1 read-alouds, Tier 3 intensive interventions, and in science and social studies instruction.

TIER 2 INSTRUCTION IN VOCABULARY

Tier 2 instruction in vocabulary is appropriate for upper elementary students with acceptable fluency. It is difficult to screen in the area of vocabulary and impossible to diagnose. Luckily, neither of these assessments is necessary. Remember that Tier 2 instruction occurs for brief intervals and is highly targeted at skills that impair comprehension. Although all students can build their vocabulary, we believe that this time is better spent shoring up fluency problems and addressing any underlying difficulties with multisyllabic decoding if students need it and by answering questions about specific vocabulary items that arise during reading or discussion. However, if fluency is not problematic, then small-group work in comprehension and vocabulary is warranted. In fact, the success of your differentiated instruction will ultimately rest on the number of students you can move from word recognition and fluency, to fluency and comprehension, and then to vocabulary and comprehension.

Content

Students who meet the fourth- or fifth-grade fluency benchmark are well served by instruction that extends their vocabulary. We recommend approaching such instruction in the context of reading selections rather than word lists. In this way, vocabulary and comprehension can be developed together, and students can see how new words are used in context. In order to make useful selections of trade books, we refer you to our discussion in Chapter 6.

There is no list of words that must be taught in Tier 2 settings. The book selections will in large part dictate which words you should teach. For fiction, these will be a small number of general vocabulary words, perhaps three per day. For nonfiction, the words will be technical terms associated with the content subject, and mindful selection of information texts will allow you to link Tier 2 instruction to subject matter topics.

Instructional Strategies

For fiction, we advise against singling out a few words to preteach. This policy may sound strange, but there are good reasons for it. To begin with, general vocabulary has relatively limited influence on comprehension. If you are unfamiliar with a few adjectives, you can still usually manage to grasp the events of a narrative. In addition, highlighting the words in advance of reading is likely to cause students to look for these words when they begin to read, possibly impairing their comprehension. We advocate studying the words after the students read, returning to the text for examples of how each is used.

For information books, different strategies are called for. The words we select for these books are central to comprehension, and we introduce them in advance. Because they are naturally clustered together, it is actually easier to teach them. We do not have to worry that their meanings are unconnected because they are always closely related. The most effective instructional strategies take advantage of these connections.

Remember that you will be applying these strategies in small groups with readers who are fluent. Your task is to introduce them quickly to key words and their relationships to each other. Your goals are twofold: (1) to help them acquire the word meanings and (2) to facilitate their comprehension of the selection. Finally, unless you are collecting data for RTI purposes, we do not recommend pretesting the students. First, it is a time-consuming process. Second, multiple exposures are required to learn the meaning of any word. This means that whether one student may have encountered the word several times already and another has no familiarity with it, both will benefit from instruction.

As you read about these techniques, keep in mind that you can also use them to teach words and concepts directly as part of whole-class content area instruction.

CONCEPT OF DEFINITION

Concept of definition (Schwartz & Raphael, 1985) is a strategy that is based on the idea that a good definition has two components. It tells the category to which a concept belongs, and it provides features that enable us to distinguish the concept from other members of the same category. A hammer is defined as a tool for driving nails. From this simple definition, we can see that hammer is a member of the category tools, and we can distinguish it from other tools is by noting what it is used for. Concept of definition utilizes these two components to directly teach important new words, especially in content subjects. This strategy relies on the creation of a semantic diagram and is sometimes called "word mapping." The word map that is created in the course of this instruction makes explicit the connections between a new word and known words. This word map might be drawn on a whiteboard, presented with an overhead projector or Elmo, or duplicated on paper for students to use. A simple word map has a space for the word in the center, a connecting line to the class to which it belongs, more lines to its characteristics or attributes, and some examples. In the example provided in Figure 7.8, the key term is *igneous rocks*. Note that this concept belongs to the larger category of rocks and that examples of igneous rocks appear below the key term. Characteristics are connected at the side, and examples of rocks other than igneous are linked to the concept of rocks but not to igneous.

This strategy is only useful when the target word is a member of a specific category. Fortunately, many content area terms are of this kind. The strategy is helpful both for developing new concepts and for teaching children to generate definitions as they are learning new words. For example, a student can look at the completed diagram and say that an igneous rock is "a rock that is volcanic in origin and was once molten." Note that this makeshift definition has the two characteristics of any good definition. It tells the category to which the igneous rocks belong, and it provides features that enable us to tell igneous rocks from other kinds.

SEMANTIC FEATURE ANALYSIS

Semantic feature analysis (feature analysis, for short) is also based on the notion of a definition. It is a very simple instructional technique. Begin with a lopsided T chart. You can

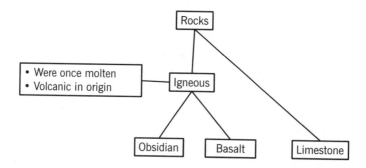

FIGURE 7.8. Example of a Concept of Definition diagram.

Planets	Has Moons	Has Rings	Rocky Surface
Mercury	–	–	+
Venus	–	–	+
Earth	+	–	+
Mars	+	–	+
Jupiter	+	+	–
Saturn	+	+	–
Uranus	+	+	–
Neptune	+	+	–

FIGURE 7.9. Example of a feature analysis chart.

also use the Table function of Microsoft Word if you want to produce a more attractive chart. Feature analysis is used to compare and contrast members of the same category. In the upper left-hand corner, write the name of the category that the students will learn about. Across the top of the chart, write "Features." In the left-hand column, list the members of the category. Each column is completed by writing either a plus or minus for each category member, depending on whether it has or lacks that feature. (You can write the letter *S* if a category member *sometimes* possesses a particular feature.) Figure 7.9 presents a sample feature analysis chart based on the planets.

Feature analysis can only be used with groups of terms that are members of the same category. Fortunately, these groups are often encountered in information books. If your responsibilities as a teacher include instruction in mathematics, science, or social studies, look for opportunities to use feature analysis in presenting and reviewing clusters of terms that are members of the same category. When you select trade books to use in Tier 2 instruction, look for books that develop knowledge associated with your content area standards. Then use feature analysis as a means of quickly introducing category members and their distinguishing features. A useful approach is to leave a portion of the chart blank and to challenge the students to complete it as they read. A key to the success of this technique is to discuss the chart after it has been constructed, together looking for similarities and differences. In the example depicted in Figure 7.9, what conclusion can you help students reach about rocky surfaces and rings?

DIAGRAMS

A diagram is a type of graphic organizer that illustrates how key concepts are related. Diagrams are another very important instructional tool for teaching clusters of related terms. They have many advantages:

- They help students "see" abstract content.
- There is little to "read."

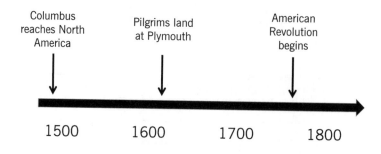

FIGURE 7.10. Time line.

■ They are easy to construct and discuss.
■ Technical terms can be taught in natural clusters.
■ They enhance recall and understanding.
■ They have an impressive research base.
■ They can be used very quickly.

We have already discussed one type of diagram, the kind used in concept of definition. Now let's examine some of the other major types of diagrams. You will be familiar with these as a proficient reader, but you may not have considered them as instructional tools for introducing and/or reviewing vocabulary.

A time line is perhaps the simplest type of diagram because it typically consists of a single straight line. Some time lines show absolute dates, as in Figure 7.10. You may be thinking that this example does not involve vocabulary. Instead, it simply labels events. We contend, however, that words like *Columbus, pilgrims,* and *Plymouth* are in every sense vocabulary words that are important for students to acquire. Time lines are also useful for depicting processes. Figure 7.11 shows how representing a repeated process is actually a more sophisticated time line.

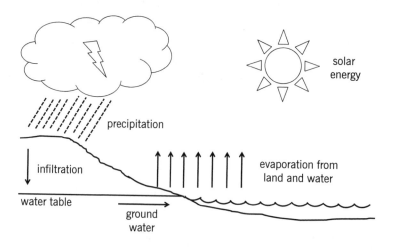

FIGURE 7.11. Example of a time line used to illustrate a process.

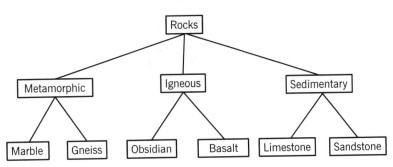

FIGURE 7.12. Example of a tree diagram.

A tree diagram shows how large concepts can be subdivided into components. They are called trees because they have branches, but in reality they appear to grow upside-down! The lower you go in a tree diagram, the smaller the concept. You might have noticed that a tree diagram is central to the concept of definition approach, but we modify it to include characteristics and we connect them laterally. We can develop our rock diagram in Figure 7.8 into a full tree diagram by deleting the features and adding more branches. Figure 7.12 demonstrates this idea. Compare it carefully with Figure 7.8. The central part is unchanged.

In a tree diagram, we deal with clear-cut categories. Concepts lie cleanly on one branch or another. In a Venn diagram, however, a concept might fall into more than one category at the same time. Venn diagrams (named for John Venn, the mathematician who created them) are useful for displaying these overlapping classifications. Two overlapping circles are the basis of what is perhaps the most common Venn diagram in schools. They permit useful comparisons and contrasts. A two-circle Venn can be used in two principal ways:

1. Each circle can represent a feature. Concepts having that feature go inside the corresponding circle. Concepts with both features go into the overlap area (called the intersection). For example, we might label one circle "Lives in Water" and the second circle "Breathes Air." We would write words like *fish* and *octopus* in the first circle but not in the second; we would write words like *cow* and *horse* in the second circle but not in the first; we would write a word like *whale* in the intersection of the two circles because a whale possesses both characteristics.
2. Each circle can represent an item or concept. We then write features inside the circles, placing shared features in the intersection. A good example is the use of a two-circle Venn to help students compare and contrast reptiles and amphibians. One circle is labeled "Reptiles" and the other "Amphibians." Various features are then categorized.

A labeled picture is a common diagram useful when the main relationship among the terms is space. The example of the water cycle in Figure 7.11 is a labeled picture with the element of time added. A simpler example appears in Figure 7.13 (compliments of Purdue University), which displays the main parts of a wasp.

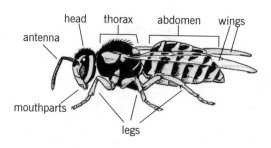

FIGURE 7.13. Example of a labeled picture. Reprinted with permission of Extension Entomology, Purdue University.

All of these strategies have some common characteristics: They allow you to introduce (and later review) words quickly; they employ a cluster approach that stresses how the words are interrelated; and they invite interaction with students. We acknowledge that there are other teaching strategies that have these qualities, but these are on our "short list" of effective approaches.

Instructional Planning

Vocabulary differs from word recognition in that there is not a clear sequence of instruction. The word meanings you teach are driven by the books you select. Instructional planning entails choosing the best method (1) for introducing the words and making time for instruction before the students read and (2) for review afterward. Planning will differ for fiction and information books for two reasons. First, we introduce the words before reading in the case of information books and afterward in the case of fiction. Second, there are more instructional approaches available to us for information books, and we will need to choose among them.

Let's examine planning for a fiction book first. Consider the example of a short trade book that the students can read in 5 days during Tier 2 time. Toward the end of each small-group session, the teacher might identify three words, providing a student-friendly

	Day 1	Day 2	Day 3	Day 4	Day 5
With Teacher	Introduce text segment	Introduce words from day 1 text segment	Review day 1 words and introduce words from day 2 segment	Review day 1 and day 2 words and introduce words from day 3 segment	Review day 1, day 2, and day 3 words and introduce words from day 4 segment
Outside Group	Students read first text segment	Students read next text segment	Students read next text segment	Students read next text segment	Students read next text segment

FIGURE 7.14. Teaching general vocabulary during Tier 2 time.

	Day 1	Day 2	Day 3	Day 4	Day 5
With Teacher	Introduce words from day 1 text segment	Review words from day 1 text segment and introduce words from day 2 segment	Review words from day 1 and day 2 text segments and introduce words from day 3 segment	Review words from day 1, day 2, and day 3 text segments and introduce words from day 4 segment	Review words from day 1, day 2, day 3, and day 4 text segments and introduce words from day 5 segment
Outside Group	Students read first text segment	Students read next text segment	Students read next text segment	Students read next text segment	Students read next text segment

FIGURE 7.15. Teaching technical vocabulary during Tier 2 time.

definition of each and returning to the point at which it was used in the text. Figure 7.14 illustrates how this process would work across the week.

This simple, repetitive structure has several advantages. It can be used with any fiction trade book. It ensures a useful routine that will allow students to develop expectations about the lesson. It also builds in cumulative review. Notice that the review each day includes words from several text segments. Their inclusion requires hardly any additional time because with each successive lesson the earlier words go faster and faster.

Now let's consider how to plan the vocabulary portion of an information book lesson. As with fiction, we usually must plan over a number of days to cover an entire trade book. We may also need to vary how we introduce each day's new words, depending on how they are related. The big difference, though, is that the words are taught prior to reading. Figure 7.15 shows how a week's small-group lessons would be structured.

CHOOSING TIER 3 PROGRAMS FOR VOCABULARY

As we did for word recognition and fluency, we stop short of recommending commercial programs because we lack sufficient empirical evidence to recommend one over another. In addition, as researchers turn their attention to the needs of young adolescent students and include those learning English within an RTI framework, improvements in the efficacy of interventions will likely be realized. When we look for evidence about the effectiveness of interventions, we turn to four Internet sources that are currently updated frequently: (1) the Institute for Education Science's What Works Clearinghouse (*www.ies.ed.gov/ncee/wwc*), (2) Center on Instruction (*www.centeroninstruction.org*), (3) Best Evidence Encyclopedia (*www.bestevidence.org*), and (4) National Center on Response to Intervention (*www.rti4success.org*). When you search for evidence on the efficacy of intensive interventions for vocabulary for upper elementary students, consider searching at a range of grade levels in order to make your search as broad as possible.

Chapter 8

Building Comprehension

In this chapter, we offer background and approaches to improving the comprehension proficiency of fourth and fifth graders. We once again follow our tiered approach, beginning with whole-class core instruction and moving to more focused applications in small groups. To accomplish this, we begin by presenting background information on the complex development of comprehension. We argue that although research can guide our efforts to develop student comprehension in both Tier 1 and Tier 2 settings, we will never fully accomplish our task; rather, comprehension development is a lifelong pursuit, building on a constantly expanding set of background knowledge, vocabulary knowledge, and strategic processes.

FOUNDATIONAL KNOWLEDGE ABOUT COMPREHENSION DEVELOPMENT

What happens when we comprehend? For proficient adult readers, the process of comprehending has become second nature. Indeed, it is so accomplished, so apparently effortless, that it is difficult to appreciate how it happens, and it is harder still to empathize with the problems encountered by struggling readers. Researchers have studied the comprehension process for decades and many questions about it remain, but we know enough to assist students in their efforts to become better comprehenders.

In order to gain awareness of how comprehension occurs, a simple, introspective example may be helpful. As you read the following sentence, think about how you make it meaningful:

> The wolf is a carnivorous mammal that inhabits much of Europe, North America, and Asia.

We suspect that you had little difficulty in understanding this sentence. There were no unfamiliar words, and the background knowledge you needed was available to you in memory. As you read, the words triggered connections in long-term memory. We might compare these connections with electrical switches that are turned to the "on" position as you read. In fact, this is not a mere metaphor. It is exactly what happens in the brain during reading. When you reached the word *wolf*, your "wolf" switch was activated, and all of the connections stored in your memory either entered your conscious thoughts or were available in the wings as needed. This bundle of connections, called a *schema*, included the pronunciation of *wolf*, visual images of wolves, definitional knowledge, and anecdotal memories such as television shows, books you might have read, visits to museums, and so on. In short, the concept of wolf is associated in your memory with an impressive array of connected information. As you read to the end of the sentence, you probably encountered information that was consistent with your prior understanding about wolves.

In an example like this one, where the information you read was well aligned with prior knowledge, the content is easily assimilated. The fact that it was easy, however, does not mean that it was simple! As you read, additional schemata were activated. You have a well-developed schema for North America, for carnivorous, and so on, and each of these concepts has its own complex network of associations in your memory. This means that many more switches were turned on as you read.

But it wasn't enough for you to turn on all of the switches. Something more was needed. Because your mind is preprogrammed to process language, you were able to perform a remarkable feat. You were able to link the concepts according to the blueprint provided by the sentence. This blueprint is governed by a set of grammatical rules that we begin to learn as infants. These rules guide us in connecting the concepts represented by words in ways that make sense. We use the same set of rules when we construct sentences as we speak or write, and we can be confident that other English speakers will use those rules to interpret what we express accurately.

In our example of the wolf, the meaning you were able to construct by using the rules of grammar to link concepts was not only consistent with your prior knowledge, it was probably contained within it. That is, the sentence told you nothing that you didn't already know. You may have found the experience reinforcing but not particularly enlightening. But let's continue our example:

> The wolf is a carnivorous mammal that inhabits much of Europe, North America, and Asia. **Wolves live in groups called packs. By working together, a wolf pack can bring down a large animal, such as an elk or a moose. When game is scarce, however, a wolf may be lucky to find a small field mouse.**

The information contained in this continuation was also easy to assimilate. It was consistent with what you already knew about wolves. This time, however, you may have encountered a fact that you did not know before, for example, that a wolf might prey upon an animal as small as a mouse. Although mildly surprising, this new information did not contradict your prior knowledge of wolves and could be rather easily added to your wolf schema. This process of assimilating new information into prior knowledge is central to learning, but there are occasional bumps in the road. One such bump involves confronting information that is clearly at odds with prior knowledge. Again, let's continue our example:

> The wolf is a carnivorous mammal that inhabits much of Europe, North America, and Asia. Wolves live in groups called packs. By working together, a wolf pack can bring down a large animal, such as an elk or a moose. When game is scarce, however, a wolf may be lucky to find a small field mouse. **Wolves are dogs. Although they are wild and difficult to domesticate, they are still dogs. They are just as intelligent as other dogs, and they are not dangerous to humans, despite the popular myth to the contrary. The fact is, there is no record of a healthy wolf ever attacking a human being in North America.**

We suspect that this continuation of the passage presented information that contradicted what you had previously believed about wolves. Most people are unaware that a wolf is a dog and most believe that wolves are dangerous. When confronted by information that contradicts prior knowledge, readers cannot simply assimilate it. If readers choose to accept the new information, their schema for wolf must be substantially altered. Piaget referred to this process as *accommodation*. It represents another kind of learning. Whether the new information is assimilated or accommodated, learning has occurred and knowledge is acquired.

Walter Kintsch (1994) offered a good description of the comprehension process. As you made your way through the passage, from clause to clause and sentence to sentence, you were building an internal representation of the passage's meaning. As you continued reading, you also expanded and refined this structure. Had you been asked a question after reading, you would have referred to this internal structure to answer. We might compare that structure to a house. You build it from the ground up, on a foundation of prior knowledge, and it has an overall design or blueprint plus numerous details such as the individual boards and bricks and shutters. Just after you have finished reading the passage, chances are you can clearly recall many of the details, in the same way that you might envision details of the house or building in which you now live. However, after a time your memory for details of the passage will fade, although you may still be able to remember its gist. Think back to a house you lived in long ago. It is likely that a similar process has occurred with respect to your memory. You still retain a general idea of what the house looked like but many of the details elude you. The same is true of the "reading house" you construct as you read. Over time, its details become fuzzy, but a general impression may remain in your memory.

We have been discussing processes that are typical of proficient readers like yourself. Now let's consider these processes from the perspective of a struggling reader. When you read the first sentence of the passage, a number of schemata were activated and you were able to link them appropriately on the basis of sentence structure. However, what if one or more of the key schemata were poorly developed or nonexistent? For example, what if you had been unfamiliar with the word *carnivorous*? What if you had only a very vague idea about the location of Europe and Asia? Your comprehension would have been seriously jeopardized. Students with limited vocabulary and prior knowledge often find themselves in this situation. Because they lack the conceptual knowledge that authors assume their readers possess, they are unable to link concepts appropriately. To put this another way, they are unable to build a solid mental structure of the content because they lacked many of the building blocks that the author required. They end up living in a reading shack!

Many of the building blocks to which we are referring here are bits of knowledge. It is important to make a distinction between vocabulary and background knowledge. Knowledge of word meanings, or vocabulary, is essential to comprehension, but it is only one component of the knowledge necessary to comprehend. Such knowledge may also include experiences and individual impressions that cannot be captured by a single word and that amplify and enrich one's definitional knowledge.

The effects of limited vocabulary and background knowledge depend on the size of the gap between what the student does know and what it is necessary to know in order to comprehend. If the gap is too large, it may not be possible for a teacher to facilitate adequate comprehension. Imagine having to read a technical research report in the field of medicine. Limitations of your prior knowledge base might well be impossible to overcome. Even with the assistance of a tutor knowledgeable about the topic, the amount of background building required might be prohibitive. In the case of a student, reading materials that contain a large number of unfamiliar words and that refer to ideas and experiences that are also unfamiliar are likely to be frustrating no matter what the teacher does. In such cases, it is better to locate alternative materials. However, in cases where that gap is not too wide, a teacher may be able to bridge it by preteaching the vocabulary and by building the prior knowledge needed to comprehend. Figure 8.1 demonstrates the relationship between prior knowledge and comprehension. As gaps in a student's prior knowledge are reduced, comprehension improves. We introduced strategies for reducing that gap through vocabulary instruction in the previous chapter.

Of course, familiarity with the topic and with the words an author has chosen is not all that is required to comprehend. In order to build a mental representation of text content, a reader needs to be able to approach the reading task strategically. Just as a carpenter must be able to strategically use a variety of tools in building a house, a reader

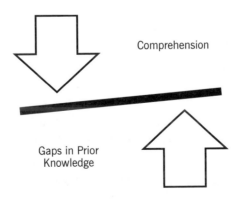

FIGURE 8.1. The relationship between prior knowledge and comprehension.

must employ a variety of strategies if a sound reading house is to be constructed. Even with assistance, the final product may be problematic. The reading house may need work. Like a master carpenter overseeing the work of a novice, a teacher can help a student improve the mental representation of text content after reading has been completed. All of this is to say that teachers have three opportunities to improve text comprehension. The actions they take before, during, and after reading can do much to ensure adequate understanding of a particular text and to demonstrate the procedures that skilled readers use to create strong mental representations.

This discussion may seem very theoretical, but the implications for the classroom are enormous. In a short story, for example, if the protagonist enters a fast-food restaurant, the author will not bore you with details about how he orders, what the restaurant looks like, how expensive it is, or how healthy the food is. The author will expect your schema for fast food to be activated instantly. However, imagine the reader who hasn't had that experience; comprehension of the text might be compromised. Anderson and Pearson (1984) used schema theory to explain the strong relationship between prior knowledge of ideas and concepts contained in a text to an individual's ability to comprehend that text. They took the restaurant example a bit further. Let's assume that the protagonist has been eating in an upscale restaurant. When does he pay for his food? A reader who has had some experience with restaurants of this kind knows that the check is paid after the meal, but readers who haven't been to this type of restaurant may not. The only restaurants they may know are fast-food establishments, where food is paid for before it is received. Their limited experience constrains their schema for the concept of a restaurant, and their comprehension is also constrained. Schemata, then, can be developed through experience in the world and through experience with text, as long as that text is understood fully.

Schema theory can also be applied to entire texts. For example, mature readers have many schemata related to the kinds of texts they may encounter. They have developed one schema for a short story, another for a novel, yet another for a news story, and so on. When they begin reading one of these forms, they activate the appropriate schema. This schema involves knowledge about how a particular genre is structured. This knowledge helps the reader form reasonable expectations, which in turn aid comprehension. As an example, read the following limerick by Anthony Euwer:

> A diner while dining at Crewe
> Found quite a large mouse in his stew.
> > Said the waiter, "Don't shout
> > And wave it about,
> Or the rest will be wanting one too."

We suspect that your schema for limericks is well developed. Because you knew that what you were about to read was a limerick, you were able to activate knowledge about how it would be structured. This knowledge included expectations about meter and rhyme scheme and also about the light tone and humorous punch line. (We hope you were not disappointed.) Think about how your attention would have been different if we told you we were presenting a haiku, where you would have expected rich evocation of emotion or imagery and a very different metrical structure. This example illustrates how important it is for readers to begin with a clear set of expectations about a given genre. This insight has led to effective instructional techniques for providing students with knowledge of text structures. It is a clear example of how theory can inform and improve practice.

To sum up, comprehension involves using prior knowledge to make sense of text. This knowledge includes word meanings, conceptual background, and an understanding of how sentences are structured and how texts are organized. The process involves extracting information from the text, interpreting it within a framework of prior knowledge, and constructing a mental representation of the text's meaning. These actions go on at the same time and the reader coordinates them purposefully. The RAND Reading Study Group (2002) defined comprehension elegantly as "the process of simultaneously extracting and constructing meaning through interaction and involvement with written language" (p. xiii).

The RAND Group's definition creates both problems and opportunities as we attempt to sort through the issues related to comprehension instruction. On the one hand, their notion of comprehension as construction opens the door to multiple interpretations of what we read, the kind appropriate to the reading of poetry and other literature. It also suggests, however, that no text has a single meaning, the one based only on an author's intention. Rather, meaning is always influenced by the particular construction process that a reader engages. This implication suggests that extensive latitude should be given to students and that assessing their comprehension exclusively in terms of how close they come to realizing the author's intended meaning is inappropriate. Most of the teachers, administrators, and policymakers whom we have met, however, prefer to think of comprehension as more a matter of extraction than construction.

An easy way to view the processes of extracting and constructing meaning is to think of comprehension as occurring at successive levels. Although several approaches have been suggested, we believe that the most straightforward involves three levels, illustrated in Figure 8.2.

At the literal level, the reader extracts ideas that have been explicitly stated. In our wolf passage, the fact that wolves are dogs is expressed clearly. It is not a point requir-

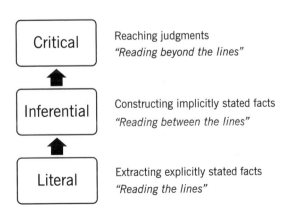

FIGURE 8.2. Levels of comprehension.

ing speculation and conjecture. Questions posed at the literal level are easy to ask and answer, but they privilege superficial comprehension rather than real understanding. This is a trap for the unwary teacher. To see just how misleading literal-level questions can be, consider the following sentence:

The thurpous twipex was bepping a purtle under a fum.

This is nonsense, of course, but you are nonetheless perfectly capable of answering questions like these:

What was the twipex bepping?
What kind of twipex was it?
Where did the bepping take place?

This is not to say that literal-level questions are not useful. They can be springboards to inferences and critical judgments. It is only when they become an end in themselves that problems arise, for it is easy to be fooled into believing that the ability to answer questions like these means that comprehension has taken place.

At the inferential level of comprehension, the reader is still concerned with factual information. However, because this information is not explicitly stated, but merely implied, the reader must construct it by logically combining the facts of a given text with each other and/or with facts that are stored in prior knowledge. You might tentatively conclude, for example, that because North America, Europe, and Asia are mentioned as wolf habitats no wolves are to be found in Africa. Africa is not mentioned in the passage, but you can construct this inference on the basis of passage content *and* prior knowledge.

In contrast, the critical level requires adequate comprehension at the levels below so that defensible judgments can be reached. Appraising the quality of an informational article is one example of a critical judgment. It would not be possible to undertake this task without having first extracted factual aspects of the article and constructed a mental representation of it. In the wolf example, imagine that you had been charged with drafting a policy statement concerning "wolf awareness"—that is, making the general public aware that wolves are not dangerous. Successfully meeting this charge would require (at a minimum) an adequate grasp of the facts expressed in the passage. Of course, critical judgments will vary considerably from reader to reader based on taste, philosophy, cultural background, and related factors. For this reason, it is inappropriate to expect all students to arrive at the same critical judgment. What is important is that they can explain *how* they arrived at their judgments. No one disputes that reaching critical judgments is a constructive process. By its nature it is divergent rather than convergent, which is why most assessments of reading comprehension tend to ignore the critical level and focus instead on the literal and inferential levels.

By the time children reach the upper elementary grades, many have begun to experience comprehension difficulties. We have discussed some of the key factors that might be to blame: limited prior knowledge and vocabulary, unfamiliar text structures, weak decoding and fluency, and ineffective use of comprehension strategies. There are other

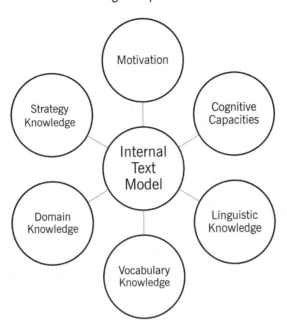

FIGURE 8.3. The RAND model of internal factors affecting comprehension.

factors as well, however, including motivation, intelligence, and the ability to attend. The RAND Reading Study Group depicts these as internal factors (see Figure 8.3). That is, they are problems that reside within the student, and, clearly, some are more susceptible than others to the efforts of teachers.

The RAND Group also reminds us of the influence of context on comprehension. They define reading comprehension as a cognitive process (the bull's-eye in Figure 8.4) that is influenced by the union of the characteristics of the text chosen, the reader's characteristics in relation to that text, and the activities that the reader will engage in before, during, and after reading. In school, all of these things happen in the classroom, which is a particular sociocultural context.

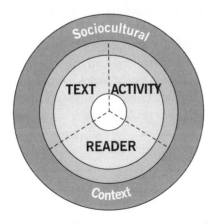

FIGURE 8.4. The RAND model of comprehension.

As an example, let's consider Peter, a fifth grader whose internal characteristics are reasonably good. That is, Peter's fluency is at benchmark, he has an average vocabulary for his age, and he is motivated to read. It is tempting to think that whenever Peter is asked to read a fifth-grade selection, his comprehension will be adequate. According to the RAND Group model, however, this expectation may be wrong. A particular text may present unfamiliar concepts or have a confusing structure despite its overall level of difficulty. The teacher may require an unusual task in response to the reading such as solving a difficult problem or writing an essay. Or Peter may be required to work with students with whom he does not get along very well. Any of these factors can impair his comprehension. Given this litany of woes, it may sound as though comprehension is a fragile flower indeed, easily plagued by a host of problems. The good news is that most of these factors can be accounted for by skillful instruction. In teaching, the key is to become aware of which factors can be addressed through instructional planning. As a teacher, you are in a position to make decisions that can take advantage of these factors in ways that help students like Peter in their quest to comprehend.

One factor over which teachers can exercise some control involves the strategies their students use to extract and construct meaning as they read. By fostering the use of a few key strategies, and by returning to these strategies repeatedly in a variety of contexts, teachers in the upper elementary grades can provide their students with the tools they need to succeed. Although writers on this subject have produced slightly different lists of strategies, there is general agreement that students must be able to visualize events and settings, to arrive at logical inferences, to make reasonable predictions, to retell the important events of a narrative, to distill main ideas, to summarize content, and to synthesize across two or more sources. Strategies such as these have replaced comprehension "skills" (e.g., noting a literal sequence of events or inferring causal relationships) in core programs. Skills like these are important, to be sure, but they eventually achieve almost automatic status, while strategies must be consciously applied. Distinguishing skills from strategies is important, and Gerald Duffy (2009) offers the following distinction:

> What is a skill and what is a strategy? A skill is something you do automatically without thought. You do it the same way every time. Tying your shoes is an example of a skill. In reading, instantly recognizing and saying a word such as "the" is a skill. You do these things automatically without thinking about them. They are automatized. A strategy, in contrast, is a plan. You are thoughtful when you do it, and you often adjust the plan as you go along to fit the situation. Planning a road trip is an example of a strategy. You are thoughtful in making decisions about what highways to take, where to spend the night, and so on. And if you run into unanticipated problems along the way (such as extensive road construction), you adjust your strategy—you change your route. Good readers use many strategies. For instance, making predictions is a strategy because readers are thoughtful in using text clues and prior knowledge to make an initial prediction when subsequent text clues provide more information. (p. 21)

As Duffy's description suggests, not every strategy is appropriate in every situation. We don't read the newspaper in the same way we read the phone book! Good teachers scaffold strategies. They model them and then support students in their attempts to apply them. But the goal is for the students to apply them on their own. Strategy use does not always come naturally, but it can be taught. Regardless of the strategies you decide to target, strategy instruction is nearly always accomplished in the same way. Teachers employ a gradual release of responsibility approach. That is, at the start, the teachers maintain most of the responsibility and control. They define and model the strategy for students, showing the strategy in action. Next, teachers move to a series of guided practice opportunities during which they share responsibility for employing the strategy. They provide students with relatively simple contexts to use the strategy, and they provide feedback to them quickly. They ratchet up the difficulty level of the context over time, still providing feedback (and noticing levels of student comfort and success). Finally, they release responsibility totally to the students, proving authentic opportunities to employ the strategy.

Research confirms that an instructional focus on comprehension strategy instruction is worth the effort! By the time students reach fourth and fifth grades, they have received instruction in the key strategies. Teachers at these grades should make it their goal to revisit them in the new and challenging texts their students face. Doing so will not only assist struggling readers but will enable readers like Peter to continue to grow as comprehenders.

Like vocabulary, comprehension is an open-ended proficiency. As Joe and his classmates progress through grades 4 and 5, they are expected to continue improving their comprehension ability. One way of estimating this positive trajectory is in grade-level terms. Because comprehension is the end product of so many components, the framers of the Common Core Standards do not attempt to delineate it. Instead, they use a grade-level index to gauge proficiency. We present these "bottom-line" standards in Figure 8.5. Note that the key difference between grades 4 and 5 is in the level of text complexity students are required to comprehend.

There are many valuable resources for building your knowledge of comprehension instruction. Whether you engage in individual professional reading or in book studies with your colleagues, we believe you will find the resources listed in Figure 8.6 helpful.

General Goal	Evidence
Grade 4	
The students demonstrate proficiency at reading texts at appropriate levels of complexity.	Students focus on reading texts independently at the fourth- through fifth-grade level of text complexity, with scaffolding likely to be required for texts at the high end of this range.
Grade 5	
The students demonstrate proficiency at reading texts at appropriate levels of complexity.	Students focus on reading texts independently at the fourth- through fifth-grade level of text complexity 70% of the time, and they are introduced to texts at a complexity level from sixth to eighth grades as "stretch" texts (30% of the time), which will likely require scaffolding.

FIGURE 8.5. Comprehension standards from the Common Core.

Duffy, G. G. (2009). *Explaining reading: A resource for teaching concepts, skills, and strategies* (2nd ed.). New York: Guilford Press.

Fuchs, D., & Fuchs, L. (2005). Peer-assisted learning strategies: Promoting word recognition, fluency, and reading comprehension in young children. *Journal of Special Education, 39*(1), 34–44.

Graesser, A. C. (2007). An introduction to strategic reading comprehension. In D. S. McNamara (Ed.), *Reading comprehension strategies: Theories, interventions, and technologies* (pp. 3–26). Mahwah, NJ: Erlbaum.

Israel, S. E., & Duffy, G. G. (Eds.). (2009). *Handbook of research on reading comprehension.* New York: Routledge.

Klingner, J.K., Vaughn, S., & Boardman, A. (2007). *Teaching reading comprehension to students with learning disabilities.* New York: Guilford Press.

McNamara, D. S. (Ed.). (2007). *Reading comprehension strategies: Theories, interventions, and technologies.* New York: Erlbaum.

Pardo, L. S. (2004). What every teacher needs to know about comprehension. *The Reading Teacher, 58,* 272–280.

Raphael, T. E., Highfield, K., & Au, K. H. (2006). *QAR now: Question answer relationships: A powerful and practical framework that develops comprehension and higher-level thinking in all students.* New York: Scholastic.

Swan, E. A. (2002). *Concept-oriented reading instruction: Engaging classrooms, lifelong learners.* New York: Guilford Press.

Sweet, A.P., & Snow, C.E. (Eds.). (2003). *Rethinking reading comprehension.* New York: Guilford Press.

Willingham, D. T. (2006–2007). The usefulness of brief instruction in reading comprehension strategies. *American Educator, 30*(4), 39–50.

FIGURE 8.6. Resources for comprehension instruction.

TIER 1 INSTRUCTION IN COMPREHENSION

A core program provides an anthology of reading selections intended for the entire class. At grades 4 and 5, the text difficulty of these selections is typically near grade level, although variations are bound to occur. The selections represent a deliberate range of genres and text structures in order to prepare students for the increasingly challenging world of text that awaits them in middle school. Typically, each selection is the focus of a week of whole-class instruction. By returning to each selection repeatedly, the core seeks to ensure that even students who would struggle if asked to read grade-level material independently will eventually comprehend and contribute constructively to discussions and activities.

Content

The selections themselves are not the essential ingredient in the core anthology. They are merely springboards used to foster continuing comprehension growth. Similar selections might do just as well for this purpose, and a comparison of two core programs is likely to reveal little or no overlap in the selections included. The real content of the core program lies in the scaffolding that teachers provide as students engage in the reading of each text. Examining how the core supports teachers in providing that scaffolding is important.

As in previous chapters, we encourage you once again to refer to the *Guidelines for Reviewing a Reading Program* (Florida Center for Reading Research, 2007). These guidelines value explicit instruction in comprehension strategies and reviewing these strategies again and again in different selections. Such strategies should include summarizing, predicting, generating questions, and grasping main ideas, among others. Students should be taught to apply these strategies, individually and in concert, depending on which ones they need to comprehend the selection. This awareness means that they should be encouraged to monitor their own comprehension and to respond appropriately when they do not. A core program should help convey the idea that reading is done for a variety of purposes and that the manner in which we read varies with purpose. The teachers' edition (TE) should suggest questions at a variety of levels and should offer think-alouds and other prompts to support students at points of difficulty. Selections should be nested within before–during–after lesson formats, and strategy use should be embedded in each of these phases. Selections should include both narrative and expository text, and the latter should provide opportunities to interpret charts, diagrams, and other graphic organizers.

Instructional Strategies

Using the TE carefully should result in a systematic application of effective instructional approaches. However, the core is a fixed resource, and its developers simply could not have foreseen all of the situations that might arise during whole-class instruction. It is often necessary to modify the lesson in order to respond to unforeseeable events. In this section, we highlight several instructional strategies that may help you make these modifications as the need arises.

Effective questioning strategies are one means of using the core program responsively. Although the core suggests questions to ask, there are many opportunities to expand on this foundation. Here are three:

- When a student cannot answer an inferential or critical question suggested by the TE, drop to the literal level and ask for an explicitly stated fact that is useful in answering the higher level question. For example, suppose a fifth-grade teacher asks why a fictional character made a particular decision. When a student is unable to answer, the teacher asks what had happened to the character just before the decision.
- Remember that higher order questions do not result in rapid-fire responses. They require thought, and when a student does not respond immediately, providing some think time can be an effective way to foster a reasonable answer.
- Turn the tables from time to time by asking students to pose questions. Question generation is a research-based way of improving comprehension, and core selections provide many chances to elicit such questions.

The TE will provide numerous think-alouds at strategic points in most selections. A think-aloud is a suggestion for modeling how a proficient reader thinks through a difficult situation in order to comprehend. For example, let's assume that our wolf selection appears as a fourth-grade nonfiction core selection. On day 1, when the teacher engages students in choral reading, think-alouds are especially appropriate because the students are unfamiliar with the selection. When the teacher reads, "and they are not dangerous to humans," a dramatic pause may follow. "Wait a minute," the teacher might muse aloud, "That can't be right. I know that wolves are dangerous animals, so that sentence doesn't make sense. Help me figure it out. What would a good reader do now?" Students, having been in this situation before, will advise the teacher to reread in order to be certain the phrase was not misread. They will then advise reading ahead to see if new information will resolve the problem. After reading aloud that there have been no reports of wolf attacks in North America, the teacher concludes the think-aloud: "Well, I guess I was wrong. Wolves aren't as dangerous as I thought. Sometimes if we just keep reading, it will solve a problem we have in understanding." This last sentence is the point of the think-aloud. The fact that students have experienced think-alouds before does not dilute their instructive power. Just the reverse, in fact. By encountering them in a wide variety of texts over the course of several years, students will internalize the fix-up strategies of rereading and reading ahead that think-alouds are designed to teach.

Although think-alouds are built into many core selections, they represent one way of creatively expanding the program. Look for additional points in the selection to craft think-alouds, perhaps tailored to the interests and background of the students you serve. Also, look for chances to build think-alouds into your daily whole-class read-aloud, a possibility we explore presently. They afford an ideal way to demonstrate how good readers resolve problems and make texts make sense.

Instructional Planning

We again use our planning templates to order the components of core instruction, turning now to the three comprehension components: the strategy introduction, the interactive read-aloud, and the core selection.

STRATEGY INTRODUCTION

As we have indicated, the comprehension strategy will not be new to fourth and fifth graders. The core will have provided many opportunities for students to learn about it in the early elementary grades. However, a quick review is useful, followed by its application. Note that the same strategy may be appropriate both in the read-aloud and in the core selection. However, these two texts may differ in important ways, making it necessary for the teacher to focus on a different strategy in each. In either case, the rationale for strategy review is that students should be scaffolded as they apply it to texts of increasing complexity.

INTERACTIVE READ-ALOUD

Planning an interactive read-aloud will require some time. It is akin to the process that the authors of your core program used to design the instruction for the week's selection. Although the process may seem daunting at first, we are actually asking that you decide what opportunities a text provides for you to highlight the importance of text structures and comprehension strategies to support understanding. Your choices will come from a small set of high-utility structures and strategies that can be used repeatedly.

You will recall that our preference is for a nonfiction read-aloud linked to curricular standards in science or social studies. We are not opposed to the occasional fiction read-aloud for balance, but preparing a nonfiction read-aloud is more involved. In Chapter 7, we began the planning process with an eye to vocabulary development. We first offered suggestions for sizing up the book and for deciding how to preteach key vocabulary. These were steps 1 and 2 of the planning process. We now turn to comprehension and continue with step 3. Figure 8.7 lists all eight steps for easy reference.

3. *Decide how to build necessary background knowledge.* As they write, authors make certain assumptions about what the reader already knows. Consider a science book that begins, "The earth's crust is made up of three basic kinds of rocks: igneous, metamorphic, and sedimentary." In introducing these terms, the author is assuming that the reader already knows what the earth's crust is. Of course, no author can possibly predict who will actually read a book or listen to it read aloud. Because prior knowledge of a topic differs greatly from reader to reader, it is possible that some students will not know what the earth's crust is. Consequently, their comprehension will be impaired because they will not be able to link the new ideas to their background knowledge. It is up to the teacher to anticipate possible gaps between what students actually know and what an author assumes they know. The teacher must then try to fill those gaps both before and during a read-aloud.

This is not a sure-fire process because knowledge levels are likely to differ greatly among students in the upper elementary grades. The teacher can nevertheless take steps to make the book comprehensible. These steps include:

---

1. Size up the book.
2. Decide how to preteach the key vocabulary.
3. Decide how to build necessary background knowledge.
4. Decide whether to highlight one or more text structures.
5. Decide whether to highlight one or more comprehension strategies.
6. Decide what to say and do during reading to model and encourage thinking.
7. Decide what to say and do after reading to deepen understanding.
8. Develop a follow-up activity in which the children write to demonstrate or deepen understanding.

FIGURE 8.7. Steps in planning an interactive read-aloud of an information book.

- Considering what content has previously been taught (Have the students been introduced to the earth's crust?)
- Choosing where to add information (Is it better situated before the read-aloud or as "asides" during the reading?)
- Choosing how to introduce background information (Is it best accomplished by simply telling important facts, by adding to the chart or diagram we discussed in Chapter 7, or by some other means?)
- Monitoring children's understanding as you read (Do they appear to have the background needed to respond to questions, make comments, pose questions?)

4. *Decide whether to highlight one or more text structures.* Text structure knowledge provides readers with a plan for how to recognize and remember the important information in a text. Over time, this knowledge also provides fourth- and fifth-grade writers with choices for how to communicate ideas. Narrative structures are generally tackled first, and your students are apt to be familiar with story maps as a means of grasping the structure of fiction. Because teachers in primary classrooms are accustomed to providing a steady diet of narratives in their read-alouds, in their shared readings, and in their student compositions, we will not spend time on planning for fiction read-alouds. At fourth and fifth grades, information texts are where the action is. Information texts are plentiful, and research indicates they have strong appeal. Their content is easily tied to science and social studies curricula, and read-alouds can serve as tune-ups for study in these areas later in the day.

Part of the trick in supporting flexible strategies for understanding the structure of information text is that the individual texts themselves often employ multiple structures; they may use cycles, chronologies, and descriptions in order to really develop a complex concept. For this reason, it is important that teachers embrace a multiple-structure approach. We have identified and defined in Figure 8.8 the most common structures, and we provide graphic organizers for each in Appendix G. It is our hope that fourth- and fifth-grade teachers will introduce (or review) *all* of them early in the year and then refer to them flexibly all year long—during read-alouds, student reading, and composition instruction. In fact, we hope that fourth- and fifth-grade classroom walls will be littered with graphic organizers that represent the structure of texts that students are reading. We have provided some attractive model organizers, easily made in our word processing program, in Appendix G.

Begin analyzing the organization of the book by looking for key patterns. It is rare for information books at fourth and fifth grades to be organized around a single pattern. Instead, you will find that they are combinations of two or more of the basic patterns. For the book you have chosen, consider whether a single structure is dominant or whether multiple structures are used in complex ways. Then decide whether highlighting the structure will afford a clear-cut lesson about text organization. There may be one portion of the book that provides a good example of an organizational pattern. Indicating the pattern to students can serve as a brief and valuable lesson about text structure. Over the course of numerous read-alouds, your students will gain an appreciation of how each pattern works through exposure to a variety of examples.

Pattern	How It Works
Ordered Listing	In this pattern the components are listed according to some characteristic. Sometimes the order matters. The components might have a natural order that makes them easier to write about and read about. For example, a book on minerals might be organized to present them to mirror the mineral hardness scale—from softness (talc) to hardest (diamond).
Topic–Subtopic	This is a pattern in which a main topic is presented by means of a series of subtopics. For instance, the topic of weather might be presented in terms of subtopics like storms, erosion, the water cycle, ways in which humans cope, and so on. This is one of the most common organizational patterns. It is used to organize most textbook chapters and is therefore important for students to grasp. It is very similar to ordered listing, depending on how the subtopics are sequenced.
Sequence	The text is organized around a simple order of events. These events are not necessarily linked by cause and effect. Left-to-right time lines are often used to illustrate this chronological relationship (e.g., geological eras).
Cause and Effect	This pattern is really a special type of sequence, in which one event causes the next to occur (e.g., a chemical reaction). Often the events are linked in chains, in which A causes B and B causes C, and so forth. Time lines can also be used to represent causal patterns, although arrows are often included to make the causal relationships clear.
Problem–Solution	A book organized with this pattern centers around a major social or scientific problem and presents possible solutions. In a book about air pollution, the author might begin by defining the problem and then outline alternative approaches to contending with it.
Cycle	A cycle is a type of causal sequence in which a number of steps make up a repeated process (e.g., water cycle, life cycle). An ordinary time line cannot capture the fact that the steps repeat, so a circular layout of arrows is usually used.
Hierarchy	In this pattern, large concepts are broken down (delineated) into components (e.g., the concept of rocks can be broken down into types of rocks). Usually, the largest concept is associated with the topic of the book (e.g., rocks). The next tier might include the three principal types of rocks, with the next tier providing examples of each. Many technical terms are organized in this way, and tree diagrams (see Chapter 7) are used to convey both the structure of the book and relationships among key terms.
Compare–Contrast	In this pattern, two or more concepts or ideas are discussed in terms of their similarities (comparison) and differences (contrast). T charts or Venn diagrams are often used either by authors or by teachers. Students tend to pick up this pattern easily, starting with two concepts and then adding more.

FIGURE 8.8. Basic text structures used in nonfiction.

5. *Decide whether to highlight one or more comprehension strategies.* Strategy instruction comprises a variety of instructional actions with shared characteristics. All strategy approaches identify and name a complex cognitive process, they all provide a series of concrete steps that an individual uses to accomplish this process, and they all explicitly identify when and why the strategy is helpful. Like text structures, strategies are more effective when they are taught as a toolbox for readers and writers. Again, as in the case of text structures, it is our hope that teachers will review *all* of the comprehen-

sion strategies early in the year, and then refer to them flexibly all year—during read-alouds and student reading.

Read-alouds are perfect contexts for strategy instruction. Modeling is simpler when the teacher is controlling the rate of text presentation. In addition, questioning facilitates guided practice of strategies. Teachers can easily identify good spots for strategy use and ask questions to guide students as they apply them. Finally, with a strong diet of truly interactive read-alouds, spontaneous comments and participation from students provide truly released responsibility for cognitive engagement in strategy use.

Planning for strategy instruction within a particular read-aloud is not difficult. Remember first that not all strategies are equally appropriate for a given text. Consider carefully when and where strategies can be applied. Look for clear-cut opportunities where understanding the text can be facilitated by a particular strategy. Do this by recalling the principal strategies and their most effective uses:

- Visualizing (building mental images that represent content)
- Inferring (logically combining stated facts or previously known facts to arrive at unstated facts)
- Predicting (using information from the text and from background knowledge to infer future events)
- Retelling (creating an informal narrative that includes key events and sufficient detail)
- Finding or inferring the main idea (distinguishing more important from less important information and arriving at the most important single fact, either by finding it explicitly stated or by inferring it)
- Summarizing (linking a series of main ideas into a coherent overview of a text)
- Synthesizing (linking information within the same book or across more than one book)

Having a text structure and comprehension strategy goal does not ensure that a read-aloud will be productive. The real test is in the clarity and appropriateness of teacher modeling. In our experience, there is a steep learning curve for this aspect of instruction. Mature readers employ comprehension strategies fairly flexibly, and it is difficult to access the procedures involved and to share them with fourth and fifth graders. We suggest that you display a chart of strategies in your classroom and refer to it often using clear, repetitive talk.

6. *Decide what to say and do during reading to model and encourage thinking.* Read-alouds afford many opportunities for a teacher to make the experience interactive. The most obvious is to pause to ask questions, but there are many alternatives that can add variety to how the children interact with the content. Just a few of these include:

- Asking for predictions
- Prompting students to *pose* questions
- Encouraging students to contribute to a summary up to a given point
- Soliciting additions to a chart or diagram that was started prior to the read-aloud

- Prompting interpretations of the chart or diagram
- Conducting think-alouds at points of possible confusion

In planning where to pause during a read-aloud and what to do at each point, we recommend these steps:

- Choose points in the text where you can think of ways to invite interaction. These points will be examples of how one or more strategies can be applied.
- Frame what you will say and consider inserting notes in your book to remind you.
- Be sure to include think-alouds at points where the author presents information that may be confusing to students or in conflict with their prior knowledge. (Remember our wolf example.) Use these opportunities to model fix-up strategies (what we call the four "Rs"): Rereading, Reading ahead, Reflecting, and Referring to outside sources.
- Make sure that the pauses involve a variety of ways for students to interact. Do not, for example, rely on questions alone.
- Be sure to include every pupil response techniques in order to maximize engagement. Asking all students to share with a partner, for example, ensures more engagement than calling on just one student.
- Include references to the graphics you have used to introduce the read-aloud. Remember that you have kept these on display. Whenever appropriate, engage students in adding to or modifying the graphics.

One confusing thing about comprehension is that it can continue once the book is closed. Often, only knowing the full picture allows a reader to realize which initial ideas were important. In addition, comprehension of text is different from memory of text; a reader may understand a text during the read-aloud but not actually do the cognitive work that is necessary to store important ideas in memory.

7. *Decide what to say and do after reading to deepen understanding.* When you reach the last page, you may be tempted to share a "the end" moment, without fostering further interaction among the students. We believe that closing the book and moving on to other lessons is a mistake. Plan for enough time to take advantage of the fact that the content is still fresh in the minds of students. Begin by conducting a discussion that focuses on inferential thinking, drawing conclusions, and "take-away" lessons. Review the completed graphic you started before the read-aloud. Then revisit the comprehension strategy you have chosen to highlight. Even a brief time for closure can ensure that students know that the read-aloud was an instructional opportunity that can help them as readers and thinkers.

8. *Develop a follow-up activity in which the children write to demonstrate or deepen understanding.* A read-aloud of this nature takes planning, and its potential for building knowledge and skills should not be wasted. Follow-up activities allow teachers to reduce the number of independent activities that must be planned to facilitate differentiated reading instruction, to build children's fluency and flexibility in writing, *and* to process text ideas deeply enough to facilitate their integration in students' memory.

To be effective, these activities must prompt students to think deeply about the content to which they have been exposed. A work sheet is unlikely to accomplish this aim. It is up to the teacher to prepare creative assignments appropriate to fourth or fifth grade. Such assignments might include:

- Listing talking points (what to tell a family member you learned in school today)
- Generating alternative titles (an excellent approach to inferring main ideas)
- Writing a blurb for a back cover (summarizing in disguise)
- Applying the content of the book (e.g., creating a poster warning about sharks)
- Writing to convert the organizer (still plainly visible!) back into prose. (This is essentially a retelling in the student's own words, using the graphic as a prompt. This activity provides practice in an important process in nonfiction writing: starting with an organizer and converting it to sentences and paragraphs.)
- Completing a new diagram or chart
- Concept sorting

Finally, you must decide how to schedule this post-read-aloud activity. How much time will it require? Should it be collaborative or individual? Should it take place during ELA time or outside the block? Can technology help? How will the results be shared?

Note that these same options for a follow-up writing activity can also be used for the core selection.

CORE SELECTION

In Figure 8.9 we begin to bring read-aloud and core selection planning together. You will recall that the same selection is used all week but that it is read aloud to the students on day 1. The first day is different in another way as well. Because the selection is unfamiliar, the teacher must introduce it. The core teachers' edition is generally very helpful in building background knowledge and piquing the interest of students. On the following days, introducing the selection is unnecessary, but brief reviews are important; they are represented in Figure 8.10.

TIER 2 INSTRUCTION IN COMPREHENSION

Because Tier 2 time is limited, we believe it is best spent filling gaps in the basic skills (e.g., word recognition and fluency) students need to comprehend, not in developing comprehension directly. We also believe that all students must be served during Tier 2, including those without appreciable gaps in reading development. Consequently, the students we target for comprehension at Tier 2 are those with adequate fluency. Remember that comprehension, like vocabulary, is an open-ended proficiency: Our students should never cease to grow as comprehenders. Tier 2 time is an opportunity to stimulate such growth for fourth- and fifth-grade students whose fluency is adequate.

Time	Activity	Description
5 min	Strategy Introduction	The teacher highlights a comprehension strategy or text structure that will be useful with the interactive read-aloud. The teacher reminds the students how to apply the strategy, why it is important, and when to use it.
15 min	Interactive Read-Aloud	The teacher chooses an interesting and challenging piece of authentic literature, either narrative or information text, to read aloud. The teacher quickly preteaches any words that are essential to the text's meaning and also provides synonyms or quick explanations of word meaning during reading. The teacher reads the book aloud, modeling fluent reading and applying a gradual release of responsibility model for teaching about the comprehension strategy or text structure.
3 min	Introduce Written Response	The teacher introduces a follow-up writing activity based on the read-aloud, to be completed later.
10 min	Vocabulary	The teacher introduces core vocabulary for the week, introducing meanings, providing multiple sentence contexts, thinking aloud about the spellings, and listing derivatives.
12 min	Choral Reading of the Story	The teacher introduces the core selection, building background and creating interest. The students and the teacher then read the selection chorally. The teacher stops when needed to monitor and develop comprehension. If the story is long, this same procedure is used again the next day, with the rest of the story.

FIGURE 8.9. Tier 1 comprehension initial planning.

Time	Activity	Description
2 min	Strategy Introduction	The teacher highlights a comprehension strategy or text structure that will be useful with the interactive read-aloud. The teacher reminds the students how to apply the strategy, why it is important, and when to use it.
10 min	Interactive Read-Aloud	The teacher chooses an interesting and challenging piece of authentic literature, either narrative or information text, to read aloud. The teacher quickly preteaches any words that are essential to the text's meaning and also provides synonyms or quick explanations of word meaning during reading. The teacher reads the book aloud, modeling fluent reading and applying a gradual release of responsibility model for teaching about the comprehension strategy or text structure.
10 min	Vocabulary Review	The teacher introduces a follow-up writing activity based on the read-aloud, to be completed later.
10 min	Partner Reading	Students reread with a partner and purpose to improve their expression and their understanding.
10 min	Whisper Reading	Students reread independently for fluency and to complete a purposeful task.
3 min	Introduce Written Response	The teacher introduces a follow-up writing activity based on the core selection.

FIGURE 8.10. Tier 1 comprehension additional planning.

Content

Unlike word recognition, comprehension does not comprise a sequence of skills that are acquired one after another. Instead, our goal is to equip students with essential strategies used by proficient readers and to facilitate their use in texts. Because we keep returning to the same cluster of effective strategies, we ensure growth by (1) varying the types of texts that students encounter and (2) gradually increasing the difficulty level of those texts. In our discussion of read-aloud planning, we reviewed the principal comprehension strategies: predicting, inferring, visualizing, using knowledge of text structure, grasping main ideas, seeking clarification, generating questions, summarizing a selection, and synthesizing content across selections. This go-to menu of strategies has been used to craft numerous approaches to instruction; we examine five in the following section. Many teachers post the strategies in chart form for quick reference. Upper elementary students must come to realize that the strategies are not limited to a few activities planned by the teacher. They are always relevant.

Instructional Strategies

We have chosen to focus on five of the most effective instructional techniques, those with the longest research "pedigrees." Each can be applied to a wide variety of texts, although we encourage you to privilege information texts with links to your science and social studies curricula. Because the students are adequately fluent and because you will support them during Tier 2 time, select challenging texts. Fourth graders should be reading texts at a fifth-grade level during these activities, and fifth graders should be reading texts at an early middle school level. This policy is consistent with the stretch texts recommended in the Common Core Standards.

Each of the following strategies can also be used on a whole-class basis in science and social studies. Instruction in these subjects provides additional opportunities to read information text and will help prepare your students for the reading they will be expected to undertake in the middle grades.

QUESTION–ANSWER RELATIONSHIPS

Taffy Raphael (1984; Raphael, Highfield, & Au, 2006) provided teachers with a simple tool for organizing and generating good questions. She began with the three levels of comprehension we have already discussed. It would be natural to suppose that her approach involves one type of question for each level. However, question–answer relationships (QARs) are of four kinds. This is because she envisioned two kinds of inferential questions. One kind is text based and involves logically linking two facts stated by an author. The other type represents another logical connection, one that links a fact provided by the author and a second fact in the reader's prior knowledge. The cognitive process of inferring the answer is the same, but the use of the text is different.

This approach uses child-friendly terms to label the four types of QARs, grouped in pairs. The first two QARs are categorized as In the Book QARs. Answering them appropriately is a text-based undertaking. Right There questions require the student to locate explicitly stated facts. These questions are, of course, at the literal level of comprehension. Think and Search questions involve linking two or more explicit facts in text in order to infer a fact that is not stated.

Raphael classifies the other two types of QARs as In Your Head QARs because prior knowledge and perspective are required to answer them. Author and You questions combine information from the text with prior knowledge. On Your Own questions rely almost entirely on prior knowledge and experience. These questions can involve critical judgments. The organizer in Figure 8.11 may help you clarify these distinctions for your students.

Why teach students these types of questions? First, doing so conveys the idea that there are different ways to comprehend, and we can get at these ways by asking different types of questions. Second, it provides students with a useful framework for generating questions. Rather than asking students to pose questions, a teacher can be more specific: "Who can suggest a Think and Search question?" Additionally, the QAR framework embodies all three levels of comprehension (both Think and Search and Author and You call for inferences) and provides a vehicle for introducing students to these levels in student-friendly terms. Finally, the QAR framework provides a vocabulary for redirecting a student who has answered a question incorrectly. When a student fails to make an inference, for example, a teacher can say, "Think again. That was actually a Think and Search question" or "You are giving me an On Your Own answer. I was asking an Author and You question."

RECIPROCAL TEACHING

The best known approach to multiple strategy instruction is reciprocal teaching. Palinscar and Brown (1984) developed a collaborative activity that involves students in four comprehension strategies on a repeated basis: (1) student-generated questions, (2) clarifying what has been read, (3) summarizing the content of a text, and (4) making predictions. Since its inception, reciprocal teaching has been the subject of numerous investigations. It is one of the most thoroughly validated instructional approaches for developing students' ability to apply comprehension strategies.

In order to implement reciprocal teaching, you must commit some time to preparing your students. They need to understand the four strategies that make up reciprocal teaching. Developing this understanding means that you will need to teach these strat-

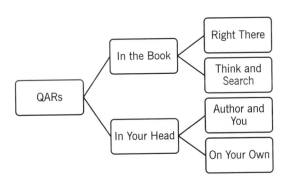

FIGURE 8.11. Four types of question–answer relationships.

egies one at a time until the students appreciate what is required. Direct explanation (Duffy, 2009) or a form of explicit teaching (Duke & Pearson, 2002) can be used.

Once the students have acquired some proficiency in these four strategies, it is time to put them together in the reciprocal teaching lesson structure. This structure involves the following steps:

1. The teacher introduces the selection. Doing so requires background building and preteaching of key terms, just as in preparing students for any assigned reading.

2. The teacher provides the students with an overall focus. For example, they might be given a chart to complete, or a postreading project might be described to them so that they can be thinking about it as they read.

3. The teacher then forms small groups. Present-day practices differ as to how to do this. Some teachers prefer groups of mixed ability, the approach used in cooperative learning (Johnson & Johnson, 1998). Other teachers use behavioral and personality considerations in forming groups. There appears to be consensus that once a group is functioning smoothly as a team, its makeup should not be altered simply for the sake of variety. In Tier 2 work, of course, you will already have a group formed homogeneously by achievement, at least insofar as the students will all be meeting grade-level fluency standards.

4. The groups meet, and each member has a copy of the selection. One of the group members has been appointed "teacher." This designation rotates among the group members. It is something of a misnomer because the group teacher is not necessarily more knowledgeable and does not undertake any kind of explicit instruction. Instead, the student designated as teacher simply leads the group through the four steps.

5. The work of the group progresses through a repeated cycle, during which the four comprehension strategies are applied to short segments of the reading selection. Some teachers use charts or a smartboard to remind the group teachers of which strategy comes next. Samples of such charts appear in Appendix D. The segments are often about a page in length and may correspond to text segments associated with subheadings. The steps the students are taught to follow in a reciprocal teaching cycle are illustrated in Figure 8.12.

You can use Tier 2 time to introduce a text and engage students in a few rounds of reciprocal teaching, eventually releasing them back to their seats to continue the reciprocal teaching discussion. Over time, that will give you a chance to listen to each group member's teaching turn, providing insights into his or her strategy knowledge and metacognitive growth.

READING GUIDES

A reading guide is a document containing questions to be answered, charts and diagrams to be completed, and other tasks that students are to undertake while reading. A reading guide may also contain page numbers and subheadings to help students keep their place

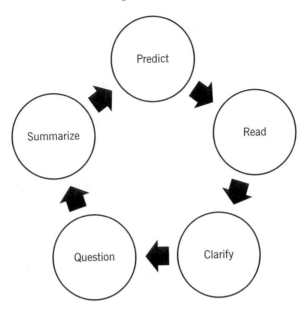

FIGURE 8.12. The cycle of reciprocal teaching.

as they read. You can use Tier 2 time to introduce both the selection and the guide and then work with other groups as the students begin to read the selection and complete the guide. At first blush, reading guides may not appear to be an inspired approach, but their advantages are considerable. McKenna, Franks, Conradi, and Lovette (2011) list the following:

- They improve comprehension by focusing students' attention on important aspects of content.
- They make reading an active rather than a passive process.
- They cause students to translate the material into their own words, phrases, and sentences.
- They are a means of integrating reading and writing.
- They produce a useful tool for review.
- They provide a blueprint for postreading discussion and give students a valuable discussion aid.
- They model strategic, purposeful reading.
- They model effective note taking.

The fear that students will only read what is needed to complete the guide is easily allayed. We certainly agree that asking questions or presenting other tasks that simply require copying verbatim information from the text will encourage students to approach the reading at a superficial level. If a teacher truly believes that students will be tempted to focus only on what the guide requires, they are admitting what a powerful tool a guide can be. The solution is to pose questions and tasks that require higher order thinking.

When students must make inferences, categorize information, and reorganize ideas and thoughts, they need to process the content rather deeply. We argue that if a teacher is satisfied that the tasks contained in a guide require adequate comprehension, then it does not matter if the students "only" read to complete those tasks.

Writing a reading guide is a straightforward task, and you will get better at it over time. Begin by closely reading the material you expect your students to read. Decide what it is you wish them to take away from the reading. Once you do this, your choice of tasks will seem much clearer. Develop your guide in a linear fashion, moving from page to page and from section to section. Be sure to include visual landmarks (page numbers and subheadings, if available). Do not avoid literal-level tasks altogether. Explicitly stated information can be useful in arriving at inferences and making critical judgments. Opportunities to engage in these higher level tasks should follow literal-level fact gathering. In this way, the guide models for students the hierarchical thinking process that is the basis of good comprehension: literal to inferential to critical.

Employing reading guides requires that you prepare students in how to complete them. You can model this process the first time your Tier 2 group uses one. Because guides are rarely used before grade 4, your students will probably need this instruction. When students begin to catch on to the way guides work, you can introduce more examples but this time provide them with their own copies. As you complete the projected guide, ask students to complete their own copy, which often means copying information into the appropriate place. Next, you can move on to guides that the students will complete with partners. At this stage, you will need to monitor their work to ensure that they are completing each guide properly. Troubleshoot whenever necessary. Finally, give students a chance to complete guides independently. Monitoring at this stage will consist of responding to raised hands and being cognizant of how guides are used by students during the postreading discussion.

Make sure that guides become a part of postreading discussions. When you return to your Tier 2 group, ask students to have their completed guides in front of them for reference. They can serve as powerful prompts. Above all, be critical of your own guides. Keep an eye out for trouble spots that can be improved the next time they are used.

TEACHING ABOUT TEXT STRUCTURE

In our discussion of read-aloud planning, we listed the basic structures used by authors to organize their writing. We suggested that a read-aloud might afford an opportunity to quickly review one or more of them, especially if they are used in combination. Tier 2 time affords another opportunity for students to examine how the basic structures are often used in combination. This time, students can observe in their own copies how complex blends of text structures are signaled in writing. Let's consider some examples in which the basic structures have been combined:

■ The author of a trade book that describes sources of energy may use simple listing to present the sources but follow these with a section that compares and contrasts them.

■ A book on the problem of the disappearing rain forest may use simple listing to present possible solutions, at the same time comparing them. In this case, simple listing is combined with problem–solution and comparison–contrast.

■ Gail Gibbons begins her book *Recycle* (fifth-grade readability) by describing the problem posed by ever-increasing amounts of trash. She does this by tracking the movement of trash from the curbside to the landfill, employing a sequential pattern to present the problem. She then turns to recycling as a major solution to this problem. However, the solution is broken down into the types of materials to be recycled. She uses simple listing to present them: paper, glass, cans, plastic, and polystyrene. A four-page section is devoted to each type. For this book, then, the overall text structure is problem–solution, but the problem component relies on a sequential structure and the solution component on simple listing.

Before we go on, it is important that we distinguish between genre and text structure. Genres are associated with text structures, of course, but text structures exist on a more basic level, as building blocks for genres. That is, a single genre may employ several text structures. A short story or fiction trade book, for example, will have an overall structure but will also have an overarching story structure that includes presenting the setting and characters, revealing a problem faced by the protagonist, and unfolding how the problem is approached and solved.

Remember that fourth and fifth graders have probably received instruction in basic text structures. The key in the upper elementary grades is to review and refine their knowledge of these structures, to teach them to recognize complex combinations, and to help them use their developing knowledge of text structures to plan their writing.

SUMMARIZING

"My goal is to say in ten sentences what everyone else says in an entire book," the philosopher Nietzsche once observed. Of course, this is easier said than done. How can you nudge your students in this direction? A good summary requires a student to make key decisions about the importance of ideas and events. This is not an easy proficiency to foster, but we describe one basic approach that has often proved successful in helping students summarize information text. It builds on the ability to infer main ideas.

The approach was developed and validated by Hare and Borchardt (1984). It does require students to write, so there is some prerequisite knowledge of spelling, which should be in place by the upper elementary years. In their approach, you will need to make a chart to review the process with children and to post as a reference as they write their own summaries. You will also need several short information texts that you can use in modeling the procedure. Finally, you will need a set of texts for scaffolding and to give children opportunities to independently apply the technique. Begin by asking the students to read the text. Next, model this procedure using the large chart you have created. Figure 8.13 includes all of the steps. These steps are easy to state but not so easy to follow. It will take time for students to think through them and to apply them to new texts they

1. Make sure you understand what you have read. Clarify what you don't understand.

2. Read it again, and this time mark the important parts.

3. Make sure that you can say the main idea of each paragraph.

4. Write each main idea as a note to yourself.

5. Write your summary by connecting the main ideas in a paragraph.

6. Check to make sure that you have avoided lists, included or created topic sentences, gotten rid of unnecessary details, and combined paragraphs.

7. Edit your summary so that it sounds natural.

FIGURE 8.13. Summarization chart for student reference.

encounter. However, instruction in summarizing can be effective, and the approach of Hare and Borchardt has the additional advantage of fostering writing ability.

Instructional Planning

Like vocabulary, comprehension instruction has no clear sequence. The text structures examined are, of course, determined by the selection. The comprehension strategies reviewed are determined both by what is appropriate for the selection and by the need to vary strategies across time and texts. In planning, we link vocabulary and comprehension. In Chapter 7, we discussed the need to choose words from the selection. Taken together, a joint focus on vocabulary and comprehension begins by carefully examining the selection to choose (1) a strategy to highlight, (2) a method of discussing the text structure, and (3) important vocabulary (general words for fiction, technical words for information text).

Because these fourth or fifth graders will be reading the selection silently, it is necessary to apply an established instructional approach that will get them started. They might generate questions according to the four QARs, they might engage in reciprocal teaching of the selection, they might complete a teacher-prepared reading guide, or they might read for the purpose of writing a summary. Note that these techniques can be combined in creative ways. During a reciprocal teaching session, the students can complete a reading guide. Likewise, the questioning phase of reciprocal teaching can be limited to a particular QAR (anything but Right There, of course!).

Merging vocabulary with comprehension instruction presents additional opportunities to blend instructional approaches. For example, a reading guide, which is primarily concerned with supporting comprehension and modeling strategies, might contain a feature analysis chart or graphic organizer to construct or complete. We hope to convey the idea that there is not a single best approach, nor is there a universal, cookie-cutter plan that will work for all groups and selections. This is good news, however, because it provides you with a chance to plan creatively by mixing and varying your approaches to instruction. Over time, your choices will keep your planning fresh and your abler students engaged. It will also give you the chance to gauge the more effective combinations of instructional approaches.

Let's consider the Tier 2 instructional sequence for vocabulary and comprehension. We begin with the planning charts presented in Chapter 7 for vocabulary instruction and expand them to their final form to include comprehension. Note that students read outside of group time. Figure 8.14 is based on a fiction selection. Note the repetitive pattern that embodies cumulative review. You will see in the Appendices H–J that we have used QARs and reading guides in our model lessons for fiction. Now let's consider how to plan for vocabulary and comprehension based on an information trade book. Remember that, as with fiction, we usually must plan over a number of days to cover an entire information book written at the fifth- or sixth-grade level. Figure 8.15 shows how a week's small-group lessons would be structured.

The plans for both fiction and nonfiction provide for cumulative review of both vocabulary and content. In comprehension, we encourage you to look for ways to bridge backward to previous content so that students can link the new with the familiar. Discussions that are cumulative (i.e., not limited to the text segment of a single day) are an excellent means of helping students forge these links (McKenna & Robinson, 2011).

Finally, we offer a few points about apportioning time. First, note that once these students begin to read, you are free to attend to other groups. You will need to schedule all of your small groups skillfully in order to take advantage of this flexibility. Also, we have assumed a 5-day plan for purposes of illustration. A specific trade book may require more or less time to complete. Further, you may find it convenient to conduct the postreading portion of these small-group lessons on the next day, blending the discussion of one text segment with an introduction to the next. Doing so provides greater flexibility, but there may be a cost in terms of the freshness of the words and content in the minds of your students.

CHOOSING TIER 3 PROGRAMS FOR COMPREHENSION

As in previous chapters, we stop short of recommending commercial programs because we lack sufficient empirical evidence to recommend one over the other. In addition, as researchers turn their attention to the needs of young adolescent students within an RTI framework, new effective interventions will be developed. When we look for evidence about the effectiveness of interventions, we turn to four Internet sources that are currently updated frequently: (1) Institute of Education Sciences' What Works Clearing-

Day 1
• Introduce text segment and build background knowledge. • Review a strategy that will be helpful in the first text segment. • Introduce an appropriate instructional approach (e.g., reciprocal teaching or a reading guide) that students will use to guide their reading.
Day 2
• Teach vocabulary from day 1 segment. • Review day 1 content in light of instructional approach. • Introduce day 2 text segment and build background knowledge. • Review a strategy that will be helpful in the next text segment. • Introduce an appropriate instructional approach (e.g., reciprocal teaching or a reading guide) that students will use to guide their reading.
Day 3
• Review vocabulary from day 1. • Teach vocabulary from day 2 segment. • Review day 2 content in light of instructional approach. • Introduce day 3 text segment and build background knowledge. • Review a strategy that will be helpful in the next text segment. • Introduce an appropriate instructional approach (e.g., reciprocal teaching or a reading guide) that students will use to guide their reading.
Day 4
• Review vocabulary from day 1 and day 2. • Teach vocabulary from day 3 segment. • Review day 3 content in light of instructional approach. • Introduce day 4 text segment and build background knowledge. • Review a strategy that will be helpful in the next text segment. • Introduce an appropriate instructional approach (e.g., reciprocal teaching or a reading guide) that students will use to guide their reading.
Day 5
• Review vocabulary from day 1, day 2, and day 3. • Teach vocabulary from day 4 segment. • Review day 4 content in light of instructional approach. • Introduce day 5 text segment and build background knowledge. • Review a strategy that will be helpful in the next text segment. • Introduce an appropriate instructional approach (e.g., reciprocal teaching or a reading guide) that students will use to guide their reading.

FIGURE 8.14. Teaching general vocabulary and comprehension for fiction during Tier 2 time.

Day 1
• Introduce text segment and build background knowledge. • Use most appropriate approach to introduce words in day 1 segment. • Review a strategy that will be helpful in the first text segment. • Introduce an appropriate instructional approach (e.g., reciprocal teaching or a reading guide) that students will use to guide their reading.
Day 2
• Review day 1 content and vocabulary in light of instructional approach. • Introduce day 2 text segment and build background knowledge. • Use most appropriate approach to introduce words in day 2 segment. • Review a strategy that will be helpful in this text segment. • Introduce an appropriate instructional approach (e.g., reciprocal teaching or a reading guide) that students will use to guide their reading.
Day 3
• Review day 1 and day 2 content and vocabulary in light of instructional approach. • Introduce day 3 text segment and build background knowledge. • Use most appropriate approach to introduce words in day 3 segment. • Review a strategy that will be helpful in this text segment. • Introduce an appropriate instructional approach (e.g., reciprocal teaching or a reading guide) that students will use to guide their reading.
Day 4
• Review day 1, day 2, and day 3 content and vocabulary in light of instructional approach. • Introduce day 4 text segment and build background knowledge. • Use most appropriate approach to introduce words in day 4 segment. • Review a strategy that will be helpful in this text segment. • Introduce an appropriate instructional approach (e.g., reciprocal teaching or a reading guide) that students will use to guide their reading.
Day 5
• Review day 1, day 2, day 3, and day 4 content and vocabulary in light of instructional approach. • Introduce day 5 text segment and build background knowledge. • Use most appropriate approach to introduce words in day 5 segment. • Review a strategy that will be helpful in this text segment. • Introduce an appropriate instructional approach (e.g., reciprocal teaching or a reading guide) that students will use to guide their reading.

FIGURE 8.15. Teaching technical vocabulary and comprehension for nonfiction during Tier 2 time.

house (*www.ies.ed.gov/ncee/wwc*), (2) Center on Instruction (*www.centeroninstruction. org*), (3) Best Evidence Encyclopedia (*www.bestevidence.org*), and (4) National Center on Response to Intervention (*www.rti4success.org*). When you search for evidence on the efficacy of intensive interventions for comprehension designed for upper elementary students, consider searching at a range of grade levels (including the middle grades) in order to make your search as broad as possible.

We encourage you to think carefully about the implications of an intensive intervention program in comprehension. Our approach, based on the cognitive model of reading assessment, is to identify the basic factors that may be impeding comprehension for particular students and to intervene at that level. Cases of comprehension difficulty when all of the factors influencing comprehension are within normal limits are mercifully rare. For this reason, most of the commercial interventions do not target comprehension exclusively but focus also on underlying causes. The assessments that accompany these programs are therefore multidimensional, and the hope is that by improving proficiency in an underlying area improvements in comprehension proficiency will follow.

Chapter 9

Creating a Climate for Extensive, Meaningful Reading and Writing

In the last four chapters of this book, we have presented background knowledge and planning strategies necessary to address whole-group and small-group instruction for your students. Before moving into the specifics of such instruction, however, it is important to consider the larger context of literacy development: the classroom context into which instruction must fit. The school day provides many opportunities to foster a classroom climate that supports literacy growth and that privileges literate activities. Teachers face what is sometimes described as the 91–9 problem. From birth until high school graduation, students will spend 91 minutes outside of school for every 9 minutes they spend in the classroom. For many students, those 91 minutes will entail very little reading and writing. The key is to take full advantage of the 9 minutes available to us. This means thinking beyond the time allocations of the ELA block and viewing the entire school day as holding the potential to foster engagement. In this chapter, we offer a variety of ways of making literacy a daylong priority.

PROMOTING LITERACY THROUGH THE PHYSICAL ENVIRONMENT

Our visits to classrooms often reveal a stark contrast between the environments in primary-grade rooms and those in grades 4 and 5. In the lower grades, it is common to see walls filled with posters, displays of student work, book covers, word walls, reminders about comprehension strategies, and the like. We see an abundance of trade books, often organized by topic, theme, and level. In grades 4 and 5, on the other hand, we are more likely to see a great deal of bare wall space and far fewer books. There is no justification for these differences. Some teachers may view the physical features of primary classrooms as somehow too childish to emulate in grades 4 and 5. We strongly disagree. The level of what students see can easily be made appropriate to their maturation and interests. The fact is, conveying the idea that literacy is important involves more than good instruction. We can reinforce it by creating an environment that invites engagement and exploration and that communicates the desirability of literate activity.

Gene Cramer (1994) suggests some highly practical guidelines for making your classroom environment more conducive to reading:

- Surround children with books. Develop a classroom library in which a variety of books are easily accessible. The library should invite browsing and selecting books to take home.
- Have a simple checkout system for children to take books home from the classroom library. Do not get bogged down in management details.
- Make the reading environment attractive. An inexpensive carpet, some colorful posters, a couple of beanbag chairs, and possibly a floor lamp or two can do much to enhance a reading corner in the classroom.
- Attend to students' physical comfort during reading sessions: adequate light, heat, ventilation, comfortable seating, and space.
- Offer healthful foods, such as raisins or crackers, as "treats" during reading and listening times. By linking a basic human need with reading, a pleasurable association with reading can be established.
- Arrange seasonal and topical displays of books in the classroom and discuss them with your students. Read sample passages and then leave the books prominently displayed. Students will pick them up to take home.
- Plan bulletin boards that reflect the joys of reading. Themes might include adventures, seasonal sports, other countries and customs, and so on. Illustrate the bulletin boards with book jackets, titles, pictures, book reviews, and comments from authors and students. Remember that critical response to reading is a hallmark of engagement and of maturing literary tastes.
- Display photographs of all students, with lists of books each has critiqued below their pictures.

Let's examine a few of these suggestions in more detail, beginning with how to display books. Most books written for students are adorned with enticing covers, expertly designed to attract buyers. Too many upper elementary teachers shelve books with only their spines showing—library style—so that the appeal of the covers is hidden. Granted, displaying books so that their front covers show requires more space. Solve this problem by rotating key books so that some of them are always presented with their covers visible. You can also use a wire rack like those seen bookstores. Angled shelving serves the same purpose. You can post book jackets on a bulletin board or suspend them as mobiles. If nothing else, lean a few books on a portion of your chalkboard ledge.

Posters promoting reading lend an excellent touch to the environment. The American Library Association offers a series depicting celebrities holding their favorite books (*www.ala.org*), but these are expensive. You can create your own posters using "celebrities" in your own room. All you need is a digital camera and Microsoft Word. Begin by photographing your students holding their favorite book. Then create the poster message

FIGURE 9.1. Teacher-made poster promoting reading.

by keyboarding it in large print. Kids can stylize their own messages. Paste a conventional (film) photo onto a printout of the poster, or place a scanned or downloaded version of the photo in the document before you print it. The result (for an example, see Figure 9.1) is a teacher-made poster encouraging reading. It's free, and it has a local relevance that commercial products cannot match.

We recommend featuring books by dedicating a portion of a wall or whiteboard for this purpose. There are many ways to call attention to the featured book. You might ask students to sign their names if they want to endorse the book, as in Figure 9.2. You can modify the practice of displaying book covers by adding an enticing fact or question. Figure 9.3 depicts one example.

Featuring books assumes, of course, that there are plenty of books to feature! We believe that the principal way to bolster a literate environment is by increasing the amount of quality reading material available to students. Doing so may appear to be an expensive proposition, but there are low-cost ways to enrich your stock of engaging materials. Enterprising teachers collect free books from their students' participation in book clubs. They team with other teachers to make requests for parent–teacher association

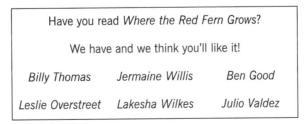

FIGURE 9.2. Student endorsements of a book.

FIGURE 9.3. Example of using a fact to lure students to a book.

funds. They mount annual book drives, which can yield a great many books. They might, for example, put out the word in a note home to parents that they are looking for donations of books their kids may have enjoyed at early ages; some parents are happy to be rid of the "clutter." They arrange for legacy books, which are contributed by their students at the end of the year. Students are asked to choose one of their own books at home, one that future students might enjoy. Students can create a label and place it on the inside front cover, identifying themselves as the contributor. Teachers find that sometimes library throwaways can still be serviceable. It is a good idea to keep abreast of the schedule the local public library uses to purge its holdings.

Don't forget magazines. Magazines designed for students can have great appeal for several reasons: They are attractively formatted and illustrated; they invite browsing rather than extended reading, and they are well suited to students' interests. Having magazines on hand in the classroom is usually not expensive. Since the *Reader's Guide to Periodical Literature* does not index sources below grade 7, elementary library media specialists often do not keep back copies. Approach your own or another school's media specialist to see if you can make an arrangement. Some magazines have content area ties that can be useful. For example, *Time for Kids* is *Time* magazine's publication for readers through grade 6. It has obvious connections with social studies and offers useful tips for teachers. Likewise, *National Geographic Kids* is the upper elementary version of *National Geographic* and has many ties to both the science and social studies curricula. These are only two examples. Find out which magazines your school library subscribes to and begin to negotiate.

Library media specialists make wonderful allies. Not only can they supply you with periodicals, but they can also make book recommendations, acquaint you with online resources, and conduct an occasional read-aloud. Another advantage to cultivating a good working relationship is the possibility of turning your classroom into a "branch library." With the cooperation of the library media specialist and careful attention to logistics, you can arrange for a rotating supply of books to enter your classroom for use by students. If you can make this happen, you can create a large and dynamic supply of good books.

LINKING READING AND WRITING

The connection between reading and writing is strong and reciprocal. Writing tends to improve reading ability, just as reading tends to improve writing ability. This is reason enough for finding ways to link the two, but there is another reason as well. By giving students opportunities to write about what they read, teachers can encourage deeper engagement with text and stimulate higher order thinking. When students are offered choices about what to write and develop a habit of responding, the classroom climate is altered. Literate activity is privileged, and a community of readers and writers begins to develop.

Providing opportunities for students to compose responses is not difficult. They can follow whole-class instruction in a common selection, they can relate to a small-group selection, or they can stem from science or social studies materials. Using a variety of structured response formats affords choice and ensures practice in writing for a range of purposes. The possibilities for response formats are almost unlimited. Here are just a few:

- *Open-ended questions.* These invite divergent thinking, speculation, and inference. ("Which character was your least favorite and why?")
- *Prompts.* Specific frames can elicit particular kinds of responses. ("My favorite part of the book was … ")
- *Diary entries.* Here the student assumes the persona of a character and writes a diary entry consistent with the text.
- *Letters to or from characters.* The student either writes to a character, perhaps to ask a question or offer advice, or assumes the persona of one character and writes to another.
- *Illustrations.* The student creates an illustration that is consistent with information contained in the text but that is not dependent on actual illustrations.
- *Cause–effect explanations.* The student infers the cause of an event in cases where the actual cause is unclear.
- *Speculations on motives.* A response similar to causal explanations is for the student to attempt to infer why a particular character takes a particular action, again in a case where motivation is ambiguous.
- *Alternate endings.* The student composes an ending that is consistent with events to a certain point but that takes an unexpected and imaginative turn.
- *Blurbs.* A blurb is a paragraph created by publishers to persuade a buyer to purchase a book. It is often filled with tantalizing facts and exaggeration.
- *"What if" predictions.* When students know the eventual outcome of a novel or story, predictions are no longer possible, *unless* a key fact is altered. ("What might have happened had the main character done this instead of that?")

MEANINGFUL COLLABORATIVE WORK

Literature Circles

Literature circles, also called literature response groups and literature study groups, are student discussion groups in which risk-free interchanges about mutually read books are invited. They create situations in which students interact with peers who may have different cultural backgrounds, and research suggests that peer interactions of this kind can lead to improved attitudes toward reading (e.g., Leal, 1993). In our model of differentiation, we have planned for all students to have 15 minutes of reading practice and 15 minutes of written response time; either or both of those segments can surely be retasked periodically to allow for a literature circle, sometimes called a book club. To support you in this, we have included materials that you can use for literature circles in Appendix F.

The rationale for literature circles is persuasive. Literature groups represent one way to model the sort of behavior that teachers should seek to foster in children if they are to participate in a literate culture. Although reading can be done on a cloistered, solitary basis, it is an inherently social act because it involves at least two individuals: reader and writer. Published works have shown that groups of multiple readers afford the opportunity of introducing a second social dimension among readers of the same work. This can be important when a student is exposed to peers whose positive attitudes may affect the perception of reading. Moreover, discussion among readers has the potential to broaden children's critical perspectives on what reading is and should be (e.g., Eeds & Wells, 1989; Leal, 1993; Schlick Noe & Johnson, 1999). Literature circles are so popular that many variations have emerged. There are many resources available online as well, such as the excellent site maintained at Seattle University (Literature Circles Resource Center: *www.litcircles.org*). Here you will find many examples for the intermediate grades.

In general, planning and conducting literature circles involves five steps, as follows.

1. *Choose a book.* If your classroom varies widely in proficiently, you will need to choose several books so that each circle can read a book of appropriate difficulty. Use your knowledge of fiction that is likely to have high appeal, and seek advice if necessary. Choosing books for students reading below level can be tricky because the content as well as the text may be too simple. Schlick Noe and Johnson (1999) recommend choosing a sequence of books for the entire year, but doing so may not be feasible. Better to get your feet wet first.

2. *Provide opportunities for students to read.* Reading is done independently, and as we have mentioned, it can be built into Tier 2 time.

3. *Provide opportunities for students to discuss.* It is important to convey what you expect to occur during a literature circle discussion. You may need to model and explain the behaviors you would like to see. Offer examples that students might bring to a discussion—for example, sharing a passage, discussing and illustration, or posing a question. Harvey Daniels (2001) recommends using role sheets to guide and support the discus-

sion, but if you choose to use these, you will not need them very long. After the discussion, debrief with students about what went well and what could have gone better.

4. *Encourage students to write about what they have read.* Early in the year, you will need to model this process. Make clear what the purpose of such writing is. Think aloud as you compose you own responses to selections the entire class has read or listened to. Provide suggestions such as those we discussed earlier in this chapter (e.g., open-ended questions, prompts, diary entries, letters to or from characters, illustrations, cause–effect explanations, speculations on motives, alternate endings, blurbs, "what if" predictions). Provide feedback and encourage depth of responses.

5. *Plan an extension project.* There are many possibilities for luring students back into the book for the purpose of engaging in a follow-up project. Examples include the creative (e.g., writing a story in a style similar to the author's or producing an original illustration), the analytical (e.g., contrasting the book with another by the same author), or the inferential (e.g., constructing a chart to contrast characters or drawing a hypothetical map of the setting). It is also important to give some thought to how the projects will be shared.

Idea Circles

Literature discussion groups bring students together to discuss *fiction* they have all read. Guthrie and McCann (1996) discovered that using *nonfiction* as the basis of these discussions can be highly motivating as well. Best of all, kids need not have read the same selection. Rather, the common element is the topic. Guthrie and McCann define an idea circle as a "peer-led, small-group discussion of concepts fueled by multiple text sources" (p. 88). In an idea circle, everyone has something unique to contribute to the discussion by virtue of having read different sources.

You can differentiate these assignments deftly, ensuring that abler readers undertake more challenging materials. You may need to take precautions, however, to guard against one or two students taking over the discussion and eclipsing others. Spelling out some simple ground rules in advance can foster balanced discussions. For example, the discussion might begin with each student sharing one fact that she or he discovered. A moderator might also be appointed, with the duty to solicit input from all participants. Next, we present a slightly modified approach to the five-step process of planning and conducting idea circles.

1. *Assemble a text set on a particular topic.* (A text set is a collection of books on the same topic but written at a variety of difficulty levels.) A topic that is part of the social studies or science curriculum makes an excellent choice. As an example, consider sound, a science topic. Some books at various levels might include:

- Connie Jankowski, *Pioneers of Light and Sound* (Lexile 980)
- Steve Parker, *Science of Sound: Projects and Experiments with Music and Sound Waves* (Lexile 840)

■ Wendy Sadler, *Science in Your Life: Sound: Listen Up!* (Lexile 790)
■ Donna Clovis, *Sound* (Lexile 460)

2. *Choose a guiding question or set of questions related to the topic.* It is a good idea to write a few questions for each book. Make sure the questions are not the same even though the content of the books may overlap. Unique questions will give everyone a chance to contribute. Consider providing students with choices of questions. More advanced students might be encouraged to write their own questions. For the easiest book in our sample text set, by Donna Clovis, we might pose a question like, What is sound? For the most challenging book, we might ask the reader to choose one pioneer and summarize his or her contribution to our knowledge of sound.

3. *Ask the students to read independently for the purpose of answering the questions you have assigned.* Encourage them to jot down a few notes as reminders. The silent reading does not need to take place in a group format. Students can read at their desks.

4. *Have the students meet as a group to discuss the topic.* It is best to begin by going from student to student, beginning with the student who will offer the most basic information. Each student reads and answers a question, and the other students respond with comments or follow-up questions. Each will be an expert on the book he or she has read, and each will know the answers to the questions that provided a focus for reading.

5. *Allow students to expand the discussion beyond the questions you provided.* You may wish to take part in this discussion as a facilitator. Pose follow-up questions, solicit additional questions, ask for clarifications, and prompt recaps from each group member.

STUDENT-CENTERED INVESTIGATIONS

Some of our preservice teachers are surprised to find that students in the upper elementary grades tend to learn best when they can interact in social contexts. They often do not do well when asked to sit at their desks and work quietly. Effective planning accounts for this tendency by providing students with opportunities to interact purposefully. A worthwhile purpose could be a problem to solve or question to investigate. An overarching goal like this will drive an activity that includes many chances to reinforce and extend the more basic skills and strategies that students are developing. This is true even when the activity stretches students by confronting them with challenging work.

Samuel Miller's work (2003) with upper elementary classrooms documents this striking fact: Even poor readers are motivated by activities that are creative and challenging, and they generally rise to the occasion when the opportunity presents itself. What clearly does not motivate them, on the other hand, is a steady diet of work sheet gruel. They can learn the routines and complete the assigned material, but their motivation to read is anything but improved.

A high-challenge language arts activity has these characteristics:

- It lasts more than a single day.
- It involves writing one or more paragraphs aimed at higher order thinking (e.g., character analysis, science research, letters to real people).
- Students work collaboratively to share ideas and give one another feedback.
- Teachers monitor closely and provide support where needed.

Tasks having these features bolster children's ability to regulate their own efforts and to work collaboratively in social settings.

Just as important is what a high-challenge activity lacks. It will not include tasks found in many work sheets, such as matching, underlining, and bubbling in answers. Nor will it target low-level word recognition and grammatical skills.

Miller (2003) found that all of the students he studied (high and low achievers alike) preferred the high-challenge activities, although low achievers lacked self-confidence *unless* such assignments were frequent. He also found that none of the teachers with whom he worked experienced a decline in achievement test scores after committing to this approach. In fact, the scores of several teachers rose significantly.

CONTENT AREA READING AND WRITING

A old metaphor suggests that an elementary teacher wears many hats during the course of the school day: a science hat, a math hat, a social studies hat, and, of course, a reading hat. A common problem arises when a teacher takes off one hat to don another. In a way, it's natural to do so, for the schedule invites us to compartmentalize our planning so that our focus regularly shifts from one subject to another. However, taking off one's reading hat and putting on a social studies or science hat can cause us to forgo an excellent opportunity to provide students with additional opportunities to read and write nonfiction. To be sure, the pressure to meet standards in science and social studies is great and can tempt us to move through a series of objectives in lecture mode. It often seems there is no time to be lost on students' reading and writing about content and we can simply tell them what they need to know. In this section, we suggest some reasons why integrating literacy activities into content area instruction is a good idea, and we present some practical ways of achieving this goal.

The Nature and Importance of Content Literacy

It is a mistake to assume that what students learn during the literacy block will transfer smoothly and seamlessly to other contexts. Reading to learn in science and social studies requires general literacy ability of course, but it also requires (1) skills and strategies that are specific to these areas (e.g., interpretation of graphics) and (2) the prior knowledge necessary to comprehend the material (McKenna & Robinson, 2011). Subject matter teachers in middle and high schools often complain about their students' inability to read assigned materials. They frequently blame elementary teachers for failing to instill in their students the basic literacy proficiencies needed to succeed. A few students do suffer from a large deficit, to be sure; however, most struggling readers possess adequate fluency but lack the content-specific strategies and the background knowledge they need. It is not the responsibility of previous teachers to impart these qualities. Only one teacher is situated to size up a reading selection, build students' knowledge in advance to the point that the content is comprehensible, and scaffold the students as they make their way through the selection. That individual is, of course, the teacher who assigns the selection. Classes and professional development in content literacy typically target teachers at the middle and high school levels, but teachers at grades 4 and 5 face exactly the same challenges.

We are not suggesting that science and social studies time be converted into an extension of the literacy block. We do, however, see these subjects as opportunities for students to engage in meaningful reading and writing activities that contribute to content learning. The pressures to meet benchmarks and standards have pushed many middle and high school teachers to the point that they reach an unfortunate conclusion—that it may be better to avoid reading and writing and to rely instead on lecture and discussion as the principal ways of building content knowledge. Our hope is that fourth- and fifth-grade teachers will not follow suit. Our case is grounded in the definition of content literacy: "the ability to use reading and writing for the acquisition of new content in a given discipline" (McKenna & Robinson, 1990, p. 184). Ironically, simply providing students with content knowledge through lecture and discussion will make them more content literate. This is because what they learn in this manner will serve as prior knowledge when they later read. However, building prior knowledge is not enough. Students must be given opportunities to apply that knowledge as they extend their learning through reading and writing. The basic conclusion—one that we hope you will share—is that literacy activities should have a place in content instruction.

Structuring Content Lessons to Facilitate Reading

The problem is how to make reading selections (textbook chapters, nonfiction trade books, articles, and the like) accessible to upper elementary students. What are the best ways of facilitating their efforts to read these materials? Fortunately, a number of research-based instructional approaches are available for helping teachers do just that. These approaches involve structuring a lesson using a before–during–after format. Within this structure, a teacher embeds approaches that help students to overcome limited prior knowledge and to focus their attention on the most important aspects of the content.

There is some irony involved in using these approaches. To begin with, many of the techniques are the same as those we would use to build overall comprehension proficiency in our students. Techniques such as effective questioning, discussing text structure, and summarizing are two-sided coins that have the effect of improving students' comprehension of a particular selection and also of improving (over the long term) their comprehension ability. This is why it is important that upper elementary teachers keep their teaching hats on all day, even when the literacy block is over and they move on to science, math, and social studies. This is also why it is crucial that teachers employ these approaches to support their students' reading of content area materials and abandon the temptation to avoid having students read, relying instead on lecture and discussion.

The fact that many instructional approaches have been demonstrated to have a double impact, on comprehending a selection and on comprehending in general, may help convince you that that they are well worth implementing. If content instruction can do double duty—building both content knowledge and reading proficiency—then surely that is a powerful argument for trying it. That said, we wish to emphasize that the lesson formats and instructional approaches we describe here are used principally to boost comprehension of an assigned selection. Improving students' overall comprehension ability is a long-term by-product.

If you want to help your students comprehend a particular text (e.g., a short story, a chapter in a science textbook, a short trade book, or an article), you would be wise to take steps to assist them. You may well need to build vocabulary and prior knowledge in advance so that they have a foundation on which to build. They may also require assistance in focusing, amid an avalanche of text, on content that is important. They may benefit from opportunities to process information in meaningful ways as they read. Scaffolding students in these ways does not need to be a daunting task. Fortunately, a number of research-based instructional approaches are available.

Directed Reading Activity

One of the first to realize that comprehension could be greatly facilitated if the right methods were employed was Emmett Betts. In 1946, he devised a basic approach to planning lessons, which he called the directed reading activity (DRA). His approach was the forerunner of later modifications and a mainstay of basal reading instruction for nearly a century. The DRA is both teacher centered and content centered. Its use is grounded in the idea that students need to extract certain kinds of information from the material they read and that the best judge of what that information should be is the teacher. The DRA is consequently a convergent approach that leads to all students completing the reading task having taken away roughly the same content. This is not to say that Betts viewed critical reading unfavorably. Indeed, critical reading can be fostered through the DRA. However, this goal was not the principal cause of its development.

■ *Before Reading.* The teacher begins by building background information. Doing so involves teaching key vocabulary—word meanings that are central to comprehension—and knowledge that the author assumes readers will possess but that the teacher is relatively certain they do not. After deciding what understandings students should take away from the reading, the teacher crafts a method of focusing their attention on the appropriate content. Doing so might involve posing questions or developing other tasks to be completed during reading. If this selection is short and the questions and tasks can be stated briefly, they might be written on the board. For longer selections, a reading guide, complete with page numbers and subheadings, might be provided.

■ *During Reading.* As they read, students are actively engaged in responding to the questions or completing the tasks. Betts believed that this approach, even though it provides students with few choices, is nonetheless preferable to the alternative of providing no guidance at all.

■ *After Reading.* When students have completed reading the selection, the teacher leads them in a discussion. Naturally, the discussion is anchored in the focus activities provided by the teacher. This does not mean that it is entirely limited to those activities, but they are used to organize the discussion. Think of the questions and tasks as a spine. The teacher may permit the reading discussion to go out onto the occasional rib, but there is always the spine to keep it moving along toward objectives the teacher has set. After the discussion, the teacher may engage students in follow-up and extension activities designed to enrich their understanding of the content. Such activities might include writing, reading further in other print sources, or using the Internet to research issues that have arisen. This follow-up step is optional, depending on the available time. We should note that in Betts's original approach, the discussion was followed by oral rereading. This step is somewhat questionable because it requires so much time (Tierney & Readence, 2004) and because it is inappropriate in content classrooms.

Figure 9.4 summarizes these steps. The DRA does not fit comfortably into an era where social interaction among learners is a preferred condition in the classroom. On the other hand, we believe that the DRA provides a useful structure into which effective techniques, such as those for developing vocabulary, can be embedded. Moreover, many teachers have found that this approach can be modified to include opportunities for student interaction.

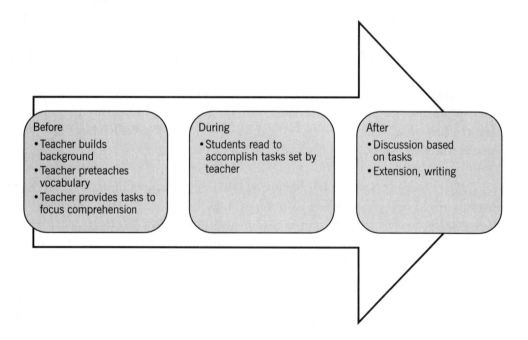

FIGURE 9.4. Steps in a directed reading activity.

Directed Reading–Thinking Activity

Russell Stauffer (1969) suggested a major modification to the classic DRA to make it more student centered and to ensure higher levels of engagement. His technique, the directed reading–thinking activity (DR-TA), begins in the same way as the DRA.

■ *Before Reading.* The teacher builds background, which includes teaching the meanings of key words before the students read. It is at this point that the DR-TA takes a student-centered turn. Instead of the teacher providing a focus for reading in the form of questions and tasks, the students form predictions. If the selection is fiction, their predictions involve subsequent events. If it is nonfiction, the predictions entail conjecture about what the facts will be.

■ *During Reading.* When students begin to read, it is not to accomplish the purposes assigned to them by the teacher (a hallmark of the DRA). Rather, it is to test their predictions. For longer selections, the teacher may break up the reading into segments. Students make a prediction for the initial segment, read to test their predictions, and engage in a brief discussion focused on the results. Then new predictions are formed for the next segment, and so forth.

■ *After Reading.* The discussion that follows reading, whether for each segment or the entire selection, is anchored in the reasons why students' predictions were confirmed or wrong.

See Figure 9.5 for a summary of these DR-TA steps. Compare it with Figure 9.4 and note the differences that distinguish the DR-TA from the DRA.

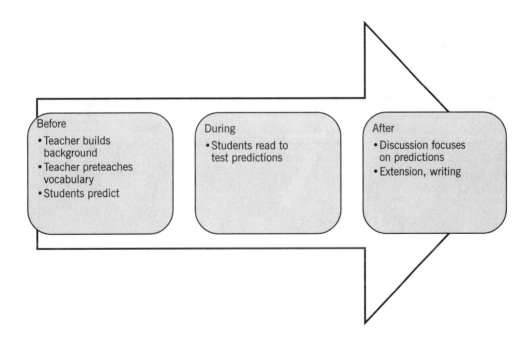

FIGURE 9.5. Steps in a directed reading–thinking activity.

When compared with other before–during–after lesson formats, the DR-TA has usually proved superior (e.g., Stahl, 2008). However, it is better suited to some materials than others, namely those that lend themselves to making predictions.

Listen-Read-Discuss

Manzo and Casale (1985) introduced another lesson format designed to support struggling students' comprehension. Their alternative, called listen–read–discuss (LRD), is based on the idea that the chief barrier to comprehension for most struggling readers is limited prior knowledge and that the patchwork approach to building prior knowledge used in the DRA and the DR-TA is inadequate to bring students to the level of background they require to understand unfamiliar material. For a summary of steps, see Figure 9.6.

■ *Before Reading.* LRD begins with the teacher presenting the content of the reading selection fully and completely. This may involve approaches such as lecture, demonstration, and discussion. Reading, however, is not involved.

■ *During Reading.* So thorough is the initial step of the lesson, during which students listen but do not read, that the subsequent reading may seem unnecessary! After all, the teacher has gone to great lengths, using effective instructional techniques, to make sure that students already know the content of the selection. Manzo and Cassale argue, however, that by "front loading" the entire selection teachers can situate their struggling students in the rare position of being able to comprehend grade-level text with

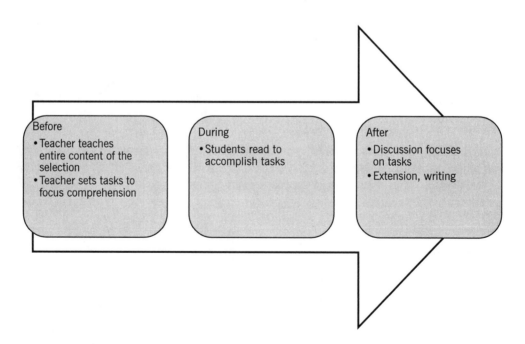

FIGURE 9.6. Steps in listen–read–discuss.

acceptable understanding. In fact, LRD has been compared favorably with other lesson formats. Reading is guided best by presenting questions and tasks, like those used in the DRA. (Predictions are inappropriate, of course.)

■ *After Reading.* Like the DRA, postreading discussion is anchored in the tasks presented by the teacher at the outset. This task serves both as a focus for discussion and as a memory prompt because students can refer to written products they have created (e.g., a chart they completed).

The use of these evidence-based before–during–after lesson formats will place reading selections within the grasp of many students who struggle. Their use will contribute to the content knowledge of all students and will help to build their proficiency by affording additional opportunities to engage in literacy activities. Best of all perhaps is that using them will signal the importance of literacy, and this message will assist you in building a classroom climate that values and rewards literacy throughout the day.

To sum up, our goal in this chapter has been to suggest ways that teachers in grades 4 and 5 can foster such a climate. We began by offering suggestions for creating an inviting classroom environment, including its physical appearance and print materials. We described approaches to making literacy activities truly interactive and socially situated. These approaches included literature circles, idea circles, and inquiry-based activities. Finally, we made our case for extending literacy approaches into content subjects not only to enhance the proficiencies of students but also to convey the message that literacy is central to all of the important dimensions of school life.

Chapter 10

Putting It All Together

Our school-based work is always motivated by a desire to embed research findings within the realities of today's classrooms. Those classrooms, and the schools and communities in which they are nested, represent more differences today than they ever did. There are meaningful differences in the needs of students and teachers. There are meaningful differences in the resources provided to them. For evidence-based instruction to become a reality in all classrooms, it has to be described clearly, and with many possible examples, and its planning and implementation must be reasonable for those teachers who are tasked to use it. It has to be presented with support, through ongoing inservice work and coaching and through fair, meaningful teacher evaluations. Once an instructional model is understood and implemented, it actually has to yield the dividends that matter: classroom communities where you can actually see teachers and students engaged in purposeful and interesting learning every day *and* where that engagement is associated with improved knowledge and skills for all, demonstrated on valid and reliable assessments.

We believe that the model for reading instruction we have presented here is a realistic one for upper elementary teachers, and in this chapter our goal is to help you see what it would mean to adopt it in its full form. Full adoption will enable you to answer the two questions that are most important:

1. Under what conditions is this model reasonable for teachers?
2. Under what conditions is this model effective for students?

Because of the rhythm of schools, we present the model within a school calendar. And because we tend to be systems thinkers, we present it with grade-level teams, rather than individual teachers, in mind.

STRATEGIC CURRICULUM DECISIONS

There is a set of basic curriculum resources (see Figure 10.1) that is required to implement our model. Time must be allocated the spring and summer before implementation to select, purchase, and organize these resources. The core program is consistent with research, which we have presented within the Florida Center for Reading Research's (2007) guidelines (with slight modifications). The other texts would be consistent with your state's content standards or with the Common Core Standards. What you do not see in Figure 10.1 is workbooks, practice books for standardized tests, or a variety of additional, layered commercial curriculum materials. In fact, one of the things that most teachers have to do when they try out our model is to take alternative curriculum materials out of their classrooms.

There are many ways that restriction of the curriculum to these most essential items is strategic. We have worked in many schools where teachers hoard old materials and pull them out when heads are turned. If those materials are truly better, then all students at a particular grade level should be using them; they should become the core. In reality, though, teachers tend to bring out these materials out of habit or to fill time. We prefer classrooms filled with books that are used for different purposes. For the teaching of reading, we emphasize connected reading rather than the skills-oriented tasks, which might be more appropriate for younger students. This emphasis saves teacher time and

Resources	Reasoning
Core program	A core program promotes consistency among classrooms at the same grade level and directs text and vocabulary selection for Tier 1 instruction.
Read-aloud texts	A rich set of single copies of authentic, interesting, challenging narratives and information texts are essential for building vocabulary, text structure flexibility, comprehension strategy flexibility, understanding of complex sentence structures, and motivation to read.
Small-group sets of narratives and information texts at different reading levels	Small-group instruction for students with needs in word recognition and fluency will likely require texts at levels below their grade-level placement; fluency and comprehension will require texts at or near grade-level placement; vocabulary and comprehension will require texts at or above grade-level placement.
Organized classroom libraries of single titles	Wide, engaged reading of interesting and diverse texts can build vocabulary, background knowledge, knowledge of sentence and text structure, and positive attitudes toward reading and writing.
Multisyllabic decoding lessons	Students with needs in word recognition and fluency in the upper elementary grades need to learn to attack complex words.
Access to intensive interventions	Students with needs in word recognition and fluency who do not respond to multisyllabic decoding instruction need intensive instruction in single-syllable decoding and will not be able to accelerate their achievement sufficiently within short small-group rotations.

FIGURE 10.1. Resources required for differentiated instruction.

district money that might be wasted on trivial, low-level resources. It compels teachers to build classroom communities where students have the personal discipline, motivation, skills, and opportunity to build their reading skills by reading.

STRATEGIC ASSESSMENT DECISIONS

As we argued in Chapter 4, very few assessments are actually needed to implement our model. What we did not mention, however, is that we are often faced with schools or districts that are committed in theory to our differentiation model but simply cannot make the break from their previous assessment systems. We have seen the problems that this causes. First, too much assessment is incredibly wasteful in terms of both time and money. It can frustrate teachers as they see instructional time being devoted to exhaustive testing. Even worse, too much assessment causes confusion, especially when the assessments yield different results.

One nonstrategic assessment decision is the commitment to use the weekly tests that are sold as part of core programs. Teachers initially tell us that they use them to assess the extent to which their students are learning the comprehension skills and strategies targeted for their grade level. The design of the tests, though, does not address this issue. Rather, when weekly tests assess student understanding of a core selection that has been read and reread collaboratively across a week, we think the test is a mere memory task and not a comprehension or strategy task. As a case in point: What if a student with intensive word recognition problems could earn a high score on that test after participating in shared reading and discussion across the week but still could not actually read the core selection? Does this mean that reading comprehension does not require decoding and fluency skills? Our experience is that, in many cases, these tests are used to generate grades rather than to influence instruction for the next week. If that is the case, it may be better to craft a new system for generating grades and to save the time it takes to give and grade the core-embedded weekly assessments.

Another nonstrategic assessment decision is to use both external screening tests with strong psychometric properties *and* teacher-made district benchmark tests with no psychometric validation. Teacher-designed tests are important. They allow individual teachers to construct performance tasks that are directly related to their instruction, and the person who creates and interprets the test is the same one who provided the instruction and who will be providing instruction in the future. Such tests can influence instruction in important ways. We know that when we make tests ourselves, in our own university classes, they are sometimes flawed. That is, there are sometimes questions that almost no one answers correctly, and we assume this is because either we taught poorly or students tested poorly. We drop those questions from the mix and reteach the material. The same applies to the teacher-generated tests, which often serve as district benchmarking. Because the items are not piloted, they are subject to multiple sources of error. We believe that they should not be used to make high-stakes decisions across classrooms.

Another nonstrategic assessment decision we often face is that districts can be quick to add additional assessments but slow to remove old ones that no longer serve any useful purpose. One example is the use of informal reading inventories to group students on the basis of their reading levels after they read orally and answer a handful of comprehension questions. This approach, although time honored, is fraught with measurement problems (Walpole & McKenna, 2006). Our system employs a more dependable approach. Students with adequate fluency receive instruction that builds vocabulary and comprehension. We assume that these students are of two types: (1) those with strong fluency and strong comprehension and vocabulary and (2) those with strong fluency and weak comprehension and vocabulary. We assume that more gains will be realized for both types of readers by providing more challenging texts, because those texts provide more authentic opportunity for teachers to build both vocabulary and comprehension.

A final nonstrategic decision we often face is a reliance on miscue analysis (again a mainstay of some informal reading inventories) to design word recognition instruction. Miscue analysis is an approach to identifying patterns of poor word recognition by categorizing the types of errors students make. It can be both time consuming and misleading (McKenna & Picard, 2006–2007), and our system avoids it in favor of something far simpler. You can see from our informal decoding inventory that we make word recognition decisions based on tests of pure word recognition. Such tasks are purposefully "inauthentic" because they strip readers of access to information (meaning and grammar), which might lead us to overestimate their performance.

To truly adopt our model, then, many classrooms (and schools and districts) will have to reduce their assessment requirements considerably. They will have to think critically about the information yielded by each assessment and the decisions made because of it. This is a task, like curriculum selection, that is best made in the spring and summer, so that policies about selection and scheduling, administering, grading, and reporting to parents can be carefully thought out in advance.

STRATEGIC MANAGEMENT DECISIONS

If you were to adopt our differentiation model, the first 2 weeks of school would be critical. It does not work to begin the year in a whole-group model and then change to a small-group differentiated model. Rather, you should begin with the end in mind. First, think about setting up a classroom environment that communicates your goals to your students. Display interesting books, as we suggested in Chapter 9. Create an organization system for your classroom library that is both attractive and utilitarian. Set up areas on your whiteboards that are always used for the same purpose. Use a chime or a bell to signal transitions between activities. Set up a computer logged on to an online dictionary and teach children to use it. Post procedures for important daily activities on chart paper: choral reading, partner reading, choosing a book from the library, or writing a thoughtful response. Post procedures for important cognitive activities on chart paper: graphic organizers, strategies for dividing words into syllables, syllable types, and common prefixes and suffixes. The goal is to reduce students' dependence on teachers to manage the classroom and to encourage them instead to develop self-monitoring and management skills.

Research has clearly shown that the most effective teachers take the time to explicitly instruct their students in the behaviors and procedures they expect (Brophy, 1983). For this reason, we suggest that even before your instruction is differentiated you begin the year by establishing the procedures that will allow your students to maximize their time in meaningful literacy tasks. Doing so will in turn allow you to maximize your time teaching small groups. Randomly assign the students in your class to groups of equal size. Then engage them in the procedures that will be essential to your instructional block. Figure 10.2 presents the goals for the first days of school.

We actually believe that it is better to hold off differentiated instruction until the procedures are comfortable both for you and for the students. It is better to spend more time on procedures than to begin differentiation with multiple distractions. If you are meeting with your class one-third at a time, you have a chance to conduct your initial attitude and interest inventories, make your first personal book recommendations, gather book reviews that you can display in the classroom environment, and conduct fluency screenings. If students are writing in response to listening, you have the chance to collect initial natural writing samples that can provide useful insights into student skills and attitudes. If they use a composition book and date their daily responses, you will have an organized, concrete record that shows their progress across time. And if you use your first small-group meetings to gather the necessary assessment data, you can begin to differentiate.

BUILDING THE DIFFERENTIATION MODEL

You will know that you are ready to begin our differentiation model in the fourth or fifth grade when you can confidently sort your students into three potential groups: students

Teacher activity	Purpose
Read aloud from an engaging trade book.	Set the expectation that the day will start with listening. Show your class that they will learn interesting things from books.
Assign a written response.	Provide a common place where students can write their response. Teach the students that writing in response to listening will be a daily expectation.
Engage in cycles of choral, partner, and whisper reading.	Establish comfortable, repetitive procedures that will not have to be reintroduced every day. Build your students' reading stamina.
Meet with each of the three groups while the other two groups either complete their written response or read from the classroom library.	Build the expectation that all students will be engaged in either reading or writing when you are working with a group. Create signals and procedures for how students will switch from one activity to another. Get to know your students as you talk with them in small groups.

FIGURE 10.2. Initial activities and their purpose.

with at least grade-level fluency, students with weak fluency but strong word recognition, and students with weak fluency and weak word recognition. If you have students in all three categories, it is almost certain that the groups will be of unequal size. This cannot be helped. It is more important for each student to obtain the instruction that is needed than for the groups to be of uniform size. Alternatively, you may only have two of these three groups represented in your class. In this case, you can differentiate further by dividing the larger of your groups into two, using data to guide you.

Although we have treated word recognition, fluency, vocabulary, and comprehension separately in previous chapters, we encourage you to choose a dual focus for each of these groups. Figure 10.3 shows each of the three groups across one instructional day. All students listen to your read-aloud, produce a written response, and engage with you in shared reading of the core selection. Then they begin their differentiation time, during which they will have two segments of independent work and one segment of small-group instruction with you. One of those segments is always to complete the written response to the day's read-aloud. If they finish the required independent tasks in either independent block, they will always choose a book to read from the classroom library.

The word recognition and fluency group includes those students whose weakness in fluency is partially explained by an inability to divide and decode multisyllabic words. For that reason, they begin their small-group lesson with targeted multisyllabic decoding practice. For fluency, they read new below-grade-level text (a segment or chapter) each day, with strong teacher support through choral reading. After their small-group lesson, they continue this fluency focus by rereading that day's selection with a partner and then again in whisper reading. The next day, in their small group, after decoding practice, they have a brief comprehension discussion before they begin the next segment in choral reading.

	Read-aloud Assign written response Shared reading of core selection		
WR/F	Written response	1. Multisyllabic decoding practice 2. Discussion of last section 3. Choral reading of new section	Partner and whisper reading of new section
F/C	1. Discussion of last section 2. Choral reading of new section	Partner and whisper reading of new section	Written response
V/C	Written response	Silent reading of new text section	1. Discussion of last section 2. Review previous vocabulary 3. Introduce new vocabulary 4. Provide comprehension focus

FIGURE 10.3. A reasonable differentiation model (WR/F, word recognition and fluency group; F/C, fluency and comprehension group; V/C, vocabulary and comprehension group).

The fluency and comprehension group includes those students whose weakness in fluency seems to stem from a lack of reading experience or practice rather than from weak decoding skills. For that reason, they read and reread texts at or near grade level. Like the word recognition and fluency group, the fluency and comprehension group reads new text (a segment or chapter) each day, with strong teacher support through choral reading. After their small-group lesson, they continue this fluency focus by rereading that day's selection with a partner and then again in whisper reading. They may also use a reading guide to focus on a series of comprehension questions. The next day, in their small group, they have a more comprehensive discussion before they begin the next segment in choral reading.

Students with no fluency problems do not need the support of choral, oral, or repeated readings. These students, moving up to the vocabulary and comprehension group, read texts at or above grade level. In this case, though, all of their small-group time is used to learn new vocabulary and to discuss the meaning of the text. There is no need for teacher support for their reading, so they do it silently and independently, away from the teacher. They could use reading guides or reciprocal teaching to prepare for their comprehension discussion. The teacher will spend time supporting students' comprehension and vocabulary rather than modeling or supporting fluency.

Taken together, and listed like this, there seem to be few differences among the groups. That is true: All three groups produce a daily written response to the read-aloud, all three groups discuss the book they are reading when they work with the teacher, and all three groups read on their own, away from the teacher. The differences, though, are the heart of differentiation.

The first difference is obvious. Only the word recognition and fluency group engages in multisyllabic decoding practice during small-group time. All three groups have engaged in this practice as part of shared reading, when the teacher has helped them identify syllable types in the vocabulary words for the core story, analyze words, and list derivatives by adding prefixes and suffixes. These words, chosen for their meanings, will be unlikely to have much in common in terms of their structure. The additional small-group practice, though, includes practice with a list of words that are similar in structure.

The second difference is less obvious. The books that the three groups are reading must be different in their level of difficulty. We have used Lexiles to identify them, but you can also use the general idea of below, at, or above grade level. The word recognition and fluency group needs a below-grade-level text so that the decoding and fluency demands will not be overwhelming. The fluency and comprehension group can read a text at or near grade level. The vocabulary and comprehension group can read a text at or above grade level. In all three cases, the text can be narrative or informational.

The modes of reading are the same for the word recognition and fluency group and the fluency and comprehension group. These students read chorally with the teacher, then reread with partners, and finally engage in independent whisper reading. This movement from choral to partner to whisper rereading is a gradual release of responsibility to the student. Within that gradual release, we embed repeated readings, a hallmark of all fluency-building programs. You should be able to see students becoming more confident and fluent across chapters, because many words are actually repeated within one book and then across books as the additional reading practice bears fruit.

When chapters in the book are too long to allow completion of choral reading within the time allotted, one of two solutions can be implemented. First, you can decide to simply break the chapter into sections, reading only as much as time allows. Second, you can decide to alternate days. On day 1, you can do only the choral reading (with follow-up partner and whisper reading). Then on day 2 students can discuss that section, but you have to decide what the students should do during their independent time that day.

The vocabulary and comprehension group reads silently. They have fluency work in the shared reading each day, and your assessments indicate that they are not struggling with fluency. Because they do not need additional fluency support, there is no reason for them to read out loud; they can read silently and independently. This also provides time for the teacher to thoroughly engage in comprehension and vocabulary support during small-group time.

Similarities among the groups is just as important as the differences. All three groups engage in discussion about the books that they are reading, sharing and deepening their comprehension. In all three cases, we favor inferential questions and prompts. There is no reason for the comprehension discussion in the word recognition and fluency group to be less meaningful. It may have to be shorter in order to accomplish the rest of the lesson in the time allowed. This will require that the teacher questions be even more carefully planned so that they are not simply low-level questions.

A final caution: Do not make your groups of equal size and do not force-fit your students into this grouping configuration. Use data to truly consider their needs. You may have three groups of word recognition and fluency students. You may have two groups of vocabulary and comprehension students and one group of fluency and comprehension. Over time, you should be aiming to reduce the number of students in the word recognition and fluency group and to increase the number in the vocabulary and comprehension group. But begin wherever the data lead you.

MEANINGFUL COLLABORATIONS

If your differentiation model is truly schoolwide, you can and should work together to do the planning necessary. Our templates for shared reading should make the planning of Tier 1 instruction fairly simple. What takes more planning is the interactive read-aloud, when you will be introducing a strategy or text structure before reading and then stopping during reading to model it or to invite the students to use it. You will also need to plan a written response, one that is engaging to the students and invites reflection on the text. We worked with a fourth-grade-level team of teachers for whom all parts of this system were new and who made planning a collaborative responsibility. For each week, the teachers selected five books that were related thematically. They took responsibility for planning for one or two books each, and they shared them. Each teacher read all five during the course of the week, but not on the same day. That way they did not need extra copies.

The second collaboration that will make differentiation easier (and the model truly schoolwide) is the lesson planning for the small-group texts. Of course, it is possible to plan for these lessons by staying one chapter ahead in all three groups. That is not ideal, though. It is better to have the whole book planned in advance. To do that, you would pick a mode (e.g., QARs or reading guides) and then write the questions for each chapter. You would also select the vocabulary words for the vocabulary and comprehension group. In our collaborative grade-level team, the teachers did just that. They began by planning for all three of their own groups, all reading different books. Then they met to discuss how those books were working. Once a group had finished a book, the teacher could either plan a new one or use a set of plans that a colleague had already tried. Besides saving time, this system allowed the teachers a reason to talk about the books and the students and to share insights they gained as they made tiered instruction work for them. It also ensured that the students were all conversant in the same body of literature. Over time, a shared book room, with the plans already made, can be established. This makes for more text choices for everyone.

AN INVITATION

We invite you to be strategic about your curriculum, your assessments, and your management. We invite you to build your differentiation model so that it is comfortable for you and your students. We invite you to collaborate with your grade-level teammates to make lesson planning simpler. To assist you, we have created a set of materials to start with. In the appendices that follow this chapter, we provide what you need to get started.

In our experience, upper elementary teachers do not have an informal decoding inventory and a set of multisyllabic decoding lessons, so we are providing them for you in Appendices B and C. There are directions for administering the informal decoding inventory, beginning with multisyllabic words. Remember that you will only give it to those students who do not meet your fluency benchmark. Those who do well on the informal inventory will be assigned to the fluency and comprehension group; those who do poorly will be placed in the word recognition and fluency group.

Next, we provide some supports for comprehension: reciprocal teaching reminders (Appendix D), QAR reminders (Appendix E), and book club reminders (Appendix F). These can be used in many ways: They can be placed in student notebooks, they can be made into posters and displayed for the class, or you can use then as samples and make your own versions. Remember that they are there as resources to help your students to be more independent.

We have also included a set of text structure graphic organizers (Appendix G). All too often, the teaching of text structures is a rare component of instruction in the upper elementary grades. Graphic organizers like these can actually link all of the parts of your day. They can be used with read-alouds, shared reading, differentiated texts, and content area texts. They can be used to document comprehension and to plan writing. Again, use them however you like. When laminated into posters, graphic organizers can be used and reused to make notes about texts that you have read together. You can also create smartboard versions that you can use and reuse interactively.

Finally, we present model lessons for each of our three groups in Appendices H, I, and J. We selected texts that differed in their reading level and that we thought fourth- and fifth-grade students would enjoy. If you would like to use our lessons, obtain the books and give them a try. These lessons may help you to focus your attention on the management and procedural aspects of differentiation at first. They may also help you to see what we mean when we say that discussions should be targeted and inferential. Surely you may decide to jump in and plan your own lessons, but ours are provided as models if you want them.

We have enjoyed our visits to classrooms this year as we have been planning and writing this book. If differentiation is new to you, please know that we are committed to a model that is reasonable for teachers as well as effective for students. We are always humbled by our work with teachers who persevere regardless of the pressures they face. We hope that this book will make their work a tiny bit easier.

Reproducible Classroom Materials

Tier 1 Planning Templates

TIER 1 INITIAL PLANNING TEMPLATE

Time	Activity	Description
5 min	Strategy Introduction	
15 min	Interactive Read-Aloud	
3 min	Introduce Written Response	
10 min	Vocabulary	
12 min	Choral Reading of the Story	

(cont.)

TIER 1 ADDITIONAL PLANNING TEMPLATE

Time	Activity	Description
2 min	Strategy Introduction	
10 min	Interactive Read-Aloud	
10 min	Vocabulary Review	
10 min	Partner Reading	
10 min	Whisper Reading	
3 min	Introduce Written Response	

Informal Decoding Inventory

DIRECTIONS FOR ADMINISTRATION

This inventory is in two parts. Part I assesses skills used to decode single-syllable words. Part II assesses skills used to decode multisyllabic words. For upper elementary students, it is best to begin with Part II, which is more challenging, and to administer Part I only for students who have difficulties with Part II.

ADMINISTERING PART I

Short Vowels

Point to **sat**. Say, "What is this word?" Go from left to right on the scoring form (top to bottom for the child), repeating this question for each word in row 1. It is fine if the student reads across the line without prompting. Repeat the procedure for row 2 (nonsense words). [**Note**: If the student cannot pass this subtest, consider placing the student in a Tier 3 intensive intervention program and using the assessments that accompany that program.]

Consonant Blends and Digraphs

Point to **blip**. Say, "What is this word?" Go from left to right on the scoring form, repeating this question for each word in row 1. It is fine if the student reads across the line without prompting. Repeat the procedure for row 2 (nonsense words).

r-Controlled Vowel Patterns

Point to **card**. Say, "What is this word?" Go from left to right on the scoring form, repeating this question for each word in row 1. It is fine if the student reads across the line without prompting. Repeat the procedure for row 2 (nonsense words).

Vowel–Consonant–*e*

Point to **stale**. Say, "What is this word?" Go from left to right on the scoring form, repeating this question for each word in row 1. It is fine if the student reads across the line without prompting. Repeat the procedure for row 2 (nonsense words).

Vowel Teams

Point to **neat**. Say, "What is this word?" Go from left to right on the scoring form, repeating this question for each word in row 1. It is fine if the student reads across the line without prompting. Repeat the procedure for row 2 (nonsense words). For nonsense words *feap* and *tead* accept either the long or short *e* sound.

(cont.)

SCORING PART I

Each subtest contains 10 real words and 10 nonsense words. Because real words might be identified at sight, a higher criterion (80%) is used for mastery. For nonsense words, the criterion is 60%. The criteria for Review and Needs Systematic Instruction differ accordingly. The following table below gives the number of correct answers that correspond to these percentages. (Note that the total percentages in the bottom row do not always equal the total of the numbers above. They were computed on a slightly different basis.)

	Real Words			Nonsense Words		
Subtest	Mastery	Review	Systematic Instruction	Mastery	Review	Systematic Instruction
Short Vowels	8–10	6–7	0–5	6–10	4–5	0–3
Consonant Blends and Digraphs	8–10	6–7	0–5	6–10	4–5	0–3
r-Controlled Vowel Patterns	8–10	6–7	0–5	6–10	4–5	0–3
Vowel–Consonant–*e*	8–10	6–7	0–5	6–10	4–5	0–3
Vowel Teams	8–10	6–7	0–5	6–10	4–5	0–3
Total	**40–50**	**30–39**	**0–29**	**30–50**	**20–29**	**0–19**

ADMINISTERING PART II

Compound Words

Point to **batman**. Say, "What is this word?" Go from left to right on the scoring form, repeating this question for each word in row 1. It is fine if the student reads across the line without prompting. Repeat the procedure for row 2 (coined and nonsense words).

Closed Syllables

Point to **dentist**. Say, "What is this word?" Go from left to right on the scoring form, repeating this question for each word in row 1. It is fine if the student reads across the line without prompting. Repeat the procedure for row 2 (nonsense words).

Open Syllables

Point to **lotus**. Say, "What is this word?" Go from left to right on the scoring form, repeating this question for each word in row 1. It is fine if the student reads across the line without prompting. Repeat the procedure for row 2 (nonsense words).

(cont.)

162

Vowel–Consonant–*e* Syllables

Point to **confine**. Say, "What is this word?" Go from left to right on the scoring form, repeating this question for each word in row 1. It is fine if the student reads across the line without prompting. Repeat the procedure for row 2 (nonsense words).

r-Controlled Syllables

Point to **fiber**. Say, "What is this word?" Go from left to right on the scoring form, repeating this question for each word in row 1. It is fine if the student reads across the line without prompting. Repeat the procedure for row 2 (nonsense words).

Vowel Team Syllables

Point to **chowder**. Say, "What is this word?" Go from left to right on the scoring form, repeating this question for each word in row 1. It is fine if the student reads across the line without prompting. Repeat the procedure for row 2 (nonsense words).

Consonant–*le* Syllables

Point to **bubble**. Say, "What is this word?" Go from left to right on the scoring form, repeating this question for each word in row 1. It is fine if the student reads across the line without prompting. Repeat the procedure for row 2 (nonsense words).

SCORING PART II

As in Part I, each subtest contains 10 real words and 10 nonsense words. Likewise, because real words might be identified at sight, a higher criterion (80%) is used for mastery. For nonsense words, the criterion is 60%. The criteria for Needs Improvement and Needs Systematic Instruction differ accordingly. The following table gives the number of correct answers that correspond to these percentages.

Subtest	Real Words			Nonsense Words		
	Mastery	Review	Systematic Instruction	Mastery	Review	Systematic Instruction
Compound Words	8–10	6–7	0–5	6–10	4–5	0–3
Closed Syllables	8–10	6–7	0–5	6–10	4–5	0–3
Open Syllables	8–10	6–7	0–5	6–10	4–5	0–3
Vowel–Consonant–*e* Syllables	8–10	6–7	0–5	6–10	4–5	0–3
r-Controlled Syllables	8–10	6–7	0–5	6–10	4–5	0–3
Vowel Team Syllables	8–10	6–7	0–5	6–10	4–5	0–3
Consonant–*le* Syllables	8–10	6–7	0–5	6–10	4–5	0–3
Total	**56–70**	**42–55**	**0–41**	**42–50**	**28–41**	**0–27**

(cont.)

READMINISTERING THE INVENTORY

The purpose of this inventory is to identify the most promising focus for targeted instruction. Following such instruction, usually over the course of several weeks, readminister just that portion of the inventory that has been the focus of instruction. It is not necessary to give the entire inventory again. If the instruction has brought a student to mastery, proceed to the next area where the inventory revealed a problem. Charting records for students over time will provide an indication of long-term progress and a tool for judging their response to instruction.

(cont.)

INFORMAL DECODING INVENTORY

Name _____   Date _____

Part I: Single-Syllable Decoding Score Sheet

Short Vowels									
sat	pot	beg	nip	cub	pad	top	hit	met	nut
								Total	
mot	tib	han	teg	fet	lup	nid	pab	hud	gop
								Total	

Consonant Blends and Digraphs									
blip	check	clam	chin	thick	frank	mint	fist	grab	rest
								Total	
clop	prib	hest	chot	slen	bund	bist	hald	slub	shad
								Total	

r-Controlled Vowel Patterns									
card	stork	term	burst	turf	fern	dirt	nark	firm	mirth
								Total	
fird	barp	forn	serp	surt	perd	kurn	nirt	mork	tarst
								Total	

(cont.)

Vowel–Consonant–*e*									
stale	hike	dome	cube	blame	chive	cute	prone	vane	brine
								Total	
bame	neme	hile	pome	rute	nube	vope	clate	vike	pene
								Total	

Vowel Teams									
neat	spoil	goat	pail	field	fruit	claim	meet	beast	boast
								Total	
craid	houn	rowb	noy	feap	nuit	maist	ploat	tead	steen
								Total	

(cont.)

INFORMAL DECODING INVENTORY

Name _____

Date _____

Part II: Multisyllabic Decoding Score Sheet

Compound Words

batman	blackmail	carpool	flashlight	baseball	corndog	crosswalk	battlefield	frostbite	bootstrap
catboy	sundog	paintrag	oatfarm	raincan	skywatch	dogrun	meatman	bluestar	hattree
								Total	
								Total	

Closed Syllables

dentist	tunnel	compact	hundred	flannel	banquet	submit	contest	blanket	gossip
sindict	pladchet	suncrip	bunpect	wunnet	blensim	pefdimp	stindam	flanpeck	winsprick
								Total	
								Total	

(cont.)

Informal Decoding Inventory, Part II *(page 2 of 3)*

Open Syllables

lotus	cupid	spiky	pony	final	spiny	ivy	rely	equal	Total
rulab	cluden	diler	slony	fodun	siny	pady	pilem	byliss	Total

Vowel–Consonant–*e* Syllables

confine	athlete	concrete	compose	stampede	suppose	endure	cascade	recline	Total
depide	repale	wranblise	mondrine	slindome	lompise	sisdike	dimcline	plinsipe	indube	Total

r-Controlled Syllables

fiber	super	furnish	serpent	varnish	jogger	surplus	servant	clergy	diner	Total
borniss	sirper	winler	wupper	sonnor	darber	burclust	perstat	birvick	biver	Total

(cont.)

Informal Decoding Inventory, Part II *(page 3 of 3)*

Vowel Team Syllables

chowder	ointment	approach	mushroom	pillow	meadow	bounty	treatment	maroon	discreet
grinlow	shoopoy	spoinap	haynick	reemin	slighnat	crainem	moanish	flaiwat	scoatal

	Total
	Total

Consonant–*le* Syllables

bubble	dandle	cattle	struggle	bugle	people	eagle	drizzle	whistle	sprinkle
buble	scanfle	fangle	baddle	magle	dafle	cogle	pubble	butle	baitle

	Total
	Total

(cont.)

SINGLE-SYLLABLE DECODING INVENTORY: STUDENT MATERIALS

sat	blip	card	stale	neat
pot	check	stork	hike	spoil
beg	clam	term	dome	goat
nip	chin	burst	cube	pail
cub	thick	turf	blame	field
pad	frank	fern	chive	fruit
top	mint	dirt	cute	claim
hit	fist	nark	prone	meet
met	grab	firm	vane	beast
nut	rest	mirth	brine	boast
mot	clop	fird	bame	craid
tib	prib	barp	neme	houn
han	hest	forn	hile	rowb
teg	chot	serp	pome	noy
fet	slen	surt	rute	feap
lup	bund	perd	nube	nuit
nid	bist	kurn	vope	maist
pab	hald	nirt	clate	ploat
hud	slub	mork	vike	tead
gop	shad	tarst	pene	steen

(cont.)

MULTISYLLABIC DECODING INVENTORY: STUDENT MATERIALS

batman	dentist	lotus	confine
blackmail	tunnel	lunar	athlete
carpool	compact	cupid	conclude
flashlight	hundred	spiky	concrete
baseball	flannel	pony	compose
corndog	banquet	final	stampede
crosswalk	submit	spiny	suppose
battlefield	contest	ivy	endure
frostbite	blanket	rely	cascade
bootstrap	gossip	equal	recline
catboy	sindict	rulab	depide
sundog	pladchet	cluden	repale
paintrag	suncrip	diler	wranblise
oatfarm	bunpect	slony	mondrine
raincan	wunnet	nicot	slindome
skywatch	blensim	fodun	lompise
dogrun	pefdimp	siny	sisdike
meatman	stindam	pady	dimcline
bluestar	flanpeck	pilem	plinsipe
hattree	winsprick	byliss	indube

(cont.)

fiber	chowder	bubble
super	ointment	dandle
furnish	approach	cattle
serpent	mushroom	struggle
varnish	pillow	bugle
jogger	meadow	people
surplus	bounty	eagle
servant	treatment	drizzle
clergy	maroon	whistle
diner	discreet	sprinkle
borniss	grinlow	buble
sirper	shoopoy	scanfle
winler	spoinap	fangle
wupper	haynick	baddle
sonnor	reemin	magle
darber	slighnat	dafle
burclust	crainem	cogle
perstat	moanish	pubble
birvick	flaiwat	butle
biver	scoatal	baitle

Word Recognition Lessons

Week 1: Compound Words

Today we will work with compound words. Compound words contain two words that are joined together to make up a new word. We will divide each compound word into its parts, read each part, and then read the parts together to read the compound word. The challenge is to figure out where to divide the word. For compounds divide after the first word.

herself	bookcase	footstep	soapstone	racehorse
anyone	doorknob	crossroad	keyhole	workshop
himself	armpit	household	afterthought	cardboard
yourself	countryside	rainstorm	manlike	gravestone
throughout	classroom	housework	likewise	swordfish
everyone	workday	storeroom	bookstore	southeast
everybody	racetrack	fireball	schoolmate	grapevine
somehow	airline	burnout	seaside	graveyard
something	farewell	cornfield	shoelace	thumbnail
somewhere	doorbell	fieldtrip	roommate	windburn

Spelling Practice

Now that we practiced reading compound words, let's try to write some compound words. Say the word to yourself. Divide it into two separate words. Spell each word. Remember to check to make sure there is at least one vowel in each word.

chopstick	catfish	dustpan	racetrack	bookstore
pitfall	boxcar	classroom	armpit	cardstock
passport	yardstick	pathway	likewise	grapevine

(cont.)

Week 2 through Week 6: Prefixes and Suffixes

Prefixes (Days 1 and 2): Today we will work with prefixes. A prefix is a word part used at the beginning of a word. You need to know a lot of prefixes. To divide and read words with prefixes, find the prefix, read the root word, and then read the prefix and root word together. Remember that the prefix changes the meaning of the root word.

Suffixes (Days 3 and 4): Today we will work with suffixes. A suffix is a word part used at the end of a word. You need to recognize suffixes when reading longer words. To divide and read words with suffixes, find the suffix, read the root word, and then read the root word and suffix together. Remember that the suffix changes the meaning of the root word.

Prefixes and Suffixes (Day 5): Today we will work with words with prefixes and suffixes. A prefix is a meaningful word part at the beginning of a word. A suffix is a meaningful word part used at the end of a word. To divide and read words with prefixes and suffixes, find the prefix, find the suffix, read the root word, and then read the prefix, root word, and suffix together. Remember that the prefix and suffix change the meaning of the root word.

(cont.)

Week 2: *un-, re-, -ful, -ly*

Day 1	Day 2	Day 3	Day 4	Day 5
un- means not. For example, the word *unable* means not able (to do something).	*re-* means again or back. For example, the word *repaint* means to paint again.	*-ful* means full of. For example, the word *painful* means full of pain.	*-ly* means in the manner of. For example, the word *suddenly* means something that happens quickly, without warning.	*un* means not. *-ful* means full of. *-ly* means in the manner of.
unscrew	rebuild	fearful	softly	ungracefully
unknown	rework	wishful	nicely	frightfully
unpack	remake	gleeful	sadly	untactful
unclean	reborn	needful	lively	unthoughtful
unplug	rewrite	thoughtful	kindly	unfaithfully
unsafe	reuse	cheerful	motherly	ungratefully
unfair	regain	boastful	fatherly	dreadfully
unkind	restate	peaceful	sisterly	peacefully
unreal	revisit	dreadful	brotherly	boastfully
Spelling Practice				
Now that we practiced reading words with prefixes and suffixes, let's practice spelling them. Say the word to yourself, break it into syllables, and spell each one. Remember to think of the parts we discussed today, and check to see that there is at least one vowel in each syllable.				
unplug	remake	cheerful	fatherly	faithfully
unreal	reuse	mindful	sadly	unmindful
unscrew	regain	thoughtful	softly	frightfully

(cont.)

Week 3: *over-, mis-, -ed, -ness*

Day 1	Day 2	Day 3	Day 4	Day 5
over- can mean in excess, or too much. For example, the word *overflow* means additional flow. *over-* is a two-syllable prefix.	*mis-* means bad or badly. For example, the word *misfortune* means to have bad fortune, bad luck.	*-ed* shows past tense and refers to something that happened in the past. *-ed* sounds like /t/, /id/, or /d/ depending on the base word.	*-ness* means with and is at the end of nouns. For example, the word *darkness* literally means with dark.	*over-* means in excess. *mis-* means bad or badly. *-ed* shows past tense and refers to something that happened in the past. *-ness* means with and is at the end of nouns.
overpower	misfit	trusted	kindness	youthfulness
overgrow	mistrust	blessed	sweetness	mistrusted
overcook	mismatch	heated	coolness	cheerfulness
overrun	misjudge	marked	chillness	colorfulness
overgrown	misread	barked	fairness	restfulness
overdo	misspell	cheered	loudness	wastefulness
overstep	mistreat	boasted	goodness	mismarked
overplant	misuse	worked	greatness	overmatched
overplay	miscount	helped	nervousness	misspelled
overstay	misplace	lifted	sickness	misguided
Spelling Practice				
Now that we practiced reading words with prefixes and suffixes, let's practice spelling them. Say the word to yourself, break it into syllables, and spell each one. Remember to think of the parts we discussed today, and check to see that there is at least one vowel in each syllable.				
overplay	misplace	cheered	sickness	restfulness
overplant	misjudge	lifted	sweetness	mismatched
overstep	mistrust	dressed	goodness	mistrusted

(cont.)

Week 4: *pre-, dis-, -able; -er, -ar,* and *-or; -ed*

Day 1	Day 2	Day 3	Day 4	Day 5
pre- means before. For example, the word *preheat* means to heat something before using it.	*dis-* means the opposite of. It means not, just like the prefix *un-*. For example, the word *disapprove* means not to approve (something).	*-able* means able to. For example, the word *manageable* refers to something that can be managed.	*-er* and *-or* can mean one who (does something). For example, the word *teacher* literally means a person who teaches.	*pre-* means before. *dis-* means the opposite of. *-able* means able to. *-ed* shows past tense and refers to something that happened in the past.
pregame	discharge	laughable	pitcher	previewed
prebake	dislike	enjoyable	banker	distractable
precook	disown	suitable	buyer	disbanded
prepay	distrust	valuable	editor	discovered
preschool	disarm	workable	actor	prescribed
preview	disagree	teachable	dancer	prejudged
prepaid	disallow	trainable	painter	disordered
preset	disinfect	washable	leader	avoidable
prescribe	disorder	wearable	worker	disarmed
prejudge	disbelief	readable	pointer	dismounted
Spelling Practice				
Now that we practiced reading words with prefixes and suffixes, let's practice spelling them. Say the word to yourself, break it into syllables, and spell each one. Remember to think of the parts we discussed today, and check to see that there is at least one vowel in each syllable.				
prepay	disagree	workable	banker	avoidable
precook	disorder	washable	pointer	disjointed
prescreen	discharge	suitable	worker	disbanded

(cont.)

Week 5: *fore-, trans-, -ing, -en, -ed*

Day 1	Day 2	Day 3	Day 4	Day 5
fore- means before, or in front of. For example, the word *forearm* refers to the part of your arm in front of the elbow.	*trans-* means across or beyond. For example, the word *transport* means to carry across a distance.	*-ing* is an ending for verbs that you are using all the time.	*-en* means to make more. For example, the word *lighten* means to make lighter.	*trans-* means across or beyond. *-ing* is an ending for verbs. *-en* means to make more. *-ed* shows past tense and refers to something that happened in the past.
foresee	transplant	flossing	blacken	toughened
forelegs	transpose	praying	sharpen	transported
foresight	transform	laughing	moisten	strengthened
forefather	transcribe	playing	strengthen	foretelling
forewarn	transport	planting	frighten	loosening
forethought	transact	throwing	lengthen	lightened
foretell	transatlantic	barking	quicken	forewarned
forehead	transverse	blasting	toughen	transfixed
foremost	transmit	tracking	brighten	transplanted
forefinger	transpire	drawing	broaden	sharpening

Spelling Practice

Now that we practiced reading words with prefixes and suffixes, let's practice spelling them. Say the word to yourself, break it into syllables, and spell each one. Remember to think of the parts we discussed today, and check to see that there is at least one vowel in each syllable.

forefather	transport	blasting	toughen	strengthened
foremost	transform	tracking	brighten	transplanted
foresight	transact	praying	moisten	sharpening

(cont.)

Week 6: *under-, after-, -some, -ment, pre-, -ful, re-, -ness*

Day 1	Day 2	Day 3	Day 4	Day 5
under- means below or less than. For example, the word *underpaid* means being paid less than you deserve. *under-* is a two-syllable prefix.	*after-* means later than a specific event or point in time. For example, the word *afternoon* means the time after 12 P.M. *after-* is a two-syllable prefix.	*-some* changes a word into an adjective. You are using words with the suffix *-some*. For example, *handsome* means good looking or attractive.	*-ment* means an action or process. For example, the word *government* means the action of governing, ruling a state.	*pre-* means before. *-ful* means full of. *re-* means again. *under-* means below, less than. *-ness* means with and is in nouns. *-ment* means action or process.
underage	aftershave	lonesome	statement	understatement
underground	afterworld	handsome	placement	repayment
understate	afterlife	fearsome	movement	underimprovement
underpants	afterthought	wholesome	payment	pretreatment
underplay	aftertaste	tiresome	treatment	gleefulness
underarm	aftereffect	awesome	improvement	resettlement
underfed	afterglow	bothersome	shipment	gracefulness
underlie	afterward	gruesome	retirement	underpayment
undereat	aftershock	loathsome	advancement	prepayment
undermost	aftermath	meddlesome	agreement	blissfulness
Spelling Practice				
Now that we practiced reading words with prefixes and suffixes, let's practice spelling them. Say the word to yourself, break it into syllables, and spell each one. Remember to think of the parts we discussed today, and check to see that there is at least one vowel in each syllable.				
underfeed	afterschool	bothersome	shipment	gracefulness
understate	aftercare	tiresome	agreement	blissfulness
underground	aftermath	troublesome	treatment	understatement

(cont.)

Week 7: Closed Syllables

Today we will work with words that have closed syllables. A syllable is called closed if the vowel is followed by one or more consonants. The word *stamp* is a closed syllable. So is the word *an*. If you find a closed syllable in a word, the vowel sound will be short. The challenge is to figure out where to divide the word. A strategy you can use is to place a dot underneath each vowel. Then decide how to divide. Remember: In a closed syllable, the vowel is followed by one or more consonants and its sound is short. So divide after the consonant. When you have double consonants, break the word between them. Blends are usually not divided and digraphs are never divided. Divide the syllables, decode them, and blend them. If your word doesn't sound right, divide it in a different way.

Practice Words (Sample Talk)

Here is my first word. I will mark the vowels. Now I will look for double consonants to help me to divide. I will divide between two consonants. I will now read each part and blend them. If the word sounds right, I have divided it correctly.

Day 1	Day 2	Day 3	Day 4	Day 5
absent	muffin	conquest	contest	puffin

Words

met	ship	dash	fluff	plump
shed	loft	stump	brush	dusk
velvet	submit	lesson	contrast	attract
bottom	gadget	blanket	fabric	affix
pilgrim	dentist	suffix	fossil	attempt
trumpet	common	insect	gallop	wisdom
cactus	faster	hammer	glutton	nostril
custom	expel	puppet	cannon	husband
blossom	basket	until	canvas	collect
ribbon	compass	pallet	falcon	pumpkin

Spelling Practice

Now that we practiced reading words with closed syllables, let's spell some words with the same patterns. Think of the vowel sound within each syllable when you spell it.

bottom	compass	blanket	canvas	wisdom
velvet	common	puppet	fabric	husband
trumpet	gadget	insect	contrast	attract

(cont.)

Week 8: Open and Closed Syllables

Today we will work with words that have open syllables. A syllable is called open if the vowel is not followed by one or more consonants. The word *he* is an open syllable. If you find an open syllable in a word, the vowel sound will be long. The challenge is to figure out where to divide the word. A strategy you can use is to place a dot underneath each single vowel. Then decide how to divide. Remember: In an open syllable, the vowel is not followed by one or more consonants and its sound is long. So divide after the vowel. Divide the syllables, decode them, and blend them. If your word doesn't sound right, divide it in a different way.

Practice Words (Sample Talk)

Here is my first word. I will mark the vowels. Now I will think if I should divide after the vowel or after the consonant. I will now read each part and blend them. If the word sounds right, I have divided it correctly.

Day 1	Day 2	Day 3	Day 4	Day 5
ivy	navy	gravy	pupil	apron

Words

be	hi	fry	eject	she
unit	event	music	equal	frugal
cozy	fever	python	recent	puma
moment	hotel	pupil	bypass	bacon
nomad	focus	aphid	human	hyphen
rely	student	raven	pilot	blatant
retry	silent	lady	stupid	mucus
moment	depend	total	evil	vacant
baby	basic	robot	brutal	program
even	bonus	result	fatal	strident

Spelling Practice

Now that we practiced reading words with open syllables, let's spell some words with the same patterns. Think of the vowel sound within each syllable when you spell it.

nomad	bonus	music	evil	strident
unit	depend	robot	brutal	bacon
baby	focus	raven	recent	frugal

(cont.)

Week 9: Closed, Open, and Vowel–Consonant–*e* Syllables

Today we will work with words that have closed syllables, open syllables, and vowel–consonant–*e* syllables. In a vowel–consonant-*e* syllable, there is a single vowel and a consonant followed by a final /e/ that indicates that the vowel is long. The word *fate* is a vowel–consonant–*e* syllable and so is the word *blame*. If you find a vowel–consonant–*e* syllable in a word, the vowel sound will be long. The challenge is to figure out where to divide the word. A strategy you can use is to place a dot underneath each vowel. Then decide how to divide. Remember: In a vowel–consonant–*e* syllable, the pattern you see is vowel–consonant–*e*. So when the vowel–consonant–*e* does not come at the end of a word, divide after the *e*. For each word, divide the syllables, decode each one, and blend them. If your word doesn't sound right, divide it in a different way.

Practice Words (Sample Talk)

Here is my first word. I will mark the vowels. Now I will look for the pattern vowel–consonant–*e*. I will now read each part and blend them. If the word sounds right, I have divided it correctly.

Day 1	Day 2	Day 3	Day 4	Day 5
collide	revise	migrate	pavement	define

Words

rake	space	frame	flute	brute
mistake	supreme	donate	pollute	stampede
estate	athlete	microbe	dictate	divide
ignite	humane	cascade	crusade	explode
conspire	reduce	chloride	refuge	precede
mandate	define	volume	deplete	inquire
compose	restate	concede	decade	expire
translate	rephrase	suffice	impede	debate
rotate	deduce	immune	extreme	acquire
divine	define	polite	before	impure

Spelling Practice

We will practice spelling some words with closed, open, and vowel–consonant–*e* syllables. Think of the vowel sound for each syllable type when you spell it.

compose	athlete	donate	refuge	stampede
ignite	supreme	volume	deplete	expire
estate	humane	immune	dictate	divide

(cont.)

Week 10: *r*-Controlled Syllables

Today we will work with words that have closed syllables, open syllables, and *r*-controlled syllables. An *r*-controlled syllable has a vowel followed by an *r* that changes the vowel sound. The word *car* is *r*-controlled. So is the word *bear*. The challenge is to figure out where to divide the word. A strategy you can use is to place a dot underneath each vowel. Then decide how to divide. Remember: In a closed syllable the vowel will be short; in an open syllable, the vowel will be long, and in an *r*-controlled syllable, the vowel will not be long or short because of the *r*. Divide the syllables, decode each one, and blend them. If your word doesn't sound right, divide it in a different way.

Practice Words (Sample Talk)

Here is my first word. I will mark the vowels. I will then decide where to divide the word. I will now read each part and blend them. If the word sounds right, I have divided it correctly.

Day 1	Day 2	Day 3	Day 4	Day 5
barber	harvest	farmer	tamper	blubber

Words

far	sir	her	fur	or
garment	letter	sermon	butter	fever
circus	thermos	after	carbon	turnip
skirmish	sturdy	marshal	rattler	afford
parchment	dinner	further	garlic	current
carpet	perhaps	barley	person	worry
monster	perfect	burden	farther	minor
worker	marker	furnish	merchant	robber
server	confirm	burlap	suburb	alert
surplus	kernel	border	hermit	thirty

Spelling Practice

Now that we practiced reading words with closed, open, and *r*-controlled syllables, let's spell some words with the same patterns. Think of the vowel sound within each syllable when you spell it.

garment	perfect	further	hermit	afford
carpet	confirm	border	garlic	alert
monster	diner	sermon	carbon	turnip

(cont.)

Week 11: Vowel Teams

Today we will work with words that have open, closed, *r*-controlled, and vowel team syllables. In a vowel team syllable, there are two vowels working together to make one sound. The word *main* has a vowel team and so does the word *clown*. Remember that *w* and *y* can work as vowels. A strategy you can use is to place a dot underneath each single vowel and an underline below a vowel team. Then decide how to divide. Remember in a closed syllable the vowel will be short. In an open syllable the vowel will be long, and in an *r*-controlled syllable the vowel will not be long or short because of the r. Divide the syllables, decode them, and blend them. If your word doesn't sound right, divide it in a different way.

Practice Words (Sample Talk)

Here is my first word. I will mark the vowels and underline the vowel teams. I will now read each part and blend them. If the word sounds right, I have divided it correctly.

Day 1	Day 2	Day 3	Day 4	Day 5
seasons	contain	steamer	retrieve	healthy

Words

glow	float	fear	bear	pearl
maintain	fairway	faucet	compound	portrait
flounder	applaud	weather	roundup	instead
allow	boarder	harpoon	coastline	relief
crayon	mistook	preacher	enjoy	mushroom
ointment	county	feather	blackout	townsfolk
raccoon	autumn	daughter	tiptoe	beneath
approach	baboon	rooster	widow	repeat
complain	tattoo	slaughter	window	pillow
balloon	ready	jawbone	willow	freedom
meadow	feedback	seesaw	mildew	campaign

Spelling Practice

Now that we practiced reading words with closed, open, *r*-controlled, and vowel team syllables, let's spell some words with these patterns. Think of the vowel sound within each syllable when you spell.

balloon	tattoo	daughter	willow	feedback

(cont.)

184

Week 12: Consonant–*le* Syllables

Today we will divide and read words that have a consonant–*le* syllable. The consonant–*le* syllable, as its names indicates, is a consonant followed by *le*. The consonant–*le* syllable type is at the end of words. The syllable before it can be any of the types we discussed. When you see a consonant–*le* syllable at the end of a word, always divide before it. Divide the syllables, decode each one, and blend them. If your word doesn't sound right, divide it in a different way.

Practice Words (Sample Talk)

Here is my first word. I will mark the vowels and underline the vowel teams. I will look for the consonant–*le* pattern and divide before it. Then I will look at the first part of the word and decide what type of syllable it is. I will now read each part and blend them. If the word sounds right, I have divided it correctly.

Day 1	Day 2	Day 3	Day 4	Day 5
candle	able	saddle	fable	cattle

Words

cripple	cable	double	eagle	noodle
grapple	noble	sprinkle	people	beetle
turtle	cycle	riddle	staple	beagle
crumble	maple	mumble	noodle	whistle
simple	title	idle	pickle	bridle
muscle	steeple	ample	freckle	riddle
ruffle	fable	rifle	poodle	giggle
drizzle	bugle	stifle	steeple	whittle
puzzle	marble	gargle	dawdle	dribble
jungle	sniffle	hurdle	wrinkle	mingle

Spelling Practice

Now that we practiced reading words with the different syllable types, we will spell them. Think of the vowel sound and pattern within each syllable when you spell.

jungle	noble	mumble	poodle	beagle
simple	title	riddle	eagle	dribble
candle	marble	sprinkle	people	whistle

(cont.)

Week 13: *-ed* and *-ing*

We have worked with the suffixes *-ed* and *-ing*. We said that these suffixes appear always in verbs. Today we will work on some of the spelling patterns for these suffixes.				
Day 1	Day 2	Day 3	Day 4	Day 5
In a verb where the base word ends in a final *e*, we will add only *d* when creating the past tense. The *-ed* will make the sound /d/, /id/, or /t/ depending on the base word.	In a verb where the base word ends in final *e*, we will drop the *e* when adding *-ing*.	In a verb where the base word ends in a short vowel followed by a single consonant, we double the final consonant before adding *-ed* or *-ing*.	In a verb where the base word ends in a long vowel followed by a single consonant, we add *-ed* or *-ing* without changing the base word.	In the following words, either the base word ends in a final *e* and the *e* was dropped, the final consonant was doubled, or there was no change. Remember what we discussed during the week and identify the base word after reading the word.
used	hoping	nodding	moaned	riding
waved	writing	hopped	boasted	smiling
skated	closing	sniffed	meeting	tuning
traded	framing	planned	mailing	shouting
shaped	waving	swimming	cleaning	waited
glazed	skating	stopped	eating	seemed
based	making	rubbing	dreaming	voted
spiked	moving	permitted	preaching	fanning
grated	having	begging	greeting	flopping
cared	taking	dropped	snowing	slipped
You may ask the students to spell some of the words after they practice reading them.				

(cont.)

Week 14: Changing *y* to *i* or No Change

We have worked with the suffixes *-ed* and *-ing*. We will examine the endings *-ies* and *-ied* as well as changes in words that end in *y*. We will work on some of the spelling patterns for these suffixes.

Day 1	Day 2	Day 3	Day 4	Day 5
In a verb that ends in a consonant plus *y*, we first change the *y* to *i* before adding *-ed* or *-es*. In a verb that ends in a vowel plus *y*, we do not need to change the *y* before adding *-s* or *-ed*.	In a singular word that ends in *y*, we add an *-s* to make it plural when there is a vowel before the *y*. If there is a consonant before the *y*, we drop the *y* and add *-ies*.	In a verb that ends in *y*, there is no change when adding *-ing*.	In a word that ends in a consonant followed by *y*, we change the *y* to *i* before adding a suffix.	Read the words and identify the root word and the changes that happened to *y*.
cried	days	crying	armies	delaying
applies	pennies	hurrying	fanciful	deliveries
occupied	juries	applying	variance	adversaries
supplies	monkeys	portraying	appliance	tendencies
conveys	abilities	studying	ordinarily	joyful
conveyed	buddies	terrifying	emptiness	accompanied
employed	families	qualifying	burial	thirstiness
qualifies	personalities	enjoying	dutiful	verified
replied	surveys	tidying	alliance	certified
horrified	delays	employing	ladies	petrifying

You may ask the students to spell some of the words after practicing reading them.

(cont.)

Week 15: Combinations of Syllable Types

You know all the syllable types, and you know how to divide and read words with two syllables. Today we will divide and read words that have more than two syllables. The challenge is to determine where to divide the word. A strategy you can use is to place a dot underneath each vowel and an underline below a vowel team. Blends and vowel teams are usually not divided. Digraphs are never divided. Remember that the real test is to ask if the word you read sounds right. If it doesn't, divide it in a different way.

Practice Words (Sample Talk)

Here is my first word. I will mark the vowels and underline the vowel teams. I will now read each part and blend them. If the word sounds right, I have divided it correctly.

Day 1	Day 2	Day 3	Day 4	Day 5
prosecute	compromise	pantomime	personalize	instrument

Words

speculate	persistent	compressor	stimulate	example
porcupine	argument	assembly	validate	ignorant
turbulent	evacuate	dictator	advocate	assignment
recorder	scholastic	fabricate	increasing	neighborhood
understand	refinement	determined	announcement	domestic
department	mechanism	technical	compromise	attainment
hibernate	synchronize	congratulate	absolute	retirement
camcorder	departure	customer	eradicate	government
delightful	dissatisfy	progressing	insulate	storekeeper
laborer	professor	murderer	singular	quadruple

Spelling Practice

Now that we practiced reading multisyllabic words, let's try to spell them. Say the word, break it into syllables and try to spell each syllable. In the end, check to see if each syllable part is represented correctly.

porcupine	departure	customer	insulate	ignorant
camcorder	refinement	dictator	singular	domestic
hibernate	evacuate	congratulate	stimulate	example

(cont.)

188

Week 16: Accent and Schwa Sound

Today we will work with the schwa sound. The schwa sound is the /uh/ sound and can be heard in the unaccented syllable of multisyllabic words. For example, in the word *about* the *a* makes the /uh/ sound. The first syllable is unaccented and it is pronounced with a schwa. We will read some multisyllabic words that have schwa syllables. Divide the words using what you know about the syllable types, decode each part, blend them, and decide if the word sounds right. Then pay attention to the unaccented syllable. Remember the schwa sound can be in any unaccented syllable regardless of the vowel letter you see.

Day 1	Day 2	Day 3	Day 4	Day 5
-al is a suffix and in multisyllabic words makes the schwa sound. Words that end in *-al* can be nouns or adjectives. The word *signal* is a noun and the *-al* is unaccented.	*-ic* is a suffix, and it can be in words that are nouns and adjectives. The accent in these words is always before the ending *-ic*.	*-ant* and *-ance* are at the end of words. These endings have the schwa sound and are unaccented.	*-ive* is unaccented and makes the schwa sound as in *active*.	In three-syllable words, the open middle syllable is unaccented and it has the schwa sound.

Words				
vital	horrific	tolerance	fugitive	pharmacy
general	terrific	attendance	captive	legacy
personal	athletic	defiant	narrative	tentacle
arrival	patriotic	abundant	relative	argument
global	pathetic	hesitant	massive	metaphor
internal	sarcastic	relevant	perceptive	singular
eternal	statistic	occupant	respective	innocent
nocturnal	angelic	reluctance	negative	alphabet
funeral	ceramic	compliance	sensitive	antelope
identical	electric	significance	massive	octopus

You may ask the students to spell some of the words after practicing reading them.

(cont.)

189

Week 17: Accent in Two- and Three-Syllable Words

Today we will work with the two- and three-syllable words and examine their accent. In words with two syllables the accent usually is on the first syllable. Sometimes, though, the accent may be on the second syllable. Divide each syllable based on its type. Then pay attention to the accent. The syllable that is mostly stressed has the primary accent. The syllable that has a less strong accent has a secondary accent.

Day 1	Day 2	Day 3	Day 4	Day 5
-it and *-et* are suffixes of multisyllabic words. They usually are pronounced as /it/.	*-ate* is a suffix and can have the /it/ or /et/ sound.	*-ate* is a suffix. It is pronounced /it/ when it is unaccented and the word is a noun or an adjective. It is pronounced with a long ā and has a secondary accent when the word is a verb.	*-ine* is an unaccented suffix and is pronounced /in/. In two-syllable words the accent is on the first syllable.	*-ain* is an unaccented suffix and is pronounced /in/. In two-syllable words the accent is on the first syllable.
Words				
poet	accurate	estimate	feminine	chieftain
planet	adequate	illuminate	masculine	captain
quiet	literate	literate	doctrine	fountain
orbit	pirate	chocolate	engine	bargain
credit	fortunate	climate	famine	chaplain
audit	private	senate	examine	certain
limit	certificate	donate	imagine	porcelain
toilet	compassionate	ornate	medicine	villain
implicit	delicate	vaccinate	Madeline	mountain
closet	desperate	validate	determine	curtain
You may ask the students to spell some of the words after practicing reading them.				

(cont.)

Week 18: Accent in Two- and Three-Syllable Words

Today we will work with the two- and three-syllable words and examine their accent. In words with two syllables the accent is usually on the first syllable. Sometimes, though, the accent may be on the second syllable. Divide each syllable based on its type. Then pay attention to the accent. The syllable that is mostly stressed has the primary accent. The syllable that has a less strong accent has a secondary accent.

Day 1	Day 2	Day 3	Day 4	Day 5
-ine can be also pronounced /en/. When it is pronounced /en/, the accent is on the second syllable for two-syllable words. For three-syllable words the first syllable has the primary accent and the last the secondary.	*-ice* is an unaccented suffix that is usually pronounced with a schwa sound and forms nouns.	*-tion* is an unaccented suffix that forms nouns. It is pronounced (shun). The syllable before *-tion* is always accented.	*-age* is an unaccented suffix. In words with more than one syllable it is pronounced /ij/.	*-ture* is an unaccented suffix. It is pronounced /chur/. *-sure* is also an unaccented suffix and it is pronounced /zhur/.

Words				
chlorine	justice	ignition	cabbage	composure
vaccine	office	repetition	garbage	pleasure
sardine	crevice	election	savage	future
figurine	apprentice	starvation	advantage	puncture
Pauline	novice	quotation	language	gesture
routine	notice	frustration	cottage	literature
magazine	practice	commotion	voyage	departure
submarine	accomplice	rotation	wreckage	adventure
marine	cowardice	perfection	shortage	mixture
machine	service	position	bandage	fracture

You may ask the students to spell some of the words after practicing reading them.

.

191

Reciprocal Teaching Reminders

Question	Who? What? When? Where? Why? How? When you read, you should ask questions about what you are reading. These questions will start your RT discussion. Questions help you share understanding of the author's meaning. Create questions using these question starters. Try to focus your questions on the most important ideas.
Clarify	I didn't understand and then … I got confused, but … It didn't make sense until … When you read you will find words or phrases that you don't know, but then you figure them out. You may also find a section that is difficult to understand. Keep track of the times that something was hard but you had to figure it out.
Summarize	What is the main idea of this section? What are the main points in this part of the reading? You end your RT discussion with a summary of the section you have been discussing. You may ask yourself these questions to help you guide the summary. Provide the main ideas without giving details.
Predict	What will the next section be about? Based on what I read so far and what I know, I predict … The author says _____, and I know _____, so I predict _____ After you have summarized, it is time to prepare the group for the next section of the reading. Get them started by making a prediction, based on what you've read so far and any clues that the author gives in the headings or illustrations.

QAR Reminders

Right There	The information to develop the question and its answer is in the same sentence.
Think and Search	The information to develop the question and its answer is not in just one sentence, but in different sentences. Look carefully in the text to create and answer the questions.
Author and You	The question comes from something that the author has given you. To answer it, you need to think about what you already know about that written information.
On Your Own	The question is related to something in the book, but the answer is based on your own knowledge and experience.

Book Club Reminders

Question Creator: In the Text	Your job is to develop questions about the section you read today. You will develop questions for which the answers can be found in the text, in one sentence, or in multiple sentences. These questions will begin with what, where, who, or when. Think of questions that will help your book club review important information.
Question Creator: In Your Head	Your job is to develop and answer questions about the section you read today. The answers will not be in the text. In order to answer these questions, you must use your personal experiences, other reading you have done, or your general knowledge. These questions will begin with why, how, or what if. Think of questions that will help your book club review important information.
Connector	Your job is to guide your club to make connections between what you just read, previous chapters, other readings, or your experiences. You should be explicit in the references you make to the text as well as to other texts so your club members will understand your connections and be able to make them.
Predictor	Your job is to guide your club to predict what will happen next in the text. In order to make an accurate prediction, you should use the information the author provided in the text. You should combine this information with other readings or with your general knowledge and then "guess" what will happen next. You will evaluate your prediction after you read the next section. Help members of your club make informed guesses.
Visualizer	Your job is help members of your club visualize the information that the author presented and describe it in your own words. Look for descriptive words that the author used and the feelings they evoked. Help members of your club to visualize in ways that deepen understanding.
Word Wizard	Your job is to select unusual or interesting words or phrases from the selection you read and explain them based on the information that the author provided. Help the members of your club find and understand new words or phrases.
Summarizer	Your job is to help your club summarize the information in the text you just read. In order to create a good summary, you should focus on the main ideas that were presented. Your summary should include the character/s and the main actions without giving any details. Help members of your club make a useful summary.

Text Structure Graphic Organizers

Sequence

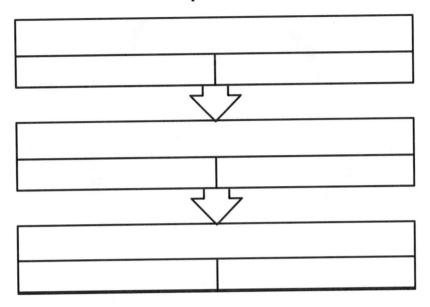

Cause and Effect

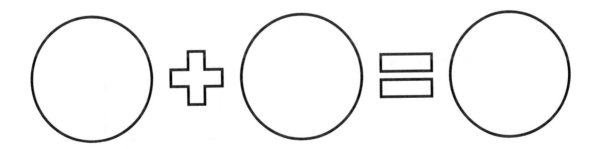

(cont.)

Cycle

Hierarchy

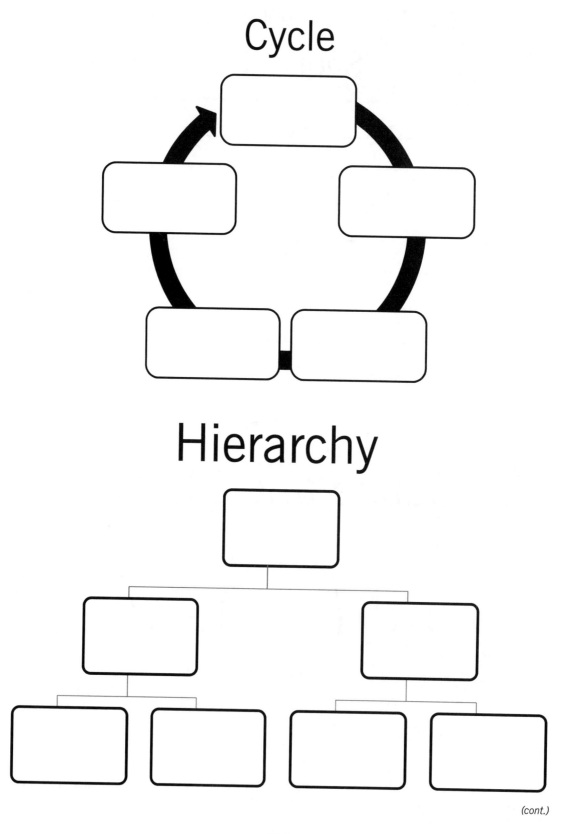

(cont.)

Topic–Subtopic

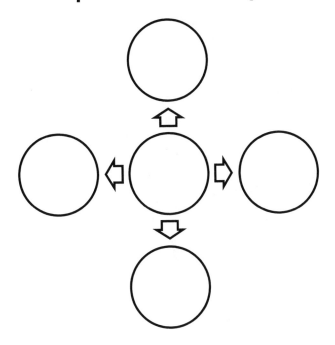

Compare–Contrast

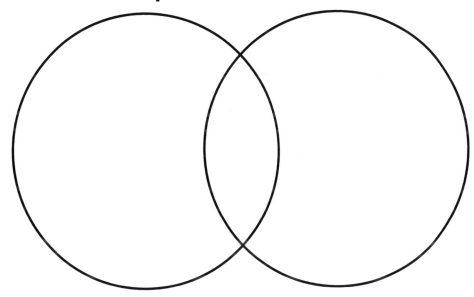

(cont.)

Compare–Contrast

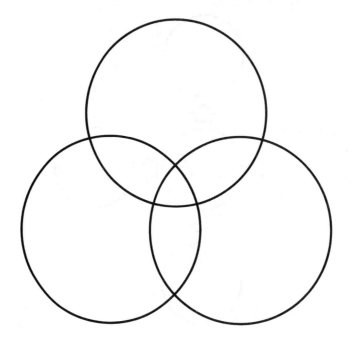

Continuum

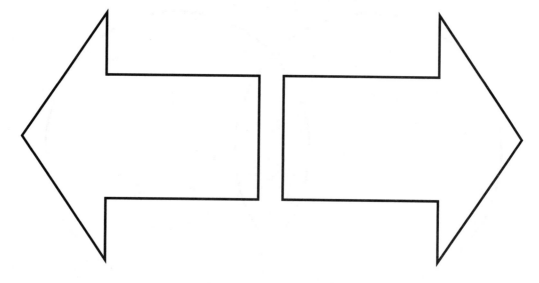

(cont.)

Story

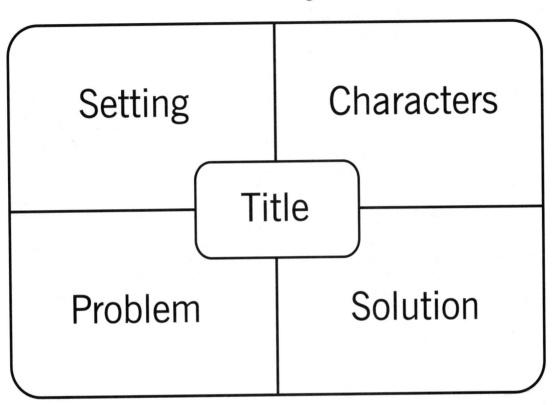

Setting

Characters

Title

Problem

Solution

Word Recognition and Fluency Sample Plans

Texts Used in Sample Lessons

	For Word Recognition and Fluency Groups	For Fluency and Comprehension Groups	Stretched Suggestions
Grade 4	600L–725L	645L–780L	770L–910L
Narrative	Howe: *Bunnicula* (700L)	Lowry: *Number the Stars* (670)	Lin: *Where the Mountain Meets the Moon* (820)
Informational	Simon: *Danger! Earthquakes* (710L)	Levine: *Hana's Suitcase* (730)	Simon: *The Brain* (900)
Grade 5	645L–780L	730L–845L	865L–980L
Narrative	Hiaasen: *Hoot* (760)	O'Dell: *Sing Down the Moon* (820)	Paulsen: *The River* (960)
Informational	Peck: *The Life and Words of Martin Luther King, Jr.* (700) Simon: *Danger! Volcanoes* (790L)	Adams: *The Best Book of Weather* (IG840)	Usborne *Introduction to Weather and Climate Change* (IG980)

Sample Lessons for a Fourth-Grade Word Recognition and Fluency Group

Bunnicula: A Rabbit Tale of Mystery, by Deborah and James Howe
Lexile Level: 700; 98 pages
All lessons take the same format.

1. Work with multisyllabic decoding.
2. What do we already know about these characters? What do we already know about the events? or Let's review what we learned in yesterday's reading.
3. Choral read the next chapter.
4. Partner and whisper read the same chapter. Work on improving expression.
5. Use the QARs for a quick discussion.

QARs
1. Right There
2. Think and Search
3. Author and You
4. On Your Own

Reading	Questions for Discussion
Chapter 1	
1	What does the family tell Harold when they go out? What is Mr. and Mrs. Monroe's job? What did they find on Toby's chair? What was in the center of the shoebox? Why did Mrs. Monroe suggest calling the bunny Bunnicula?
2	Why didn't Harold want to go to the movies? How do the Monroes show they are thoughtful toward their pets? In what room of the house did Mr. Monroe decide that the rabbit would stay? Why did Pete suggest naming the rabbit Mr. Johnson?
3	Why did the mother ask Toby to take off his boots? Why did the note say, "Take good care of my Baby?" What was the reason for Pete and Toby's argument?
4	Why would someone leave their child in a blanket with a note asking whoever found it to take care of it? What do bunnies eat?
Chapter 2	
1	How did Chester come into the house? How could gypsies tell your fortune?
2	How do gypsies travel?
3	Why can't Chester be considered an ordinary cat?
4	Would you expect a bunny to have fangs?

(cont.)

Reading	Questions for Discussion
Chapter 3	
1	How does a cat change a subject it finds uncomfortable? When was the rabbit waking up?
2	Why did Harold have no one to talk to? Why couldn't Harold understand why the children would play with Bunnicula?
3	How was Chester "gone" for 45 minutes? What could have happened to the tomato and caused it to turn white?
4	What would you expect a tomato to look like?
Chapter 4	
1	According to Chester, why does Bunnicula bite vegetables?
2	Why would Harold say that Toby has a rotten sense of humor? Why did Toby find the book *Treasure Island* hard to read? What did Harold think that a parrot was? Why does Chester think that Bunnicula is a vampire? What similarities exist between Bunnicula and vampires?
3	Who do you think is smarter, Harold or Chester? Why? How do you think the zucchini turned white?
4	How would a vampire feed himself? Where is Transylvania?
Chapter 5	
1	What does Toby say can happen as a result of the use of chemicals in food?
2	Why does Harold think that Mr. Monroe has been bitten by Bunnicula? What explanations does the family give about the white vegetables? How does the family interpret Chester's awkward behavior?
3	Why did Chester wear the towel as a cape? Why was Chester embarrassed?
4	What is DDT and how is it used?
Chapter 6	
1	On what did Harold trip as he entered the living room? Where had Bunnicula buried the nose? When does Chester find the bunny to be a threat?
2	What was the strange odor that Harold smelled? What did Chester throw at the rabbit? What happened to the steak?
3	Why did Chester place garlic everywhere? Why didn't Chester enjoy the bath that Mrs. Monroe gave him? What is the mistake that Chester made in regard to the book's suggestion?
4	What are some of the uses of garlic?

(cont.)

Reading	Questions for Discussion
Chapter 7	
1	What was Harold determined to do the next day?
2	Why was Chester not talking to Harold? What signs did Harold notice about the bunny that made him think it was sick? Why was the bunny so tired looking?
3	Why was Chester wearing a piece of garlic around his neck?
4	How could you tell if someone was sick?
Chapter 8	
1	What did Harold do when he went to the front door?
2	Why wasn't Bunnicula eating the food that Pete and Toby left for him in his cage? How did Harold carry Bunnicula to the dining room table? Why did Harold take the rabbit out of his cage?
3	Why was Chester sleeping during the day? Why did Chester attack the bunny?
Chapter 9	
1	From what did Bunnicula suffer? What was Bunnicula given immediately? What is sibling rivalry? What does Chester read now?
2	Why did the vegetables never turn white again? How does Chester "find himself"?
3	Why was Harold concerned about his injection? Why does Harold wish that Toby would cover two chocolate cupcakes? Why is Toby allowed to stay up late on Friday?
4	What kind of juice is nutritious? Why would someone go to a psychiatrist? What is the difference between a psychologist and a psychiatrist?

Sample Lessons for a Fourth-Grade Word Recognition and Fluency Group

Danger! Earthquakes, by Seymour Simon
Lexile Level: 710; 29 pages
All lessons take the same format.

1. Work with multisyllabic decoding.
2. What do we already know about these characters? What do we already know about the events? or Let's review what we learned in yesterday's reading.
3. Choral read the next chapter.
4. Partner and whisper read the same chapter. Work on improving expression.
5. Use the QARs for a quick discussion.

QARs
1. Right There
2. Think and Search
3. Author and You
4. On Your Own

Reading	Questions for Discussion
pp. 1–9	
1	What do earthquakes cause the ground to do? How long do earthquakes last? How many earthquakes happen every year around the world? What is the Richter scale? What is the Mercalli scale?
2	What kinds of destruction are caused by earthquakes? What is the difference between the Mercalli and the Richter scales?
3	How would people react to a magnitude 7 earthquake as measured by the Richter scale?
4	How would people have reacted during the San Francisco earthquake?
pp. 10–17	
1	What is the zone where most earthquakes take place called? What is the earth's crust?
2	How does the movement of the plates connect to earthquakes?
3	Why does California have so many earthquakes annually?
4	Would places with volcanic eruptions also have earthquakes?

(cont.)

Reading	Questions for Discussion
pp. 18–29	
1	What state has the most earthquakes?
2	What happened in 1811 in the Mississippi valley? What were the effects of the earthquake in Anchorage in 1964? What is the safest ground for building? What would make a building safe from earthquakes? What are some of the benefits and drawbacks of scientific assistance in regard to earthquakes? What are some of the things you need to know in case of an earthquake?
3	What materials would people use in the rebuilding efforts?
4	Have you ever experienced an earthquake? Do people get trapped in a building during earthquakes? How do they survive?

Sample Lessons for a Fifth-Grade Word Recognition and Fluency Group

Hoot, by Carl Hiaasen
Lexile Level: 760; 292 pages
All lessons take the same format.

---

1. Work with multisyllabic decoding.
2. What do we already know about these characters? What do we already know about the events? or Let's review what we learned in yesterday's reading.
3. Choral read the next chapter.
4. Partner or whisper read the same chapter. Work on improving expression.
5. Use the reading guide questions below for a quick discussion.

Chapter	Questions for Discussion
1	How did Dana Matherson ambush Roy? Why was Dana treating Roy like that? What was the running boy wearing? Why wouldn't the running boy wear shoes? Why couldn't the officer report the incident as vandalism? What did the removal of the survey stakes cause in the construction plans? Why did Curly pretend he didn't know that there were owls on the property? What was Garett's most popular trick? What explanations did Garett give for the shoeless boy?
2	Who was Dana tormenting? Why was Roy trying to get to the door of the school bus? How did Roy escape from Dana? What happened at the golf course? Why was Roy called "cowgirl"? What was Roy's favorite place of all the places he had lived? What did Roy do when his father told him that they would move to Florida? Why wouldn't Mrs. Hennepin believe Roy's story initially? How was Mrs. Hennepin convinced that Roy was telling the truth? What did Mrs. Hennepin ask Roy to do? Why did the girl confront Roy? Why did Roy feel uncomfortable when the girl confronted him?
3	Why was the police officer delayed? What vandalism was performed at the property? How did the alligators come to be in the potties? Why didn't Roy's father get upset when he was told that Roy hit another student? Why did Mr. Eberhardt ask his wife to call the school the next morning? Should Dana also be disciplined by the school? Were the tone and the content of the letter that Roy wrote appropriate? Why did Roy's father ask Roy to look at the dictionary? What explanation did the police give for the alligators?

(cont.)

Chapter	Questions for Discussion
4	How did Garett get all the inside information? What did Beatrice do to the linebacker? Was it appropriate for Beatrice to act in that manner? What was Officer Delinko's motive for working on a volunteer basis? What was the officer's career goal? What did the owls that the officer saw look like? What had happened to the officer's car? Why did Roy approach and speak to Beatrice? Why did Roy visit Dana? Was the behavior between Dana and his mother ordinary?
5	Why did Trace Middle decide not to take disciplinary action against Dana? What did Roy find at the bottom of the ditch? What was inside the bag that Roy turned over? Why didn't Roy move when he encountered the bear? Why did the boy tie Roy and cover his head?
6	How would the officer feel if he knew the information that was published in the newspaper? What explanation was given by the chief for the officer's mistake? Why would the chief give false information? Why did Roy go to the construction site? Why did Roy feel guilty for sneaking away from the house? Why was Roy walking in the rain instead of riding his bike?
7	Where did Beatrice lead Roy? Why did Roy carry the shoebox? Who was the running, shoeless boy? Why was the officer glad to find Roy? Why was the running boy called Mullet Fingers? How did Beatrice create an excuse for Roy's delay? Why did the officer want Roy's father to write a letter for him? How did the officer feel and what did he think when Roy's mother mentioned the article in the newspaper?
8	Why was Roy allowed to ride the school bus so early? Who was Chuck Muckle? Why was Chuck Muckle upset about the newspaper article and why did he scold Curly? Who is Kimberly Dixon? Why did the pancake company have no time for any additional delays? Why did Curly bring the dogs to the construction site? Why did the dog owner say not to feed the dogs? What did Dana do to Roy when he saw him at the bus? Why didn't the bus driver see what was happening between Roy and Dana?

(cont.)

207

Chapter	Questions for Discussion
9	Why did Garett insist that Roy pretend to be sick? Why didn't Roy ask for the vice principal's support? Do you think that the school handled the bullying issue appropriately? What did Curly witness when he arrived at the site? Why did the dog owner become so upset? How did the dog owner threaten Curly? Why? Why wasn't the reptile wrangler able to locate the snakes? How did Dana ambush Roy? How did Roy escape from Dana's menace?
10	Who saved Roy? What favor did Beatrice ask of Roy? Why did Beatrice tell Roy's mother that the experiment would be messy? Who was Leon Leep? What differences did Lonna and her son have? Why did Lonna send her son to the military prep school? How did Roy treat the running boy? Is it safe for the running boy to rely only on the ointment that Roy put on his wound? Why weren't the cottonmouths able to hurt the dogs or a human? Why shouldn't they build a Mother Paula at that construction site?
11	What did the officer find at the top of the fence? Why did Roy wave to the police car? Who did Curly shoot at his trailer? Why did the officer visit the house of the Eberhardts? Why hasn't Roy told his father about the letter that the officer had requested?
12	How did the running boy manage to get treated at the hospital without notifying his family? What did Beatrice and Roy tell the doctor? Why did Beatrice leave Roy and go home? Why didn't Beatrice share the running boy's true name with Roy? Why didn't Roy want to be at the emergency room when he heard the siren? Why did Roy's father insist on going to see his "wounded son"? What happened when the grownups entered the room of the wounded boy? Where do you think the wounded boy went?
13	Why did Roy show the bird book to his father? Why was Roy worried about the owls? Do you think that what Roy did for the running boy was correct?

(cont.)

Chapter	Questions for Discussion
14	What news did Garett share with Roy? Why did Roy visit Beatrice's house? Was it nice the way that Beatrice's mother spoke to Roy? Why did Roy lie? How did Beatrice's mother treat Beatrice? Why did Dana's father want to pay Roy? Why did Dana try to hit Roy? What do burrowing owls mostly eat? Would you say that the running boy is bitter? Why? What efforts did the running boy make to inform the pancake company about the existence of the owls? Why did Roy say that he was planning on doing his homework that night? Where did the running boy take Roy? What did the boys do at the creek?
15	How did Roy insult Dana? Why wasn't Roy running as fast as he could? What information did Roy give to Dana? What did Dana promise Roy? Why did Curly have a gun with him? Who did Curly catch at the company's property? How did Dana end up at the pancake company's property? Why did Dana say that his name was Roy? Why did the officer stop the teenager? How did Dana react when he was caught by the police officer?
16	What did Garett tell Roy about Dana? Why did Roy lure Dana to the property? Why didn't Roy tell Garett that he had lied to Dana and led him to the property? What would be the consequences for Dana? Why? What efforts did Curly make to locate his gun? What had happened to the machines on the property? Who had done it? Where was Curly's gun? How could Roy check whether the actions of the pancake company were legal? Who did Roy find under his bed? Why?
17	Why did Curly exaggerate in his description of how the teenager was caught? What decision did Chuck Muckle make? Why didn't Beatrice go to school that day? Why wasn't Officer Delinko sure that the boy he arrested was the vandal they were looking for? How was the officer convinced that Dana was not the vandal? Why did Roy go to the building and zoning department? Why did Curly and Roy argue?

(cont.)

Chapter	Questions for Discussion
18	What did Officer Delinko think when he saw the owls and the bulldozer? What did Roy read in the newspaper that morning? Why did Beatrice bite the ring on her stepmother's toe? Why didn't Mullet Finger want to involve Roy and Beatrice? Why did Roy give Mullet Finger the camera? What did Roy share with his class?
19	Why did Curly refuse to admit the existence of owls on the property? Why did Roy ask his parents for a note? What did Chuck Muckle ask from the officer? How did the crickets end up on the property?
20	What preparations were made at the construction site? Who else appeared at the site besides Roy and Beatrice? Why did Beatrice say that these people needed a life? What did Roy say while "Mother Paula" was talking? Who was in the ground? Why did Chuck Muckle ask that the boy be arrested for trespassing? Why didn't Officer Delinko say that the snakes were not real? What did Chuck Muckle do to the "snakes"? Why did Roy, Beatrice, and the rest of the children stand? What did Lonna do in front of the cameras? Why?
21	What was the running shoeless boy's name? What did the lady from the *Gazette* want from Roy? Who had taken the pancake company's file from the building department? Why? Why did Roy give the file to the reporter?
Epilogue	What scandal was revealed in the next weeks? What did the EIS report find? What were the consequences for the pancake company's stock? Why? What happened to Chuck Muckle? What did the president of Mother Paula's announce? How did Dana and Mullet Fingers escape? Why did Mullet Fingers choose Dana to accompany him? Why did Roy return to the creek? Who caught the mullet and placed it in Roy's sneaker?

Sample Lessons for a Fifth-Grade Word Recognition and Fluency Group

The Life and Words of Martin Luther King, Jr., by Ira Peck
Lexile Level: 700; 96 pages

1. Work with multisyllabic decoding.
2. What do we already know? or Let's review what we learned in yesterday's reading.
3. Choral read the next chapter.
4. Partner or whisper read the same chapter. Work on improving expression.
5. Use the reading guide questions below for a quick discussion.

Chapter	Questions for Discussion
pp. 7–9	Where did the life of Martin Luther King, Jr., end? What was Martin Luther King, Jr., doing at the Baptist church in Montgomery? How were the Negroes trying to win equality and dignity? How did King serve the civil rights movement?
Chapter 1	What was the separation of the races called? What jobs were offered to King? What were some of the things that King wanted? What happened in Montgomery on December 1, 1955? Why was Rosa Parks's refusal an unusual act? Why did King want to care for more than the souls of his parishioners?
Chapter 2	How did King, Sr., show his feelings toward the Jim Crow system? Why was the police officer shocked by King, Sr.'s, response? Why wouldn't the children next door play with Martin? What kind of student was King? Why couldn't Martin decide what direction to take in his studies?
Chapter 3	Why did Martin think that segregation and poverty went together? What did Mahatma Gandhi achieve? How? Why was nonviolence not a coward's way?
Chapters 2–4	What events are described from 1929 to 1953?
Chapter 4	Why was peace wearing thin on the city's bus lines? Who was E. D. Nixon? How was the bus boycott organized?
Chapter 5	Why didn't the Negroes of Montgomery ride the buses? How did King suggest they protest? What propositions were made by Ralph Abernathy?
Chapter 6	How did the police department end the 10-cent service offered by taxis? Why? What were some problems that could affect the boycott? Why were the car pool drivers arrested? Why was King threatened?

(cont.)

Chapter	Questions for Discussion
Chapter 7	Why was school segregation unconstitutional? What was the decision of the U.S. Supreme Court? What was the Ku Klux Klan? What were its beliefs? Why was King feeling guilty about the acts of violence?
Chapter 8	Why did King refuse any other job offer? What attempts against King were made in September 1958? What were the sit-ins? Why did J. F. Kennedy call Coretta King? Why was King grateful to J. F. Kennedy?
Chapters 5–8	What events are described from 1953 to 1960?
Chapter 9	What were the life conditions for the Negroes in Birmingham? What were the efforts of Project C?
Chapter 10	Why was King arrested in Birmingham? Why wasn't Coretta, his wife, in Birmingham? Why did Coretta call J. F. Kennedy? What criticisms did King receive from white ministers? How did King respond to the white ministers? How was the nonviolence movement different than black nationalism? How did Bull Connor attempt to end the march?
Chapter 11	How did J. F. Kennedy try to end segregation? What were the things that King wanted to happen, which he included in his speech at the Lincoln Memorial? What happened on November 22, 1963? What were the components of the Civil Rights Act of 1964?
Chapter 12	What efforts were made to prevent the Negroes of Selma, Alabama, from voting? What was the result of the march?
Chapter 13	What was the reason for the riots? What were the beliefs of the black power movement? Why was King against the war in Viet Nam?
Chapter 14	How did King die? For what did King want to be remembered? What is written on King's gravestone?
Chapters 9–14	What events are described from 1960–1968?

Sample Lessons for a Fifth-Grade Word Recognition and Fluency Group

Danger! Volcanoes, by Seymour Simon
Lexile Level: 790; 28 pages

1. Work with multisyllabic decoding
2. What do we already know? or Let's review what we learned in yesterday's reading.
3. Choral read the next chapter.
4. Partner or whisper read the same chapter. Work on improving expression.
5. Use the QAR questions below for a quick discussion.

QARs
1 Right There
2 Think and Search
3 Author and You
4 On Your Own

Reading	Questions for Discussion
pp. 1–5	
1	What is the biggest explosion in nature? What is the origin of the word *volcano*? What is magma?
2	What is a volcano? What are the effects of volcanoes on humans and nature? How does magma reach the surface of the earth?
3	Why would people leave their homes?
4	Where would you find volcanoes? What would you see in an area where a volcano had erupted?
pp. 6–15	
1	What is the magma called when it reaches the surface of the earth? What happens to magma when it reaches the surface? How many active volcanoes are in the world? What is the Ring of Fire?
2	What happened at the Mount St. Helens volcano? What is the procedure for the formation of a cinder cone volcano?
3	What would happen if lava moved quickly?
4	What happened at Pompeii in the eruption of Vesuvius?
pp. 16–28	
1	What is a dome volcano? What happened in 1902 at Mount Pelée? What are composite volcanoes?
2	What is the procedure for the formation of a shield volcano? How do volcanoes support the growth of the earth?
3	What would the conditions of life be around a dormant volcano?
4	What type of volcano is Columbus in Santorini, Greece?

Fluency and Comprehension Sample Plans

Sample Lessons for a Fourth-Grade Fluency and Comprehension Group

Number the Stars, by Lois Lowry
Lexile Level: 670; 137 pages

All lessons take the same format.

1. What do we already know about these characters? What do we already know about the events? or Let's review what we learned in yesterday's reading.
2. Choral read the next chapter.
3. Partner and whisper read the same chapter. Work on improving expression.
4. Use the inferential questions below as a reading guide and then for a quick discussion.

Reading	Questions for Discussion
Chapter 1	Why did Annemarie want to race with Ellen? Why did the soldiers stop the girls? Why do you think the soldier laughed at Kristi's reaction? Why did Mrs. Rosen ask Ellen to use a different route to school? How do you think Mrs. Johansen and Mrs. Rosen felt when Kristi described their encounter with the soldiers?
Chapter 2	How was King Christian different from the other kings? Why didn't King Christian need any bodyguards? How did Denmark's and Norway's resistance to the Nazis differ? How do you think Peter Nielsen felt after the loss of Lise? Why do you think Mr. and Mrs. Rosen never spoke of Lise?
Chapter 3	Why did Ellen's father complain? Why did Kristi and Ellen sleep together? Why were citizens not allowed out after 8:00 P.M.? Why was the button shop closed by the Germans? Why was Annemarie awakened in the middle of the night by her mother? How would you feel about your friend if you were in Annemarie's place?
Chapter 4	Why was Kristi upset? Why did the Danes destroy their own naval fleet? Why did the Nazis take the synagogue list of the Jewish people's names? How does Ellen feel with her parents being away? Why is Ellen with the Johansen family?

(cont.)

Reading	Questions for Discussion
Chapter 5	How did Lise lose her life? Why did Annemarie break Ellen's necklace? Why was the soldier suspicious of Ellen? How did the father prove to the soldier that Ellen was his daughter? Why did the soldier tear Lise's picture? How do you think Ellen and Annemarie felt about the presence of the soldiers?
Chapter 6	Why didn't her father let Ellen go to school? How did Ellen feel about school and how did she react when told she wouldn't go that morning? Why did the father speak in code with Uncle Henrik? What did father mean by "cigarettes"? What did Annemarie think that Kristi would say to the soldier?
Chapter 7	Why did the mother tell the girls to stay away from people? What did Annemarie do with Ellen's necklace? Why couldn't Ellen overhear any laughter between her mother and Uncle Henrik?
Chapter 8	Why did the soldiers take the butter from the farmers? What did the girls and the mother do after they had breakfast? Why did the mother insist that Uncle Henrik get married? Why did the mother move the furniture in the living room?
Chapter 9	How could Annemarie be brave without knowing the entire truth? Who was Great Aunt Birte? How did Ellen feel when she walked away with Uncle Henrik?
Chapter 10	What was the reason the soldiers entered Uncle Henrik's house? Why was the officer curious about the closed casket? What was the explanation that the mother gave to the officer about the closed casket? How did the officer react to the mother's explanation? What did Peter do after the soldiers left?
Chapter 11	What was inside the casket? Why did Peter insist that the baby drink the drops of liquid he gave? Why didn't Mr. Rosen ask what was in the packet and why didn't Peter explain?
Chapter 12	How did Annemarie feel when Ellen and her family left? What did Annemarie think when her mother was not at home? How did Annemarie feel when she saw her mother lying on the ground?
Chapter 13	What happened to the mother? Why wasn't the packet that Peter gave to Mr. Rosen delivered to Uncle Henrik? How did Annemarie prepare the packet?
Chapter 14	How is Annemarie similar to and different from Little Red Riding Hood? Describe the path that Annemarie was traveling.

(cont.)

Reading	Questions for Discussion
Chapter 15	Why was Annemarie copying Kristi's behavior while talking to the soldiers? What did the soldiers do with Annemarie's lunch? How did Annemarie feel when the soldier lifted the napkin? Why were the dogs focused on the basket? How did the soldier react to the view of the handkerchief? How did Uncle Henrik feel when he saw the packet inside the basket?
Chapter 16	Why did Annemarie—and not the mother or Uncle Henrik—milk the cow? Why did the soldiers search the fishermen's boats? How were the soldiers using the dogs? What was the importance of the handkerchief?
Chapter 17	How did the people of Denmark react to the end of the war? Why wasn't Peter with the Johansen family? What was the truth about Lise's death?
Afterword	What aspects of the story are based on true events? What aspects of the story are fictional?

Sample Lessons for a Fourth-Grade Fluency and Comprehension Group

Hana's Suitcase, by Karen Levine
Lexile Level: 730; 109 pages

All lessons take the same format.

1. What do we already know about these characters? What do we already know about the events? or Let's review what we learned in yesterday's reading.
2. Choral read the next chapter.
3. Partner or whisper read the same chapter. Work on improving expression.
4. Use the QAR questions below as a reading guide and then to structure a discussion.

QARs
1. Right There
2. Think and Search
3. Author and You
4. On Your Own

Reading	Questions for Discussion
Introduction	
1	What kind of a story is *Hana's Suitcase*?
2	What were some of the actions of the Nazi dictator Adolf Hitler?
3	How do children have the power to create peace in the future?
4	What is a genocide? What other genocides—besides the Nazi genocide in World War II—have been recorded in history?
pp. 2–4	
1	Where is the suitcase?
2	What does the suitcase look like? Who is the owner of the suitcase?
3	How could the owner of the suitcase end up in Auschwitz?
4	What could the contents of a suitcase be?
pp. 5–9	
1	Where was Nove Mesto? How many days did the father work? What did Hana's mother do once a week?
2	What were some of the activities that people could do at Nove Mesto? Describe the town of Nove Mesto. How did Hana and George help at the store?

(cont.)

Reading	Questions for Discussion
3	Why would Hana's family be charitable? Why would being Jewish become very important in their life?
4	What subjects do students study in public schools? What are the basic principles of the Jewish religion?
pp. 10–14	
1	What does Fumiko want the young people of Japan to learn?
2	What were some of Fumiko's actions in her effort to collect physical objects?
3	How would actual items from people of the Holocaust assist Fumiko in her goal?
4	What was Zyclon gas?
pp. 15–19	
1	What was Hana's greatest love?
2	What did Hana look like? What did Mr. Rott suggest?
3	What prediction could be made about Hana's future based on her walnut? Why would Mr. Rott make such a suggestion?
4	Were the Jewish people the only ones who were under attack during Hitler's reign?
pp. 20–21	
1	What did 10-year-old Akira wonder about?
2	Where did Fumiko write seeking information on Hana Brady?
3	Why were the children encouraging Fumiko to proceed with her efforts?
pp. 22–27	
1	What did the Nazis declare about the Jews?
2	What were some of the new rules that the Nazis applied to the Jews of Nove Mesto? Why was Hana lonely?
3	Why would the Brady family's items be safe with gentiles but not with them?
4	What is the purpose of list keeping?
pp. 28–29	
1	What terrible things had happened in Theresienstadt?
2	What was the history of Terezin?
3	Why would the captive Jews teach, learn, and perform while in captivity?
4	What is a ghetto?

(cont.)

Reading	Questions for Discussion
pp. 30–32	
1	What did Hana always dream about? What happened in March 1941?
2	How did Hana and George continue their education? What happened to Hana's mother?
3	Did Hana and George enjoy homeschooling? Why?
4	What are the benefits and drawbacks of homeschooling?
pp. 33–34	
1	Where were many of the drawings displayed? Whose name was on the drawings?
2	What was depicted on the drawings that Fumiko received?
3	How did Fumiko feel when she saw Hana's name?
4	What were some materials used to draw?
pp. 35–39	
1	What did the Nazi officer declare?
2	Why did Hana miss her mother at night? What was the content of the package sent to Hana?
3	Why did Hana's mother send her the package? Why did Hana's family have to wear the Star of David? Why was Hana's father also arrested and removed from his home?
4	What was the Gestapo?
pp. 40–42	
1	What did the children name their club? How often did the children meet to plan their newsletter?
2	Why was Fumiko enchanted by Hana's drawings? What did the newsletter include?
4	Why do people write newsletters? Who would write a newsletter?
pp. 43–48	
1	How did Boshka try to distract the children? Why wasn't Uncle Ludvik an obvious target for the Nazis? Where was the father imprisoned?
2	What items did the children take with them when they left for Uncle Ludvik's place? How did the children spend their time at Uncle Ludvik's home?

(cont.)

Reading	Questions for Discussion
3	Why couldn't Hana and George stay at their house?
4	Why are dogs said to be "man's best friend"? What were the conditions for the prisoners of the Gestapo?
pp. 49–52	
1	Where were Hana and George to report on May 14, 1942? For how long did Hana and George stay at the warehouse? How did Hana celebrate her 11th birthday?
2	What did the children take with them?
3	Why was Uncle Ludvik heartbroken?
4	What was the purpose of the concentration camps?
pp. 53–54	
1	To whom did Fumiko write? Where did Fumiko decide to go?
2	What parts of the exhibit drew the visitors' attention?
3	Why were the visitors mostly interested in these items?
4	What would you find in a museum?
p. 55	
1	What happened on the morning of the fourth day?
2	What orders did the German soldier give to the people?
3	Why couldn't the people leave the warehouse on their own?
4	What were the main means of transportation in the 1940s?
pp. 56–58	
1	Where was Fumiko invited to go?
2	How would Fumiko get to Terezin?
3	What was the purpose of the conference that Fumiko would attend?
4	What is a conference? Why do people attend conferences?
pp. 59–61	
1	What did the soldier ask at the front of the line?
2	What happened after the train stopped?
3	Why wasn't the soldier interested in conversation? Why did the soldier search the suitcases for money and jewelry?
4	Why were people separated in the concentration camps?

(cont.)

Reading	Questions for Discussion
pp. 62–63	
1	Why was Fumiko upset?
2	How did Fumiko locate Ludmila?
4	How would you locate someone whose tracks were lost for a long time?
pp. 64–70	
1	Why wasn't Hana allowed to leave the building?
2	What were the life conditions in Kinderheim? What classes did Hana attend at the camp? How was the game of Smelina played?
3	Why did the girls hold secret classes? Why did Hana get upset by the lady who wanted to call her mother?
4	What was the diet of the people in the concentration camps?
pp. 71–73	
1	What was next to Hana's name?
2	What did Fumiko and Ludmila find?
4	When would you place a checkmark next to a written word?
pp. 74–82	
1	Who had given Hana and George the scooters?
2	How did Grandmother look when Hana and George found her in the attic? What did George tell Hana before he left? How did Ella prepare Hana to see George?
3	Why were the Nazis systematic in the lists they kept?
4	Where is Auschwitz located?
pp. 83–85	
1	For what did Ludmila and Fumiko look for an hour?
2	What was the meaning of the checkmark next to Hana's name?
3	Why was Hana's life ended unjustly?
4	What exhibits are in the Jewish Museum of Prague?
pp. 86–88	
1	Where was Mr. Kotouk leaving for?
2	What information did Mr. Kotouk give to Fumiko?
3	Why did Fumiko want to meet Mr. Kotouk?
4	What is the job description of an art historian?

(cont.)

Reading	Questions for Discussion
pp. 89–91	
1	What copies had Fumiko made?
2	What surprise did Fumiko have for the children in Japan?
3	Why would the Holocaust survivors refuse to talk about their experiences?
4	How many people survived the Holocaust?
pp. 92–96	
1	How old was George Brady? What were George Brady's plans? How old was George Brady when Auschwitz was liberated in January 1945?
2	What was the fate of George's parents?
3	Why did George faint?
4	Why would someone faint? How would you share bad news with someone?
pp. 97–99	
1	What did George do when he moved to Toronto?
2	What did Fumiko ask of George?
3	Why would George help Fumiko?
4	What is the purpose of photo albums?
pp. 100–102	
1	What happened as Fumiko unfolded the pages?
2	What did Fumiko learn from George's letter?
3	Why did Fumiko get so excited?
4	Where is Canada?
pp. 103–107	
1	Who did George Brady bring with him?
2	How did Hana finally become a teacher? What was the reason that Hana was killed?
3	How had Fumiko's actions given honor to Hana?
4	Are there Nazi survivors now?
pp. 108–109	
1	What had happened to Hana's original suitcase?
4	What is a "replica"?

Sample Lessons for a Fifth-Grade Fluency and Comprehension Group

Sing Down the Moon, by Scott O'Dell
Lexile Level: 820; 135 pages

All lessons take the same format.
1. What do we already know about these characters? What do we already know about the events? or Let's review what we learned in yesterday's reading.
2. Choral read the next chapter.
3. Partner or whisper read the same chapter. Work on improving expression.
4. Use the inferential questions below as a reading guide and then to structure a discussion.

Chapter	Questions for Discussion
1	How did spring change everything in one night? Why is it bad luck to be happy? How did the gods punish the girl's brother? Why should the girl have left the meadow instead of staying? Why did the girl leave the sheep and return alone to her house? Why didn't her mother speak to her that night? Where is the girl living?
2	What lesson did the girl learn from the experience of the past spring? How is the trail to the mesa used by the girl and her tribe? Why would Tall Boy's parents want him to marry the girl? Why did the girl feel better after she commented on her friends' sheep?
3	How many warriors left that morning and how did they prepare for the hunt? How did Tall Boy get his name? Why were the white men called Long Knives by the Indians? How would the Long Knives break the peace with the Indians based on what they said to "Old Bear"?
4	How was the girl able to tell which sheep were hers? Why was the girl's dog barking? How did the girl know that the men who approached her were slavers? Why did the Spaniards abduct the two girls?
5	What plan did the girls devise to escape from the Spaniards? Was the girls' plan successful? Why? Why did the Spaniards insist that the girls eat?
6	How many days did the walk to the south take? How did Running Bird's grandfather describe the place where the white people live? What had the woman cooked, and how did the Navaho girls respond to her invitation to eat? Why did the girl have her dog sleep by her? How did the girl interpret the sweeping girl's glance?

(cont.)

Chapter	Questions for Discussion
7	How did the woman greet the girl? What does the woman need the girl for? Why did the girl find it hard to describe Canyon de Chelly to Rosita? Why did Rosita say that the lady would pay more money for the girl than she did for her?
8	Why was Rosita going over the chilies carefully? Why did Nehana tell the girl not to trust Rosita? What did the girls do at the house when people arrived? What had Nehana done in the past? What information did Nehana share with the girl and what did it mean?
9	Why did they go to church that day? How did the girl manage to leave the house? Why did the girls cover their faces with the blanket?
10	Why did the man ask the girls for their destination? Why did the girls follow the stream instead of going on land?
11	Who did the girls find in the woods? How did the girl feel at the sound of the Indian war cry? What happened to Tall Boy?
12	How did the medicine man take care of Tall Boy's wound? Why was the girl's mother opposed to her visiting Tall Boy? Why did Running Bird and the girl's mother feel pity for Tall Boy?
13	What was the Womanhood Ceremony? What was the girl doing during this time? How was the girl to become "industrious" and "obedient"? How was the girl to become a good runner? How was the girl to become comely? Why was the girl not running fast when Tall Boy was chasing her with the other boys?
14	What did the Long Knives announce to the Navaho people? How did the Navaho people react? What was Tall Boy's reaction? Where did the Navahos lead their sheep? Why didn't they take them with them? What did the white men do when they arrived at the Canyon? Why was Tall Boy left behind by the other warriors? What were the Navaho people hoping that the white men would do?
15	What did the white soldiers do to the houses, the trees and the crops? Why? Was the Long Knives' intention to leave the village? Why?
16	How did the village people find shelter and water? What did the tribe people do on the first night of the full moon? Was Tall Boy successful in his attack? Why?

(cont.)

Chapter	Questions for Discussion
17	Where were the tribes heading? Why did the girl take Little Rainbow's girl? Were the girl's mother and sister happy that she was carrying Little Rainbow's child?
18	How many wagons were there and what were they carrying? What were the life conditions? What happened to Little Rainbow's child? How did Little Rainbow react?
19	How are the Apaches different from the Navahos? How did the Navaho men spend their time in Bosque Redondo? What had happened at Sand Creek and why?
20	How did Tall Boy's father acquire a horse? How did Tall Boy use the horse? Why was the girl's mother pleased with Tall Boy? How was the wedding ceremony performed? What advice was given to the girl by the relatives? Where did Tall Boy and his wife stay? Why did Tall Boy not want to think of the Canyon? Why did the girl not want her baby to be born at the camp?
21	What preparations did the girl make for her escape with Tall Boy from the camp? How did Tall Boy react when the girl shared her plan with him? What did the Apache ask for when he met Tall Boy and how did Tall Boy react? Why did Tall Boy hit the Apache? What happened to Tall Boy that day? Why did the girl say that it was the Apache's fault and not her husband's?
22	How did Tall Boy manage to escape and return home? Why did the girl call Tall Boy an old woman and her mother an old man? Why didn't the girl's mother look Tall Boy in the face? Where did the girl and Tall Boy decide to go that day? What did the couple do when they reached Elk-Running Valley?
23	Why did the couple leave Elk-Running Valley? What did Tall Boy say that the girl's sheep looked like? Why? Why did Tall Boy give his son a spear? What song did Tall Boy teach his son? Why did the girl step on the spear?
Postscript	What happened in June 1863? What is the "Long Walk"? What happened to the Navahos in 1868? Who was preacher Chivington and what did he do?

Sample Lessons for a Fifth-Grade Fluency and Comprehension Group

The Best Book of Weather, by Simon Adams
Lexile Level: IG840; 31 pages

All lessons take the same format.
1. Let's review what we learned in yesterday's reading.
2. Choral read the next chapter.
3. Partner or whisper read the same chapter. Work on improving expression.
4. Use the QAR questions below as a reading guide and then to structure a discussion.

QARs
1. Right There
2. Think and Search
3. Author and You
4. On Your Own

Reading	Questions for Discussion
pp. 1–5	
1	What is the atmosphere? What is the exosphere? What is the thermosphere? What is the mesosphere?
2	What are the layers of the earth's atmosphere? How is weather made?
3	What are some of the benefits of clouds?
4	How can the weather affect people?
pp. 6–7	
1	What is meteorology?
2	How do scientists make a weather forecast? What are weather balloons used for? What are some of the instruments that humans use to measure weather phenomena? How can weather be an alternative energy source?
3	Why do people seek natural energy that does not cause pollution?
4	Why would people need to look for alternative sources of energy?
pp. 8–9	
1	During what periods did parts of the earth turn into desert? How do scientists discover what the weather was like in the past?
2	What are some of the reasons that dinosaurs became extinct? What did the earth look like 10,000 years ago?

(cont.)

Reading	Questions for Discussion
3	What would happen to the earth's climate if the sky were covered in dust?
4	How would it be possible for the dinosaurs to have become extinct because of a meteorite?
pp. 10–11	
1	What is winter?
2	What are the different climates in the different areas of Earth?
3	Why would some places on Earth have two seasons instead of four? What is a monsoon?
4	How many seasons are there?
pp. 13–16	
1	What can harmful rays from the sun cause on the skin? On what scale is wind measured?
2	How does the sun support life on Earth? What are some of the effects of the sun? What is the wind? What is the Coriolis effect?
3	What resources might people have for survival during droughts?
4	What are some of the most common skin diseases caused by the sun? What are some of the things that people do for enjoyment on windy days?
pp. 17–21	
1	What is a downpour? What is a cirrus cloud? How can you tell how far away a storm is?
2	How do clouds turn into water? How is water on Earth recycled? What are the different types of clouds? How are thunderstorms formed?
3	Why would buildings need to be equipped with lightning rods? Why should electricity be transferred through the rods to the earth?
4	What are the benefits of water for life? Why are thunderstorms scary?

(cont.)

Reading	Questions for Discussion
pp. 22–25	
1	What is fog? Where does snow form? What is snow made of?
2	How would fog affect transportation? What are the similarities and differences between smog and fog? How does mist form? What is the shape of snowflakes?
3	Why would driving in fog be dangerous?
4	How is fog formed? What is an avalanche? What can people do on snowy days?
pp. 26–30	
1	How do hurricanes form? In what direction do typhoons, hurricanes, and cyclones move in the Northern and Southern Hemispheres? Why are palm trees able to stand in the wind? What are hailstorms? Why is the level of carbon dioxide increasing on earth?
2	How do tornadoes form and how fast can they move? How are the aurora borealis and aurora australis formed? How are rainbows formed? What are the effects of air pollution on sea levels?
3	How do sun rays and rain form the colors of the rainbow? How does the greenhouse effect affect our planet?
4	What are some of the effects of hurricanes on the economy of a city? What are the colors of the rainbow? What are the effects of acid rain on forests?

Vocabulary and Comprehension Sample Plans

Sample Lessons for a Fourth-Grade Vocabulary and Comprehension Group

Where the Mountain Meets the Moon, by Grace Lin
Lexile Level: 820; 278 pages

All lessons take the same format. Remember: We recommend that students in this group do their reading and complete the guide independently, returning to the teacher the following day.

1. What do we already know about these characters? What do we already know about the events? or Let's review what we learned in yesterday's reading.
2. Have the students read and complete the reading guide.
3. Review Tier 2 vocabulary from the previous day.
4. Use the inferential questions below as a reading guide and then to structure a discussion.

Chapter	Questions for Discussion
1	Why did the villagers call the black mountain Fruitless Mountain? Why did everything in the village have the color of dried mud? What did Minli look like? Was Minli's mother happy? Why? Why wasn't the family spending the two copper coins? Why was Jade Dragon offended by the villagers? What could happen to a place because of lack of rain? Why didn't Ma approve of Ba's stories?
Vocabulary	The first word is **impulsive**. What word? *Impulsive*. *Impulsive* means tending to act suddenly and without thought. The author said, "When people saw her lively and impulsive spirit they thought her name, which meant quick thinking, suited her well." Let's discuss what that sentence means. I'll read it again. [Reread and discuss, focusing on the word and connecting the sentence to the narrative context.] Here is another example with the word *impulsive*: "She is very impulsive and every day is as adventurous as the previous one." Can you think of other examples using the word *impulsive*? What is the word? *Impulsive*. Related words: *impulse, impulsively, impulsiveness*. The second word is **reverence**. What word? *Reverence*. *Reverence* means a feeling of great respect. The author said, "She was very proud of her power and of the reverence the people of earth paid her." Let's discuss what that sentence means. I'll read it again. [Reread and discuss, focusing on the word and connecting the sentence to the narrative context.] Here is another example using the word *reverence*: "The children were brought up with reverence for nature and life." Can you think of other examples using the word *reverence*? What is the word? *Reverence*. Related words: *reverent, reverently, irreverence, revere*.

(cont.)

Chapter	Questions for Discussion
2	What did Minli's parents do as soon as the sun began to set? Was it wise for Minli to spend her money on a goldfish? How would Ma feel after returning from the field? Why?
Vocabulary	The first word is **exhaustion**. What word? *Exhaustion. Exhaustion* means extreme weakness. The author said, "and many times she wanted to stop in irritation and exhaustion." Let's discuss what that sentence means. I'll read it again. [Reread and discuss, focusing on the word and connecting the sentence to the narrative context.] Another example using the word *exhaustion* would be "Farmers leave sections of land unused for some period of time to avoid the exhaustion of the soil." Can you think of other examples using the word *exhaustion*? What is the word? *Exhaustion.* 　　Related words: *exhaust, exhausted, exhausting, exhaustingly, exhaustible.* The second word is **discouraged**. What word? *Discouraged. Discouraged* means losing the confidence and will to do something. The author said, "But Minli was not discouraged and she held out her copper coins to the goldfish man." Let's discuss what that sentence means. I'll read it again. [Reread and discuss, focusing on the word and connecting the sentence to the narrative context.] Another example of the word *discouraged* would be "My nephew was discouraged after falling off his bicycle and didn't want to ride any more." Can you think of other examples using the word *discouraged*? What is the word? *Discouraged.* 　　Related words: *courage, courageous, encourage, encouraged, encouraging, encouragingly, discourage, discouraging, discouragingly.*
3	How did Minli's family react to her purchase? How was the magistrate described in the story? How do people find their partners in life? Why wouldn't the magistrate approve his son's marriage to the grocer's daughter? What did the magistrate brag about the day of his son's wedding?
Vocabulary	The first word is **resentfully**. What word? *Resentfully. Resentfully* refers to doing something when you don't really want to. The author said, "More stories! Ma said and her chopsticks struck the inside of her empty bowl resentfully." Let's discuss what that sentence means. I'll read it again. [Reread and discuss, focusing on the word and connecting the sentence to the narrative context.] Another example with the word *resentfully* would be "Most citizens paid the fee resentfully." Can you think of another example using the word *resentfully*? What is the word? *Resentfully.* 　　Related words: *resent, resentful, resentfulness, resentment.* The second word is **acceptance**. What word? *Acceptance. Acceptance* means approval, being approved for something. The author said, "every manipulation was part of a strategy to achieve acceptance into the imperial family." Let's discuss what that sentence means. I'll read it again. [Reread and discuss, focusing on the word and connecting the sentence to the narrative context.] Another example using the word *acceptance* would be "After acceptance of his proposal, they signed the contract immediately." Can you think of other examples using the word *acceptance*? What is the word? *Acceptance.* 　　Related words: *accept, accepted, accepting, acceptable, unacceptable.*

(cont.)

Chapter	Questions for Discussion
4	Why did Minli leave the house with the goldfish? Why can't most people hear the fish talking? What did Minli realize that was very unusual? How did the goldfish end up at the goldfish man's cart? Why did the goldfish reveal his ability to talk to Minli?
Vocabulary	The first word is **realized**. What word? *Realized. Realize* means to suddenly understand something clearly. The author said, "As the sound faded into the night, Minli realized it was an echo of her mother's impatient, frustrated noise." Let's discuss what that sentence means. I'll read it again. [Reread and discuss, focusing on the word and connecting the sentence to the narrative context.] Another example using the word *realized* would be "As she drove away, she realized that she had finally been hired in her first job and she was independent." Can you think of other examples using the word *realized*? What is the word? *Realized.* Related words: *realizing, realization.* The second word is **despaired**. What word? *Despaired. Despair* means to give up hope. The author said, "I despaired in his cart, for I have seen and learned much of the world, including the way to Never-Ending Mountain." Let's discuss what that sentence means. I'll read it again. [Reread and discuss, focusing on the word and connecting the sentence to the narrative context.] Another example using the word *despaired* would be "She despaired because the wild, black sea seemed too rough to sail upon." Can you think of other examples using the word *despaired*? What is the word? *Despaired.* Related words: *despair, despairing.*
5	Why was Minli's planting slow that day? Why did Minli leave her house? Would it be safe for her away from home?
Vocabulary	The first word is **obedient**. What word? *Obedient. Obedient* refers to someone who follows directions and rules and never objects to others' requests. The author said, "Love, your obedient daughter." Let's discuss what that sentence means. I'll read it again. [Reread and discuss, focusing on the word and connecting the sentence to the narrative context.] Another example using the word *obedient* would be "He was the most obedient student in the classroom, who never gave his teacher a reason to scold him." Can you think of other examples using the word *obedient*? What is the word? *Obedient.* Related words: *obey, obedience, disobedient, disobedience.* The second word is **uneasy**. What word? *Uneasy. Uneasy* means troubled or worried. The author said, "But she shook away her uneasy feelings and prepared for her journey." Let's discuss what that sentence means. I'll read it again. [Reread and discuss, focusing on the word and connecting the sentence to the narrative context.] Another example with the word *uneasy* would be "She felt uneasy about betraying her friends, but in her heart she knew they had to face the consequences of their actions." What is the word? *Uneasy.* Related words: *unease, uneasiness.*

(cont.)

Chapter	Questions for Discussion
6	Why didn't the neighbors notice Minli as she was leaving? How did Minli make a compass? How would Minli use the compass?
Vocabulary	The first word is **refused**. What word? *Refused. Refuse* means to say no to a request or command. The author said, "when the mother called them for dinner both refused to move, each clinging to their dishes of wet dirt." Let's discuss what that sentence means. I'll read it again. [Reread and discuss, focusing on the word and connecting the sentence to the narrative context.] Another example with the word *refused* would be "The patient refused to take the pills that the doctor suggested." Can you think of other examples using the word *refused*? What is the word? *Refused.* 　　　Related words: *refusing, refusal.* The second word is **foolishness**. What word? *Foolishness. Foolishness* means the lack of careful thought, carelessness. The author said, "Minli had to smile at their foolishness." Let's discuss what that sentence means. I'll read it again. [Reread and discuss, focusing on the word and connecting the sentence to the narrative context.] Another example using the word *foolishness* would be "It was due to her foolishness and careless driving that she ended up with a flat tire." Can you think of other examples using the word *foolishness*? What is the word? *Foolishness.* 　　　Related words: *fool, foolish, foolishly.*
7	What did Minli's parents notice at the house? Why did Ma accuse Ba about Minli's leaving the house? Why would Minli's parents try to find her?
Vocabulary	The word is **uncertainly**. What word? *Uncertainly. Uncertain* means without being sure. The author said, "But when they reached the mountain they looked at each other uncertainly." Let's discuss what that sentence means. I'll read it again. [Reread and discuss, focusing on the word and connecting the sentence to the narrative context.] Another example using the word *uncertainly* would be "When he began putting up the tent he looked uncertainly at the directions." Can you think of other examples using the word *uncertainly*? What is the word? *Uncertainly.* 　　　Related words: *certain, certainly, certainty, uncertain, uncertainty.*
8	Why didn't Minli have any water left? Who did Minli find in the stream of salt water?
Vocabulary	The word is **contain**. What word? *Contain. Contain* means to hold something inside and can refer to objects or feelings. The author said, "And unable to contain her curiosity, Minli forgot about her thirst and began to follow it." Let's discuss what that sentence means. I'll read it again. [Reread and discuss, focusing on the word and connecting the sentence to the narrative context.] Another example using the word *contain* would be "She could not contain her sadness and wept by the side of her car" or "I am not sure you are allowed to bring a bottle that contains liquids to the airport." Can you think of other examples using the word *contain*? What is the word? *Contain.* 　　　Related words: *contained, containing, container, uncontained.*

(cont.)

Chapter	Questions for Discussion
9	Why was Ma resentful?

Vocabulary	The first word is **resentment**. What word? *Resentment. Resentment* means anger or ill will. The author said, "Her resentment seemed to darken with the fading moon." Let's discuss what that sentence means. I'll read it again. [Reread and discuss, focusing on the word and connecting the sentence to the narrative context.] Another example using the word *resentment* would be "It was her resentment about living in the city that caused his decision to apply for a different job." Can you think of other examples using the word *resentment*? What is the word? *Resentment.*
	     Related words: *resent, resentfully, resentfulness.*
	
	The second word is **miserable**. What word? *Miserable. Miserable* means terribly unhappy or uncomfortable. The author said, "Making her believe she could change our miserable fortune with an impossible story!" Let's discuss what that sentence means. I'll read it again. [Reread and discuss, focusing on the word and connecting the sentence to the narrative context.] Another example using the word *miserable* would be "We were miserable when the cold rain soaked our clothes." Can you think of other examples using the word *miserable*? What is the word? *Miserable.*
	     Related words: *misery, miserably.*

10	How was the dragon Minli found different from the dragons in Ba's stories? How did the dragon end up in this condition? Why did the monkey act in such a way?
Vocabulary	The word is **unreasonable**. What word? *Unreasonable. Unreasonable* means without fairness or common sense. The author said, "I have been trying to make them let me pass peacefully for days but they are so unreasonable." Let's discuss what that sentence means. I'll read it again. [Reread and discuss, focusing on the word and connecting the sentence to the narrative context.] Another example of the word *unreasonable* would be "Her decision to raise the rent by $1,000 was unreasonable." Can you think of other examples using the word *unreasonable*? What is the word? *Unreasonable.* Related words: *reason, reasoning, reasoned, unreasoning, reasonable.*
11	Why doesn't the dragon have a name? Why did the artist create the dragon? How was the dragon the artist made different from other dragons? Why? Why didn't the dragon want to belong to Magistrate Tiger? Why didn't the artist paint the dragon's eyes? Why did the dragon say it was not real? What similarities and differences exist between Minli and the dragon and Dorothy from the *Wizard of Oz*?

(cont.)

Chapter	Questions for Discussion
Vocabulary	The first word is **conceited**. What word? *Conceited. Conceited* means having a high opinion of oneself. The author said, "A conceited, self-important man, who when only the imperial family is allowed to use the image of a dragon commissions one." Let's discuss what that sentence means. I'll read it again. [Reread and discuss, focusing on the word and connecting the sentence to the narrative context.] Another example using the word *conceited* would be "You are so conceited and think that your life is more important than anyone else's." Can you think of other examples using the word *conceited*? What is the word? *Conceited.* Related word: *conceit.* The second word is **procession**. What word? *Procession.* A *procession* is a group of people or vehicles moving in an orderly way, as in a march or a parade. The author said, "I heard footsteps coming toward me, many of them, so I knew it was a whole procession of people." Let's discuss what that sentence means. I'll read it again. [Reread and discuss, focusing on the word and connecting the sentence to the narrative context.] Another example using the word *procession* would be "The elephants slowly passed by in a grand procession." Can you think of other examples using the word *procession*? What is the word? *Procession.* Related words: *proceed, proceeding, proceedings, process.*
12	Why did Ma and Ba feel ashamed? Why was Lao Lao moaning in her room? How could the goldfish man change his fortune? Why was the old man willing to change the goldfish man's fortune? What did Ma think was impossible and what did the goldfish man find possible?
Vocabulary	The first word is **inexplicably**. What word? *Inexplicably. Inexplicably* means happening in a way that cannot be explained. The author said, "Inexplicably, they felt ashamed." Let's discuss what that sentence means. I'll read it again. [Reread and discuss, focusing on the word and connecting the sentence to the narrative context.] Another example using the word *inexplicably* would be "Inexplicably, the judge decided not to punish the criminal." Can you think of other ways to use the word *inexplicably*? What is the word? *Inexplicably.* Related words: *explicable, inexplicable.* The second word is **engrossed**. What word? *Engrossed. Engrossed* means being completely focused on something. The author said, "And even though the old man was engrossed in his book, he must have smelled them as well because without lifting his eyes from the page he began to eat." Let's discuss what that sentence means. I'll read it again. [Reread and discuss, focusing on the word and connecting the sentence to the narrative context.] Another example using the word *engrossed* would be "He was so engrossed in the baseball game that he didn't hear his daughter leaving." Can you think of other examples using the word *engrossed*? What is the word? *Engrossed.* Related words: *engross, engrossing.*
13	What did the dragon look like? Why did Minli feel pity for the dragon? Why wouldn't the monkeys let Minli and the dragon pass through the peach trees?

(cont.)

Chapter	Questions for Discussion
Vocabulary	The first word is **doubtful**. What word? *Doubtful. Doubtful* means not being sure. The author said, "Minli was a little doubtful about riding the dragon." Let's discuss what that sentence means. I'll read it again. [Reread and discuss, focusing on the word and connecting the sentence to the narrative context.] Another example using the word *doubtful* would be "When she arrived late her mother was doubtful about her excuse." Can you think of other examples using the word *doubtful*? What is the word? *Doubtful.* Related words: *doubt, doubted, doubting, doubtfully.* The second word is **clamoring**. What word? *Clamoring. Clamoring* means making a loud and continued noise. The author said, "Minli could still see the monkeys clamoring in the trees." Let's discuss what that sentence means. I'll read it again. [Reread and discuss, focusing on the word and connecting the sentence to the narrative context.] Another example using the word *clamoring* would be, "The principal observed the clamoring of students at the front entrance." Can you think of other examples using the word *clamoring*? What is the word? *Clamoring.* Related words: *clamor, clamored.*
14	How did Minli use the monkeys' greediness to her benefit?
Vocabulary	The first word is **pretended**. What word? *Pretended. Pretend* means to make believe. The author said, "Minli and the Dragon no longer pretended to be asleep." Let's discuss what that sentence means. I'll read it again. [Reread and discuss, focusing on the word and connecting the sentence to the narrative context.] Another example using the word *pretended* would be "She pretended not to understand the situation when in reality she was fully aware of it." Can you think of other examples using the word *pretended*? What is the word? *Pretended.* Related words: *pretend, pretending, pretence.* The second word is **violently**. What word? *Violently. Violently* refers to using physical force. The author said, "The heavy pot of rice shook as the monkeys fought violently to get free." Let's discuss what that sentence means. I'll read it again. [Reread and discuss, focusing on the word and connecting the sentence to the narrative context.] Another example using the word *violently* would be "The volcano erupted violently and steaming lava began to flow into the valley." Can you think of other examples using the word *violently*? What is the word? *Violently.* Related words: violent, violence, nonviolence, nonviolent.
15	What was the proof that the family the emissary observed was truly happy? How was the paper of happiness lost? Why didn't any of the soldiers read the paper with the secret?
Vocabulary	The first word is **exaggerated**. What word? *Exaggerated.* To *exaggerate* means to describe something as bigger or better than it really is. The author says, "The stories are exaggerated." Let's discuss what that sentence means. I'll read it again. [Reread and discuss, focusing on the word and connecting the sentence to the narrative context.] Another example using the word *exaggerated* would be "He exaggerated when he said that he caught a 40-foot tuna." Can you think of other examples using the word *exaggerated*? What is the word? *Exaggerated.* Related words: *exaggerate, exaggerating, exaggeration.*

(cont.)

Chapter	Questions for Discussion
	The second word is **enraged**. What word? *Enraged. Enraged* means very angry. The author said, "As he relayed the story, Magistrate Tiger not surprisingly was enraged." Let's discuss what that sentence means. I'll read it again. [Reread and discuss, focusing on the word and connecting the sentence to the narrative context.] Another example of the word *enraged* would be "He became enraged when he saw his best baseball cards torn up by his younger sister." Can you think of other examples using the word *enraged*? What is the word? *Enraged.* Related words: *enrage, enraging.*
16	How did Minli cope with her family's worries about her departure? Why did the fish mistake the dragon for Aunt Jin? Why did the fish suggest that the dragon hide?
Vocabulary	The first word is **determined**. What word? *Determined. Determined* means having made up your mind and sticking to it. The author said, "But Aunt Jin was determined to find out." Let's discuss what that sentence means. I'll read it again. [Reread and discuss, focusing on the word and connecting the sentence to the narrative context.] Another example using the word *determined* would be "The coach was determined to lead the team to a win this season." Can you think of other examples using the word *determined*? What is the word? *Determined.* Related words: *determine, determining, predetermine, undetermined.* The second word is **discomfort**. What word? *Discomfort. Discomfort* means lack of ease. The author said, "'He can't fly,' Minli answered for the Dragon when she saw his discomfort." Let's discuss what that sentence means. I'll read it again. [Reread and discuss, focusing on the word and connecting the sentence to the narrative context.] Another example using the word *discomfort* would be "The shoes were too small and caused her great discomfort." Can you think of other examples using the word *discomfort*? What is the word? *Discomfort.* Related words: *comfort, comforting, comforted, comfortable, uncomforting, uncomforted, uncomfortable.*
17	Why wasn't Minli able to see the King?
Vocabulary	The first word is **occurrence**. What word? *Occurrence.* An *occurrence* is an event, something that happens. The author said, "A large, muddy water buffalo led by a boy perhaps a year or two older than Minli wandered through and was ignored as a commonplace occurrence." Let's discuss what that sentence means. I'll read it again. [Reread and discuss, focusing on the word and connecting the sentence to the narrative context.] Another example using the word *occurrence* would be "They realized that the meteor they saw was a rare occurrence." Can you think of other examples using the word *occurrence*? What is the word? *Occurrence.* Related words: *occur, occurring, occurred.*

(cont.)

Chapter	Questions for Discussion
	The second word is **lingering**. What word? *Lingering. Lingering* means staying in a place longer than expected. The author said, "By this time the Inner City guards had seen them lingering by the gate." Let's discuss what that sentence means. I'll read it again. [Reread and discuss, focusing on the word and connecting the sentence to the narrative context.] Another example using the word *lingering* would be "The food left a lingering odor in the kitchen." Can you think of other examples using the word *lingering*? What is the word? *Lingering.* Related words: *linger, lingered.*
18	What did the buffalo boy's house look like? How did the buffalo boy meet his friend? Is his friend an ordinary friend? Who could be his friend's grandfather?

Vocabulary	The first word is **ashamed**. What word? *Ashamed. Ashamed* means feeling embarrassed or guilty about something. The author said, "As I lifted it, the softness made me ashamed of my rough hands." Let's discuss what that sentence means. I'll read it again. [Reread and discuss, focusing on the word and connecting the sentence to the narrative context.] Another example using the word *ashamed* would be "The boy was ashamed when the teacher found out he had cheated." Can you think of other examples using the word *ashamed*? What is the word? *Ashamed.*
	    Related words: *shame, shameful.*
	
	The second word is **vaguely**. What word? *Vaguely. Vaguely* means in an uncertain or unclear way. The author said, "It was funny how the buffalo boy's whole manner changed when he talked about her—his vaguely mocking attitude and tough expression washed away and he lit up like a lantern." Let's discuss what that sentence means. I'll read it again. [Reread and discuss, focusing on the word and connecting the sentence to the narrative context.] Another example using the word *vaguely* would be "She vaguely remembered the conversation she had had with her mother last week." Can you think of other examples using the word *vaguely*? What is the word? *Vaguely.*
	    Related words: *vague, vagueness.*

19	Why didn't the buffalo boy want to know more about his friend? Where would the King be the next morning?
Vocabulary	The first word is **graceful**. What word? *Graceful. Graceful* means having elegance and beauty. The author said, "The bag she held in her graceful hand seemed to be made out of the same silk." Let's discuss what that sentence means. I'll read it again. [Reread and discuss, focusing on the word and connecting the sentence to the narrative context.] Another example using the word *graceful* would be "She was so graceful when she danced that it almost seemed she was flying." Can you think of other examples using the word *graceful*? What is the word? *Graceful.* Related words: *grace, gracefully, ungracefully, gracefulness.*

(cont.)

Chapter	Questions for Discussion
	The second word is **mysterious**. What word? *Mysterious*. *Mysterious* refers to something that cannot be explained. The author said, "Don't you think it's mysterious that you only see her once in a while?" Let's discuss what that sentence means. I'll read it again. [Reread and discuss, focusing on the word and connecting the sentence to the narrative context.] Another example using the word *mysterious* would be "It was mysterious to me how she managed to finish all the chores within two hours." Can you think of other examples using the word *mysterious*? What is the word? *Mysterious*. Related words: *mystery, mysteriously*.
20	Why did Minli's parents decide to return home? How was Ma changed?
Vocabulary	The word is **ignorant**. What word? *Ignorant*. *Ignorant* refers to someone who is not aware of something or may not have enough knowledge about a matter. The author said, "She stood waiting, clearly ignorant of the fish's words." Let's discuss what that sentence means. I'll read it again. [Reread and discuss, focusing on the word and connecting the sentence to the narrative context.] Another example using the word *ignorant* would be "I was surprised that the substitute was ignorant of the rules we used in the classroom." Can you think of other examples using the word *ignorant*? What is the word? *Ignorant*. Related words: *ignorance, ignorantly*.
21	Why did Minli offer to pay the buffalo boy? Was the grocer merciful toward the old man? Why? Why did Minli give her last coin to the beggar to buy a peach? What trick did the beggar perform?

Vocabulary	The first word is **extraordinary**. What word? *Extraordinary*. *Extraordinary* means very unusual. The author said, "Now in the daylight the buffalo boy's friend didn't seem as extraordinary." Let's discuss what that sentence means. I'll read it again. [Reread and discuss, focusing on the word and connecting the sentence to the narrative context.] Another example using the word *extraordinary* would be "She wore an extraordinary hat that caused people to stare." Can you think of other examples using the word *extraordinary*? What is the word? *Extraordinary*.
	  Related words: *ordinary, ordinarily, extraordinarily*.
	
	The second word is **amused**. What word? *Amused*. *Amused* means feeling entertained by something humorous. The author said, "He was watching with an amused look, and suddenly Minli saw that the beggar wasn't really that old at all." Let's discuss what that sentence means. I'll read it again. [Reread and discuss, focusing on the word and connecting the sentence to the narrative context.] Another example using the word *amused* would be "The monkey amused the crowd by jumping from tree to tree and holding its hat." Can you think of other examples using the word *amused*? What is the word? *Amused*.
	  Related words: *amuse, amusing, amusement, amusingly*.

22	How did the beggar-King return to the Inner City? Why did the King hide Minli? How would the King honor the spirit of the moon?

(cont.)

Chapter	Questions for Discussion
Vocabulary	The first word in **intricate**. What word? *Intricate*. *Intricate* means complex, complicated. The author said, "Intricate dragons and multicolored clouds that matched the designs of the gold bracelet he wore . . . " Let's discuss what that sentence means. I'll read it again. [Reread and discuss, focusing on the word and connecting the sentence to the narrative context.] Another example using the word *intricate* would be "This map and its explanations were the most intricate things I had ever seen." Can you think of other examples using the word *intricate*? What is the word? *Intricate*. Related words: *intricately, intricacy.* The second word is **decisively**. What word? *Decisively*. *Decisively* refers to making a choice and then not changing your mind. The author said, "Yes, the King said decisively." Let's discuss what that sentence means. I'll read it again. [Reread and discuss, focusing on the word and connecting the sentence to the narrative context.] Another example using the word *decisively* would be "The president always thought carefully about his choices, and then he acted decisively." Can you think of other examples using the word *decisively*? What is the word? *Decisively*. Related words: *decide, decision, decided, deciding, decisive, indecisive, indecisively.*
23	What did Minli and the King have for dinner? What was the King's guess about the borrowed line Minli was looking for? How did the city come to be called the City of the Moonlight? Why did the King give the paper to Minli?
Vocabulary	The first word is **elaborately**. What word? *Elaborately*. *Elaborately* refers to something done with lots of detail. The author said, "At the center, the two stools and small table of elaborately carved gingko wood waited for them." Let's discuss what that sentence means. I'll read it again. [Reread and discuss, focusing on the word and connecting the sentence to the narrative context.] Another example using the word *elaborately* would be "That was the most elaborately decorated birthday cake I had ever seen." Can you think of other examples using the word *elaborately*? What is the word? *Elaborately*. Related words: *elaborate, elaborating, elaborated, elaborative, elaborateness.* The second word is **fascinated**. What word? *Fascinated*. *Fascinated* means being very interested. The author said, "Minli watched fascinated as the king took from the gold pouch a delicate folded piece of paper." Let's discuss what that sentence means. I'll read it again. [Reread and discuss, focusing on the word and connecting the sentence to the narrative context.] Another example using the word *fascinated* would be "I was fascinated to see how the carpenter built the beautiful cabinet." Can you think of other examples using the word *fascinated*? What is the word? *Fascinated*. Related words: *fascinate, fascinating, fascinatingly.*
24	How were the lion statues unique? What is the lions' responsibility? How did the Old Man of the Moon help the lions keep the city together?

(cont.)

Chapter	Questions for Discussion

Vocabulary	The first word is **attained**. What word? *Attained. Attain* means to reach or achieve something you want. The author said, "'And you still have not attained wisdom,' the father lion told him." Let's discuss what that sentence means. I'll read it again. [Reread and discuss, focusing on the word and connecting the sentence to the narrative context.] Another example using the word *attained* would be "She attained the recognition of her friends after she solved the mystery." Can you think of other examples using the word *attained*? What is the word? *Attained.*
	    Related words: *attain, attaining, unattained.*
	
	The second word is **marvelous**. What word? *Marvelous. Marvelous* means excellent. The author said, "It was a marvelous gift." Let's discuss what that sentence means. I'll read it again. [Reread and discuss, focusing on the word and connecting the sentence to the narrative context.] Another example using the word *marvelous* would be "I attended a marvelous show last week." Can you think of other examples using the word *marvelous*? What is the word? *Marvelous.*
	    Related words: *marvel, marveling, marveled, marvelously.*

25	What did Ba say the word on the paper of happiness was? Has Ma's attitude changed?
Vocabulary	The word is **occasionally**. What word? *Occasionally. Occasionally* means from time to time, once in a while. The author said, "Ba stroked her hair as she wept, occasionally closing his eyes as he fought his own gloom." Let's discuss what that sentence means. I'll read it again. [Reread and discuss, focusing on the word and connecting the sentence to the narrative context.] Another example using the word *occasionally* would be "I drink coffee only occasionally because it is not good for my stomach." Can you think of other examples using the word *occasionally*? What is the word? *Occasionally.* Related words: *occasion, occasional.*
26	How did Minli and the dragon end up with two borrowed lines?
Vocabulary	The first word is **disastrous**. What word? *Disastrous. Disastrous* means causing great damage. The author said, "Part of her was tempted to explore the mosaic walkways through the jewel colored leaves but she knew being discovered by the king's counselors would be disastrous." Let's discuss what that sentence means. I'll read it again. [Reread and discuss, focusing on the word and connecting the sentence to the narrative context.] Another example using the word *disastrous* would be "The earthquake was disastrous for the people who lived nearby." Can you think of other examples using the word *disastrous*? What is the word? *Disastrous.* Related words: *disaster, disastrously.*

(cont.)

Chapter	Questions for Discussion
	The second word is **explore**. What word? *Explore*. *Explore* means to look into something closely or to look with the purpose of discovering. The author said, "Part of her was tempted to explore the mosaic walkways through the jewel colored leaves ..." Let's discuss what that sentence means. I'll read it again. [Reread and discuss, focusing on the word and connecting the sentence to the narrative context.] Another example using the word *explore* would be "Through this class we will have the opportunity to explore the world of literature." Can you think of other examples using the word *explore*? What is the word? *Explore*. Related words: *explored, exploring, explorer, unexplored*.
27	How did Minli and Dragon manage their hunger? Why did Minli feel guilty?
Vocabulary	The word is **confusion**. What word? *Confusion*. *Confusion* means not understanding or knowing what to do. The author said, "But just as Minli shook her head with confusion, there was a sudden sound outside the cave." Let's discuss what that sentence means. I'll read it again. [Reread and discuss, focusing on the word and connecting the sentence to the narrative context.] Another example using the word *confusion* would be "The way the question was worded led to confusion among the students." Can you think of other examples using the word *confusion*? What is the word? *Confusion*. Related words: *confused, confusing*.
28	What could be the fear that the goldfish sensed?
Vocabulary	The first word is **soundless**. What word? *Soundless*. *Soundless* means very quiet, silent. The author said, "Ba looked at Ma and saw her soundless lips move as she gazed at the moon." Let's discuss what that sentence means. I'll read it again. [Reread and discuss, focusing on the word and connecting the sentence to the narrative context.] Another example using the word *soundless* would be "She slipped into the water raising a soundless wave." Can you think of other examples using the word *soundless*? What is the word? *Soundless*. Related words: *soundlessly, soundlessness*. The second word is **implored**. What word? *Implored*. *Implore* means to beg for help. The author said, "'Please,' he implored the moon silently, 'please watch over Minli.'" Let's discuss what that sentence means. I'll read it again. [Reread and discuss, focusing on the word and connecting the sentence to the narrative context.] Another example with the word *implored* would be "I implored her to leave me alone in order to avoid a fight." Can you think of other examples using the word *implored*? What is the word? *Implored*. Related words: *implore, imploring*.
29	Why did Minli begin to cry? Why was Minli worried about the dragon?

(cont.)

Chapter	Questions for Discussion
Vocabulary	The first word is **viciousness**. What word? *Viciousness. Viciousness* means extreme cruelty. The author said, "The tiger was large, but Dragon was bigger—though the viciousness of the tiger's expression made them seem evenly matched." Let's discuss what that sentence means. I'll read it again. [Reread and discuss, focusing on the word and connecting the sentence to the narrative context.] Another example with the word *viciousness* would be "The viciousness of the evil queen's true personality was revealed in time." Can you think of other examples using the word *viciousness*? What is the word? *Viciousness.* Related words: *vicious, viciously.* The second word is **grimaced**. What word? *Grimaced.* To *grimace* means to make a face that shows disapproval or pain. The author said, "Every time she unwrapped the blanket, she grimaced—the ugly wounds had turned black and evil looking liquid was starting to seep." Let's discuss what that sentence means. I'll read it again. [Reread and discuss, focusing on the word and connecting the sentence to the narrative context.] Another example using the word *grimaced* would be "She grimaced when she saw my black eye." Can you think of other examples using the word *grimaced*? What is the word? *Grimaced.* Related words: *grimace, grimacing.*
30	Why did the little girl approach the tiger? How did the girl explain her brother's absence?
Vocabulary	The first word is **immense**. What word? *Immense. Immense* means huge or great. The author said, "It was a high price but we knew with your immense power and strength we could not disobey." Let's discuss what that sentence means. I'll read it again. [Reread and discuss, focusing on the word and connecting the sentence to the narrative context.] Another example using the word *immense* would be "The woman showed immense courage when she entered the flaming building." Can you think of other examples using the word *immense*? What is the word? *Immense.* Related words: *immensely, immensity.* The second word is **seething**. What word? *Seething. Seething* means being very angry. The author said, "The tiger nodded at the girl with narrowed eyes seething with fury." Let's discuss what that sentence means. I'll read it again. [Reread and discuss, focusing on the word and connecting the sentence to the narrative context.] Another example using the word *seething* would be "She was seething when she saw the mess on the kitchen floor." Can you think of other examples using the word *seething*? What is the word? *Seething.* Related words: *seethe, seethed.*
31	Why did the girl lead the tiger to the well? Why did the tiger get upset at the thought that someone was mocking him?

(cont.)

Chapter	Questions for Discussion
Vocabulary	The first word is **ferociously**. What word? *Ferociously. Ferociously* refers to acting in a fierce or violent way. The author said, "The tiger glowered ferociously, stalked to the edge of the well and snarled into the blackness." Let's discuss what that sentence means. I'll read it again. [Reread and discuss, focusing on the word and connecting the sentence to the narrative context.] Another example using the word *ferociously* would be "The mother bear roared ferociously when she thought her cub was threatened." Can you think of other examples using the word *ferociously*? What is the word? *Ferociously.* 　　Related words: *ferocious, ferocity.* The second word is **overwhelmed**. What word? *Overwhelmed. Overwhelmed* means feeling overpowered by something. The author said, "And when the roar echoed back it overwhelmed him with wild rage." Let's discuss what that sentence means. I'll read it again. [Reread and discuss, focusing on the word and connecting the sentence to the narrative context.] Another example using the word *overwhelmed* would be "I was overwhelmed by the beauty of the mountainside." Can you think of other examples using the word *overwhelmed*? What is the word? *Overwhelmed.* 　　Related words: *overwhelm, overwhelming.*
32	Why were the boy and the girl celebrating? How did the children use the tiger's anger against him? Why was A-Gong in a hurry?
Vocabulary	The word is **immediately**. What word? *Immediately. Immediate* means right away, without any delay. The author said, "She was grateful for its warmth but even more grateful that the man wanted to help immediately." Let's discuss what that sentence means. I'll read it again. [Reread and discuss, focusing on the word and connecting the sentence to the narrative context.] Another example using the word *immediately* would be "The students left the classroom immediately when the fire alarm sounded." Can you think of other examples using the word *immediately*? What is the word? *Immediately.* 　　Related word: *immediate*
33	What was the tonic A-Gong used? Was the medicine effective?
Vocabulary	The first word is **weariness**. What word? *Weariness. Weariness* means tiredness. The author said, "The man turned and looked at her wind-burned face, tangled hair and eyes shadowed with weariness." Let's discuss what that sentence means. I'll read it again. [Reread and discuss, focusing on the word and connecting the sentence to the narrative context.] Another example of the word *weariness* would be "After marching all day, the soldiers felt great weariness." Can you think of other examples using the word *weariness*? What is the word? *Weariness.* 　　Related words: *weary, wearily.*

(cont.)

Chapter	Questions for Discussion
	The second word is **protested**. What word? *Protested. Protest* means to express disapproval or to object to something. The author said, "'I want to stay with Dragon,' Minli protested." Let's discuss what that sentence means. I'll read it again. [Reread and discuss, focusing on the word and connecting the sentence to the narrative context.] Another example using the word *protested* would be "The workers protested against the reduction of their pay." Can you think of other examples using the word *protested*? What is the word? *Protested.* Related words: *protest, protester, protesting.*
34	Why did the villagers use their baskets to catch what fell from the sky? How did the Village of the Moon Rain come to have its name?
Vocabulary	The first word is **merriness**. What word? *Merriness. Merriness* means cheerfulness. The author said, "Their every other word seemed to be mixed with merriness." Let's discuss what that sentence means. I'll read it again. [Reread and discuss, focusing on the word and connecting the sentence to the narrative context.] Another example using the word *merriness* would be "The student was full of merriness after receiving a good grade." Can you think of other examples using the word *merriness*? What is the word? *Merriness.* Related words: *merrily, merry, merriment.* The second word is **unforgiving**. What word? *Unforgiving. Unforgiving* means harsh and not allowing mistakes. The author said, "and Minli saw that the flowering trees were the only things that grew easily from the unforgiving rough soil." Let's discuss what that sentence means. I'll read it again. [Reread and discuss, focusing on the word and connecting the sentence to the narrative context.] Another example using the word *unforgiving* would be, "It was her unforgiving nature that led to the end of their friendship." Can you think of other examples using the word *unforgiving*? What is the word? *Unforgiving.* Related words: *forgive, forgiving, forgivable, forgiveness, unforgivable.*
35	What happened after the storm? Why were Minli's parents laughing and crying?
Vocabulary	The first word is **shamefacedly**. What word? *Shamefacedly. Shamefaced* means showing shame or embarrassment. The author said, "A cross look streaked across Ma's face but as she looked at Ba rubbing his ear shamefacedly she did something she hadn't done in years." Let's discuss what that sentence means. I'll read it again. [Reread and discuss, focusing on the word and connecting the sentence to the narrative context.] Another example using the word *shamefacedly* would be "She gave her apology shamefacedly because she had never acted so badly before." Can you think of other examples using the word *shamefacedly*? What is the word? *Shamefacedly.* Related words: *shame, shamefaced, shameful.*

(cont.)

Chapter	Questions for Discussion
	The second word is **intertwined**. What word? *Intertwined*. Twine is a type of rope. *Intertwined* means mixed together the way pieces of twine might be woven together to form a rope. The author said, "Their laughter intertwined but when they looked at each other they could see the tears forming were not from joy." Let's discuss what that sentence means. I'll read it again. [Reread and discuss, focusing on the word and connecting the sentence to the narrative context.] Another example using the word *intertwined* would be "Their futures were intertwined and even if they tried to separate from one another they always met again." Can you think of other examples using the word *intertwined*? What is the word? *Intertwined*. Related words: *intertwine, intertwining*.
36	How was the Green Tiger created? How was the cure for Tiger's poison discovered? What was the meaning of the Green Tiger's message?

Vocabulary	The first word is **tormented**. What word? *Tormented*. *Torment* means to cause great suffering. The author said, "A-Gong my husband studied furiously trying to find out more about this powerful monster who tormented us." Let's discuss what that sentence means. I'll read it again. [Reread and discuss, focusing on the word and connecting the sentence to the narrative context.] Another example using the word *tormented* would be "The little girl was tormented by the bullies in her classroom." Can you think of other examples using the word *tormented*? What is the word? *Tormented*.
	    Related words: *torment, torments, tormenting, tormenter*.
	
	The second word is **peculiar**. What word? *Peculiar*. *Peculiar* means strange or odd. The author said, "He was standing in front of our gate doing something peculiar." Let's discuss what that sentence means. I'll read it again. [Reread and discuss, focusing on the word and connecting the sentence to the narrative context.] Another example using the word *peculiar* would be "Hearing the baby talk sounded like the most peculiar thing." Can you think of other examples using the word *peculiar*? What is the word? *Peculiar*.
	    Related word: *peculiarly*.

37	How did the family treat the dragon? Why did Minli's goodbyes freeze in her throat?
Vocabulary	The first word is **marveled**. What word? *Marveled*. To *marvel* means to feel wonder and admiration. The author said, "As she put it on she marveled at its warmth." Let's discuss what that sentence means. I'll read it again. [Reread and discuss, focusing on the word and connecting the sentence to the narrative context.] Another example using the word *marveled* would be "I marveled at the grown-up responses of the 5-year-old child." Can you think of other examples using the word *marveled*? What is the word? *Marveled*. Related words: *marvel, marveling, marvelous*.

(cont.)

Chapter	Questions for Discussion
	The second word is **fluttered**. What word? *Fluttered. Flutter* means to wave or beat rapidly. The author said, "Minli nodded—and as she waved a grateful goodbye to the village, a sea of ruined sleeves fluttered back at her." Let's discuss what that sentence means. I'll read it again. [Reread and discuss, focusing on the word and connecting the sentence to the narrative context.] Another example using the word *fluttered* would be "The flags fluttered to welcome the visitors as they entered the building." Can you think of other examples using the word *fluttered*? What is the word? *Fluttered.* Related words: *fluttering, flutter.*
38	How did the family decide to spend their time together before the Magistrate's arrival? How did their houses move to safety?

Vocabulary	The first word is **delightful**. What word? *Delightful. Delightful* means giving great pleasure. The author said, "And they had a delightful time." Let's discuss what that sentence means. I'll read it again. [Reread and discuss, focusing on the word and connecting the sentence to the narrative context.] Another example using the word *delightful* would be "We all had a delightful year and we will keep our memories forever." Can you think of other examples using the word *delightful*? What is the word? *Delightful.*
	        Related words: *delight, delighted, delighting.*
	
	The second word is **disappeared**. What word? *Disappeared. Disappear* means to vanish from sight. The author said, "One by one the butterflies and dragons disappeared as if flying home to the moon." Let's discuss what that sentence means. I'll read it again. [Reread and discuss, focusing on the word and connecting the sentence to the narrative context.] Another example using the word *disappeared* would be "A great number of pencils seem to have disappeared from the cabinet." Can you think of other examples using the word *disappeared*? What is the word? *Disappeared.*
	        Related words: *appear, appeared, appearing, appearance, disappear, disappearing, disappearance.*

39	What did New Ending Mountain look like? How did Minli, Dragon, and Da-A-Fu try to send a message to the Old Man of the Moon? Why did the string turn into a bridge?
Vocabulary	The first word is **succession**. What word? *Succession. Succession* means the coming of one person or action after another. The author said, "Each of them in succession had tried to break it." Let's discuss what that sentence means. I'll read it again. [Reread and discuss, focusing on the word and connecting the sentence to the narrative context.] Another example would be "He heard several loud knocks in succession." Can you think of other examples using the word *succession*? What is the word? *Succession.*

(cont.)

Chapter	Questions for Discussion
	The second word is **impressed**. What word? *Impressed. Impress* means to create a favorable impression. The author said, "'You may be destined to meet him then,' A-Fu said, impressed." Let's discuss what that sentence means. I'll read it again. [Reread and discuss, focusing on the word and connecting the sentence to the narrative context.] Another example would be "I was impressed to see that you cleaned up your room without my asking you to do so." Can you think of other examples using the word *impressed*? What is the word? *Impressed.* Related words: *impress, impressing, unimpressed.*
40	Why was Ba surprised at Ma's request to hear the story? Why did the Queen Mother of the Heavens send him to steal the Dragon's pearl? How did Dragon find out who stole his pearl? Who ended the quarrel between Dragon and the Queen Mother of Heavens? How?
Vocabulary	The first word is **accomplish**. What word? *Accomplish. Accomplish* means to achieve a goal or a purpose. The author said, "The servants were able to accomplish this quite easily as the Dragon—weary from his many years of work—slept quite long and soundly." Let's discuss what that sentence means. I'll read it again. [Reread and discuss, focusing on the word and connecting the sentence to the narrative context.] Another example using the word *accomplish* would be "We will accomplish our goals only if we devote time and effort." Can you think of other examples using the word *accomplish*? What is the word? *Accomplish.* Related words: *accomplished, accomplishing, accomplishment, unaccomplished.* The second word is **impetuously**. What word? *Impetuously. Impetuous* means acting quickly without thought or care. The author said, "'My dear friends,' she said impetuously, 'Your gifts and words are fine, indeed, but I have something that far outshines them.'" Let's discuss what that sentence means. I'll read it again. [Reread and discuss, focusing on the word and connecting the sentence to the narrative context.] Another example using the word *impetuously* would be "She always acted impetuously without thinking beforehand about the results of her words and actions." Can you think of other examples using the word *impetuously*? What is the word? *Impetuously.* Related words: *impetuous, impetuousness*
41	Why was Dragon disappointed?
Vocabulary	The word is **downcast**. What word? *Downcast. Downcast* means looking downward because of sadness. The author said, "Minli looked at Dragon's downcast eyes and read the years of sadness and frustration in his face." Let's discuss what that sentence means. I'll read it again. [Reread and discuss, focusing on the word and connecting the sentence to the narrative context.] Another example using the word *downcast* would be "He wore a downcast look that made him look much older than he was." Can you think of other examples using the word *downcast*? What is the word? *Downcast.*

(cont.)

Chapter	Questions for Discussion
	The second word is **loom**. What word? *Loom*. To *loom* means to appear in a way that suggests that something bad may happen. The author said, "'Then I better get going,' Minli said, but her smile faded as she looked at the bridge in front of her that seemed to loom into nothingness." Let's discuss what that sentence means. I'll read it again. [Reread and discuss, focusing on the word and connecting the sentence to the narrative context.] Another example using the word *loom* would be "When dark clouds loom overhead we know that it might rain." Can you think of other examples using the word *loom*? What is the word? *Loom*. Related words: *looming, loomed.*
42	Why did Minli find the cutting of the tree a shame? Why was Wu Kang unmoved by what the Old Man of the Moon taught him? How was the Old Man of the Moon teaching Wu Kang contentment and patience? What causes the moon rain at the Da-A-Fung's village?
Vocabulary	The first word is **astonished**. What word? *Astonished*. *Astonished* means amazed or very surprised. The author said, "Minli was too astonished to speak." Let's discuss what that sentence means. I'll read it again. [Reread and discuss, focusing on the word and connecting the sentence to the narrative context.] Another example using the word *astonished* would be "I was astonished to see how just one rainstorm benefitted my garden." Can you think of other examples using the word *astonished*? What is the word? *Astonished*. Related words: *astonish*, astonishing, astonishment. The second word is **inconvenient**. What word? *Inconvenient*. *Inconvenient* means causing trouble, difficulties, or discomfort. The author said, "It was crowded and inconvenient in the smaller house, but Wu Kang was able to apprentice himself to a furniture maker and his family began to adapt to their cramped home." Let's discuss what that sentence means. I'll read it again. [Reread and discuss, focusing on the word and connecting the sentence to the narrative context.] Another example using the word *inconvenient* would be "No one came to our meeting because the time was inconvenient for everyone." Can you think of other examples using the word *inconvenient*? What is the word? *Inconvenient*. Related words: *convenient, convenience, inconvenience.*
43	Who was supplying the red string of destiny to the Old Man of the Moon? What was Minli's dilemma? How did Minli reach her decision?
Vocabulary	The first word is **expectantly**. What word? *Expectantly*. *Expectantly* refers to thinking or acting as if something is likely to happen. The author said, "The Old Man of the Moon looked at her expectantly, his black eyes as unreadable as the night sky." Let's discuss what that sentence means. I'll read it again. [Reread and discuss, focusing on the word and connecting the sentence to the narrative context.] Another example using the word *expectantly* would be "The crowd looked expectantly at the speaker, awaiting his announcement." Can you think of other examples using the word *expectantly*? What is the word? *Expectantly*. Related words: *expect, expected, expecting, expectant, unexpected.*

(cont.)

Chapter	Questions for Discussion
	The second word is **invisibly**. What word? *Invisibly. Invisible* means not in sight. The author said, "Yet now the paper was invisibly fastened in the book, with only a thin line, like a scar, showing that it had ever been moved." Let's discuss what that sentence means. I'll read it again. [Reread and discuss, focusing on the word and connecting the sentence to the narrative context.] Another example using the word *invisibly* would be "The servants did their best to work invisibly so that the king would not be bothered." Can you think of other examples using the word *invisibly*? What is the word? *Invisibly.* Related words: *visible, visibility, invisible, invisibility.*
44	How did Ma come to the conclusion that Minli's running away was her fault?

Vocabulary	The first word is **discontent**. What word? *Discontent. Discontent* means a feeling of not being satisfied. The author said, "The woman was so caught up in her dissatisfaction that she did not realize that she was planting seeds of discontent in her daughter as well." Let's discuss what that sentence means. I'll read it again. [Reread and discuss, focusing on the word and connecting the sentence to the narrative context.] Another example using the word *discontent* would be "The harsh new rules led to lots of discontent." Can you think of other examples using the word *discontent*? What is the word? *Discontent.*
	     Related words: *content, contenting, contented, discontented.*
	
	The second word is **compassion**. What word? *Compassion. Compassion* is a feeling of deep sympathy and sadness for someone who may be in a difficult situation. The author said, "She did not know if she would receive compassion for either, but she vowed she would wait for it." Let's discuss what that sentence means. I'll read it again. [Reread and discuss, focusing on the word and connecting the sentence to the narrative context.] Another example using the word *compassion* would be "Due to the group's compassion, the people whose houses burned received the support they needed." Can you think of other examples using the word *compassion*? What is the word? *Compassion.*
	     Related words: *compassionate, compassionately.*

45	Why couldn't Dragon fly? What was the meaning of true fortune that Minli had in mind?
Vocabulary	The word is **embraced**. What word? *Embraced. Embrace* means to accept something willingly or to hug. The author said, "The silver clouds embraced them and then parted as the dragon flew through as if her wings were rippling the sky." Let's discuss what that sentence means. I'll read it again. [Reread and discuss, focusing on the word and connecting the sentence to the narrative context.] Another example using the word *embraced* would be "She embraced the challenge with enthusiasm and excitement." Can you think of other examples using the word *embraced*? What is the word? *Embraced.* Related words: *embrace, embracing.*
46	Who could be the orange dragon? How was Dragon acting strange?

(cont.)

Chapter	Questions for Discussion

Vocabulary	The first word is **distracted**. What word? *Distracted. Distracted* means unable to concentrate because you are thinking about something else. The author said, "He returned her hug warmly, but she could tell he was distracted." Let's discuss what that sentence means. I'll read it again. [Reread and discuss, focusing on the word and connecting the sentence to the narrative context.] Another example using the word *distracted* would be "I was distracted by the noise and I made a mistake on my assignment." Can you think of other examples using the word *distracted*? What is the word? *Distracted.*
	
	    Related words: *distract, distracting, distractingly, distraction.*
	
	The second word is **absentmindedly**. What word? *Absentmindedly. Absentmindedly* refers to doing things without paying attention. The author said, "'No,' Dragon glanced at her absentmindedly." Let's discuss what that sentence means. I'll read it again. [Reread and discuss, focusing on the word and connecting the sentence to the narrative context.] Another example using the word *absentmindedly* would be "He was usually careful but sometimes he worked absentmindedly." Can you think of other examples using the word *absentmindedly*? What is the word? *Absentmindedly.*
	
	    Related words: *absentminded, absentmindedness.*

47	Why did the villagers shout? What could explain the unexpected awakening of life at Fruitless Mountain?

Vocabulary	The first word is **translucent**. What word? *Translucent. Translucent* refers to a surface that allows light to come through, but not clearly. The author said, "To Minli's great surprise the grayness of the stone began to smudge away and a translucent lustrous glow seemed to shine through." Let's discuss what that sentence means. I'll read it again. [Reread and discuss, focusing on the word and connecting the sentence to the narrative context.] Another example using the word *translucent* would be "He could not see the children behind the *translucent* glass in the dining room door." Can you think of other examples using the word *translucent*? What is the word? *Translucent.*
	
	    Related words: *translucence, translucently.*
	
	The second word is **transformed**. What word? *Transformed. Transformed* means changed into something different. The author said, "As the day dawned, the mountain had transformed." Let's discuss what that sentence means. I'll read it again. [Reread and discuss, focusing on the word and connecting the sentence to the narrative context.] Another example using the word *transformed* would be "Inside the cocoon, a caterpillar is transformed into a butterfly or moth." Can you think of other examples using the word *transformed*? What is the word? *Transformed.*
	
	    Related words: transform, transforming, transformer.

(cont.)

Chapter	Questions for Discussion
48	What did the goldfish man see at the village that was different from his previous visit? How did the King reward the village? Why didn't the family take any payment from the King? Why would Minli's home have the picture of a little boy and girl at its entrance? How was the goldfish man greeted differently? Why? What could Minli be thinking?
Vocabulary	The first word is **indulgently**. What word? *Indulgently*. *Indulgently* refers to giving in to someone's mood and requests. The author said, "Parents walked over and smiled indulgently at their children and by the time the sun disappeared the goldfish man had sold out of his wares." Let's discuss what that sentence means. I'll read it again. [Reread and discuss, focusing on the word and connecting the sentence to the narrative context.] Another example using the word *indulgently* would be "The mother treated the child indulgently and bought the new toy." Can you think of other examples using the word *indulgently*? What is the word? *Indulgently*. Related words: *indulge, indulging*. The second word is **indicated**. What word? *Indicated*. *Indicate* means to point something out or to show. The author said, "The goldfish man wheeled his empty cart to the indicated gate." Let's discuss what that sentence means. I'll read it again. [Reread and discuss, focusing on the word and connecting the sentence to the narrative context.] Another example using the word *indicated* would be "The sign indicated that we could not dive into the pool." Can you think of other examples using the word *indicated*? What is the word? *Indicated*. Related words: *indicate, indicating, indicative*.

Sample Lessons for a Fourth-Grade Group in Vocabulary and Comprehension

The Brain, by Seymour Simon
Lexile Level: 900; 32 pages

All lessons take the same format. Remember: We recommend that students in this group do their reading and complete the guide independently, returning to the teacher the following day.
1. What do we already know about these topics? or Let's review what we learned in yesterday's reading.
2. Have the students read and complete the reading guide.
3. Review Tier 2 vocabulary from the previous day.
4. Use the inferential questions below as a reading guide and then to structure a discussion.

Pages	Questions for Discussion
1–7	What are some of the actions you can perform with the help of your brain? What are the two main parts of the nervous system? How are neurons and glial cells similar and different? (Compare and contrast them using the compare–contrast graph.) Title: Compare–Contrast Neurons and Glial Cells **Neurons** • Messenger cells ○ Signal from the brain to other body parts **Microscopic cells** **Glial Cells** • Do not carry messages • Outnumber neurons • Supply nutrients • Repair the brain • Attack bacteria
Vocabulary	The word is **invading**. What word? *Invading* means entering using force. The author said, "They support the neurons by supplying nutrients and other chemicals repairing the brain after an injury and attacking invading bacteria." Let's discuss what that sentence means. I'll read it again. [Reread and discuss, focusing on the word and connecting the sentence to the narrative context.] Another example using the word *invading* would be "The termites were invading the entire space behind the wall." Can you think of another example using the word *invading*? What is the word? *Invading.* Related words: *invade, invaded, invasive, invader.*

(cont.)

Pages	Questions for Discussion
8–9	What makes a nerve? What is the function of nerves? What do nerves look like? What is the function of dendrites and the axon?
Vocabulary	The word is **surrounded**. What word? *Surround* means to be on all sides of an object, to enclose something. The author said, "Axons are often surrounded by a fatty covering called a myelin sheath." Let's discuss what that sentence means. I'll read it again. [Reread and discuss, focusing on the word and connecting the sentence to the narrative context.] Another example using the word *surrounded* would be "The intruder was surrounded by police officers within seconds." Can you think of other examples using the word *surrounded*? What is the word? *Surrounded*. Related words: *surround, surrounding*.
10–13	How are messages carried from one nerve to another? Using a sequence graph, show how a message is delivered through synapses. An electrical impulse reaches the axon of a nerve and moves to dendrites on the next nerve cell. The dendrites create an electrical signal. The message reaches the end of the axon. The message passes from one neuron to the next to reach its destination. What are some kinds of stimuli? What are the sensory neurons? Why do you react when touching something hot?

(cont.)

Pages	Questions for Discussion
	Stimulus: You touch something hot.
	⇩
	The signal reaches the relay nerves on the spinal cord.
	⇩
	The signal transfers through nerves to your brain.
	⇩
	Your brain "feels" the touch.
	⇩
	Signals are sent from the brain to your spinal cord and motor nerves.
	⇩
	Motor nerves notify muscle cells, and your arm moves.
Vocabulary	The word is *respond*. What word? *Respond* means to answer in words or through a reaction. The author said, "A single touch may make thousands of them respond." Let's discuss what that sentence means. I'll read it again. [Reread and discuss, focusing on the word and connecting the sentence to the narrative context.] Another example using the word *respond* would be "I could not respond to his questions." Can you think of other examples using the word *respond*? What is the word? *Respond*. Related words: *responded, responding, response, responder, responsive.*
14–19	In the text we find the word *hemisphere*. The word *hemisphere* means half a sphere, and in this book Seymour Simon uses the word to refer to the structure of the brain. There is a left and a right hemisphere. How many bones protect the brain? How big is the brain? When does the brain stop growing? Is the human brain the biggest animal brain? What are the main sections into which the brain is divided? How many neurons are in the cerebral cortex? What is the function of the right and left hemispheres?
Vocabulary	The word is **divided**. What word? *Divide* means to break down into parts. The author said, "The cerebrum is divided into four parts called lobes." Let's discuss what that sentence means. I'll read it again. [Reread and discuss, focusing on the word and connecting the sentence to the narrative context.] Another example using the word *divided* would be "The group was divided in two opposing teams." Can you think of other examples using the word *divided*? What is the word? *Divided*. Related words: *divide, dividing, division, undivided.*

(cont.)

Pages	Questions for Discussion
20–27	What is the cerebellum? How does the cerebellum support your everyday actions? What are the functions of the thalamus and hypothalamus? What are the functions of the midbrain and the pons? How many bones make up the spinal cord? How do messages travel to and from the brain? What is the difference between vertebrates and invertebrates?
Vocabulary	The word is **adjusting**. What word? *Adjusting* means changing something slightly so that it is better or more comfortable. The author said, "It constantly receives messages about the body's actions and position, then sends back commands to the muscles, adjusting the way the body moves." Let's discuss what that sentence means. I'll read it again. [Reread and discuss, focusing on the word and connecting the sentence to the narrative context.] Another example using the word *adjusting* would be "She was just adjusting to the new country's customs when she had to move again." Can you think of other examples using the word *adjusting*? What is the word? *Adjusting*. Related words: *adjust, adjusted, adjustment, readjust, readjusting, readjusted, readjustment.*
28–32	What are some examples of how short-term memory works? What is long-term memory? What can injuries to the spinal cord cause? How do doctors examine what happens in the brain and the nervous system?
Vocabulary	The word is **regulates**. What word? *Regulate* means to control how something works. The author said, "It regulates many of the important automatic functions of your body." Let's discuss what that sentence means. I'll read it again. [Reread and discuss, focusing on the word and connecting the sentence to the narrative context.] Another example using the word *regulates* would be "She regulates her actions when she is at school." Can you think of other examples using the word *regulates*? What is the word? *Regulates*. Related words: *regulate, regulating, regulator, regulatory.*

Sample Lessons for a Fifth-Grade Group in Vocabulary and Comprehension

The River, by Gary Paulsen
Lexile Level: 960; 132 pages

All lessons take the same format. Remember: We recommend that students in this group do their reading and complete the guide independently, returning to the teacher the following day.

1. What do we already know about these characters? What do we already know about the events? or Let's review what we learned in yesterday's reading.
2. Have the students read and complete the reading guide.
3. Review Tier 2 vocabulary from the previous day.
4. Use the inferential questions below as a reading guide and then to structure a discussion.

Chapter	Questions for Discussion
1	Why was the press so interested in Brian Robeson? Why did Brian have offers to advertise products? How did the press influence Brian's relationship with Deborah?

Vocabulary	The first word is **decent**. What is the word? *Decent. Decent* means appropriate or fair. The author said, "They were large, but not fat, well built, with bodies in decent shape." Let's discuss what that sentence means. I'll read it again. [Reread and discuss, focusing on the word and connecting the sentence to the narrative context.] Other examples using the word *decent* would be "I found the wallpaper I was looking for at a decent price" and "I couldn't go out with them because I did not have any decent clothes." Can you think of other examples using the word *decent*? What is the word we learned? *Decent.*
	    Related words: *decently, indecent.*
	
	The second word is **noticing**. What is the word? *Noticing. Noticing* means paying attention, observing. The author says, "He was only too glad when people stopped noticing him." Let's discuss what that sentence means. I'll read it again. [Reread and discuss, focusing on the word and connecting the sentence to the narrative context.] Another example using the word *noticing* would be "She was glad to see that no one was noticing her torn dress." Can you think of other examples using the word *noticing*? What is the word we learned? *Noticing.*
	    Related words: *notice, noticed, unnoticed.*

2	Why did the visitors want Brian to repeat his survival adventure? How did the visitors expect to learn from Brian? What impact did the adventure have on Brian after his return to safety? Why did Brian's parents insist that he talk to a counselor?
Vocabulary	The word is **evasive**. What word? *Evasive* means avoiding something, such as not answering a question. The author said, "In all his dealings with the new world around him since he was reborn in the woods—as he thought of it—he had to be evasive, hold back." Let's discuss what that sentence means. I'll read it again. [Reread and discuss, focusing on the word and connecting the sentence to the narrative context.] Another example using the word *evasive* would be "She felt ashamed so she was evasive in her answers." Can you think of other examples using the word *evasive*? What is the word? *Evasive.* Related words: *evade, evading, evasiveness, evasively.*

(cont.)

Chapter	Questions for Discussion
3	What were some things that Brian discovered about himself after the Time? Why was Brian's mother hesitant about the men's proposal?
Vocabulary	The first word is **precaution**. What word? *Precaution*. A *precaution* is an action that protects against something that could happen. The author said, "'We would control the operation closely,' he said, 'and take every precaution possible.'" Let's discuss what that sentence means. I'll read it again. [Reread and discuss, focusing on the word and connecting the sentence to the narrative context.] Another example using the word *precaution* would be "I used every precaution as I passed by the mad dog." Can you think of other examples using the word *precaution*? What is the word? *Precaution*. Related words: *caution, precautionary*. The second word is **insane**. What word? *Insane. Insane* means senseless or crazy. The author said, "To want to go back was insane." Let's discuss what that sentence means. I'll read it again. [Reread and discuss, focusing on the word and connecting the sentence to the narrative context.] Another example would be "She seemed insane when she talked back to her parents." Can you think of other examples using the word *insane*? What is the word? *Insane*. Related words: *sane, sanity, insanely, insanity*.
4	Why was it Derek who accompanied Brian and not another man? Why did the view of the pilot make Brian feel relaxed? Why did Brian say that Hunger was the main problem during the Time? Why did Brian think that the survival gear they had with them was too much?
Vocabulary	The first word is **aspect**. What word? *Aspect. Aspect* means a part of something. The author said, "Derek had decided he should be the one to go—even though he had little or no survival knowledge—because he was a psychologist and that was the aspect they wished to learn about." Let's discuss what that sentence means. I'll read it again. [Reread and discuss, focusing on the word and connecting the sentence to the narrative context.] Another example would be "I found this aspect of the problem to be the most interesting one." Can you think of other examples using the word *aspect*? What is the word? *Aspect*. The second word is **approaching**. What word? *Approaching. Approach* means to start to deal with something. The author said, "Like it was all a game and Derek was approaching this whole business that way." Let's discuss what that sentence means. I'll read it again. [Reread and discuss, focusing on the word and connecting the sentence to the narrative context.] Another example using the word *approaching* would be "She was approaching the problem with caution to avoid mistakes." Can you think of other examples using the word *approaching*? What is the word? *Approaching*. Related words: *approach, approached*.
5	How did Brian change once he stepped on land? Why? Why did Brian refuse to unload the gear? Why did Brian agree to keep the radio?

(cont.)

257

Chapter	Questions for Discussion
Vocabulary	The first word is **clambered**. What word? *Clambered. Clamber* means to climb with difficulty using both your hands and feet. The author said, "The pilot stayed in his seat and Brian moved the passenger seat forward and clambered out of the plane." Let's discuss what that sentence means. I'll read it again. [Reread and discuss, focusing on the word and connecting the sentence to the narrative context.] Another example would be "Peter and I clambered to the top of the steep hill within half an hour." Can you think of another example using the word *clambered*? What is the word? *Clambered.* 　　　Related word: *clamber.* The second word is **hesitated**. What word? *Hesitated. Hesitate* means to pause before acting. The author said, "Brian hesitated, then sighed." Let's discuss what that sentence means. I'll read it again. [Reread and discuss, focusing on the word and connecting the sentence to the narrative context.] Another example would be "She hesitated to open the door because she was not sure what she would find." Can you think of other examples using the word *hesitated*? What is the word? *Hesitated.* 　　　Related words: *hesitate, hesitatingly, hesitant, hesitance.*
6	How did Brian and Derek prepare for the night? Why was Derek constantly exposed to the mosquitoes? Why did Derek come to realize that having the gear was wrong?
Vocabulary	The first word is **especially**. What word? *Especially. Especially* is a word used to single out a person, group, or thing. The author said, "The truth was, it wasn't much—especially for two people." Let's discuss what that sentence means. I'll read it again. [Reread and discuss, focusing on the word and connecting the sentence to the narrative context.] Another example would be "Summer is a time that is especially good for getting more exercise." Can you think of another example using the word *especially*? What is the word? *Especially.* The second word is **overrode**. What word? *Overrode.* To *override* means to have dominance over something else, to have final authority. The author said, "Somehow the beauty overrode the mosquitoes." Let's discuss what that sentence means. I'll read it again. [Reread and discuss, focusing on the word and connecting the sentence to the narrative context.] Another example would be "The importance of his goal overrode his feelings of fear about getting started." Can you think of another example using the word *overrode*? What is the word? *Overrode.* 　　　Related words: *override, overriding, overridden.*
7	What were the priorities that Brian had set for the day? Why?

(cont.)

Chapter	Questions for Discussion
Vocabulary	The word is **externalize**. What word? *Externalize. Externalize* means to direct something outward, to put it outside. The author said, "You have to tell me everything, externalize it all for me, so I can write it." Let's discuss what that sentence means. I'll read it again. [Reread and discuss, focusing on the word and connecting the sentence to the narrative context.] Another example would be "She tried to externalize her feelings, but it was difficult to make sense of them." Can you think of another example using the word *externalize*? What is the word? *Externalize.* Related words: *external, internal, internalize.*
8	Why did Brian suggest that Derek not look into a bear's eyes? Why did Brian fall? How did Brian make fire? Why was having fire an important aspect of their survival?
Vocabulary	The word is **depression**. What word? *Depression. Depression* means a sunken part or dent. The author said, "The tree was long rotted and gone to worms, the soil had filtered somewhat back into the hole and taken grass seeds, and what was left was a large depression in the side of the hill with an overhanging shelf of rock." Let's discuss what that sentence means. I'll read it again. [Reread and discuss, focusing on the word and connecting the sentence to the narrative context.] Another example would be "The depression in the couch cushions revealed where she spent the night." Can you think of another example using the word *depression*? What is the word? *Depression.*
9	How did Brian and Derek catch fish? How does Brian think that survival should be taught? Why?
Vocabulary	The word is **enhanced**. What word? *Enhanced. Enhance* means to make something bigger or better. The author said, "Then they had enhanced the beds and made them deep and soft with more boughs, there was enough firewood for a month, and they had made birch-bark containers to hold extra hazelnuts and berries." Let's discuss what that sentence means. I'll read it again. [Reread and discuss, focusing on the word and connecting the sentence to the narrative context.] Another example would be "Planting trees enhanced the value and beauty of the property." Can you think of another example using the word *enhanced*? What is the word? *Enhanced.* Related words: *enhancing, enhancement.*
10	What had awakened Brian? How did the lightning strike them?

(cont.)

Chapter	Questions for Discussion
Vocabulary	The first word is **brilliance**. What word? *Brilliance*. *Brilliance* can refer to bright light or to excellence. The author said, "He knew that he opened his mouth, that he made sound, but he could hear nothing except the whack-track of the thunder, see nothing but images frozen in the split-instants of brilliance from the lightning." Let's discuss what that sentence means. I'll read it again. [Reread and discuss, focusing on the word and connecting the sentence to the narrative context.] Other examples would be "It was her brilliance that led to the discovery of the medicine" and "The brilliance of the light made her cover her eyes." Can you think of other examples using the word *brilliance*? What is the word? *Brilliance*. Related words: *brilliant, brilliantly*.
	The second word is **concentrating**. What word? *Concentrating*. The word *concentrating* means to focus your thoughts on something. The author said, "Then he was leaning forward and his hand was out, reaching for his briefcase and radio next to the bed, one finger out, his face concentrating, and Brian thought, no, don't reach, stay low ... " Let's discuss what that sentence means. I'll read it again. [Reread and discuss, focusing on the word and connecting the sentence to the narrative context.] Another example would be "She was concentrating on solving the math problem." Can you think of other examples using the word *concentrating*? What is the word? *Concentrating*. Related words: *concentrate, concentrated, concentration*.
11	Why did Brian smell something burnt? Was Derek sleeping? Why didn't Brian want to accept that Derek was dead?
Vocabulary	The first word is **indication**. What word? *Indication*. *Indication* means a sign of something. The author said, "There was no answer, no indication that Derek had heard him." Let's discuss what that sentence means. I'll read it again. [Reread and discuss, focusing on the word and connecting the sentence to the narrative context.] Other examples would be "There was an indication of annoyance in her voice" or "His high fever was an indication of his infection." Can you think of other examples using the word *indication*? What is the word? *Indication*. Related words: *indicate, indicated, indicative*.
	The second word is **transpose**. What word? *Transpose*. *Transpose* means to change something from one place to another or to change the order of two things. The author said, "He tried to time it, but couldn't transpose the number of beats per minute measures on his digital watch into a pulse rate because he couldn't think." Let's discuss what that sentence means. I'll read it again. [Reread and discuss, focusing on the word and connecting the sentence to the narrative context.] Another example would be "I got the phone number wrong because I transposed the last two numbers." Can you think of another example using the word *transpose*? What is the word? *Transpose*. Related words: *transposing, transposed, transposition, transposable*.
12	Why couldn't Brian call headquarters for help? What had happened to Derek? Why couldn't Brian feed Derek?

(cont.)

Chapter	Questions for Discussion

Vocabulary	The first word is **severe**. What word? *Severe*. *Severe* means very serious, extreme. The author said, "He knew almost nothing of medical terms or what happened to people with severe shock, and knew less than nothing about comas." Let's discuss what that sentence means. I'll read it again. [Reread and discuss, focusing on the word and connecting the sentence to the narrative context.] Other examples would be "She was in severe pain after the extraction of her tooth" and "The punishment seemed too severe to me." Can you think of other examples using the word *severe*? What is the word? *Severe*.
	        Related words: *severely, severity*.
	
	The second word is **consciousness**. What word? *Consciousness*. *Consciousness* means mental awareness or wakefulness. It can also mean understanding. The author said, "If he stayed and Derek did not regain consciousness, how long would he . . . last?" Let's discuss what that sentence means. I'll read it again. [Reread and discuss, focusing on the word and connecting the sentence to the narrative context.] Other examples would be "Consciousness of her mistake caused her to worry" and "She regained her consciousness after her fall." Can you think of other examples using the word *consciousness*? What is the word? *Consciousness*.
	        Related words: *conscious, consciously, unconscious, unconsciously, unconsciousness*.

13	Why did Brian think that it was important for Derek to drink water? How did Brian try to establish some type of communication with Derek? Did it work? Why?
Vocabulary	The word is **exasperation**. What word? *Exasperation*. *Exasperation* means great irritation or annoyance. The author said, "He threw the stick down in exasperation." Let's discuss what that sentence means. I'll read it again. [Reread and discuss, focusing on the word and connecting the sentence to the narrative context.] Another example would be "His exasperation with her constant phone calls was understandable." Can you think of other examples using the word *exasperation*? What is the word? *Exasperation*. Related words: *exasperate, exasperated*.
14	Why couldn't Brian leave Derek behind in his search for help?
Vocabulary	The first word is **considerable**. What word? *Considerable*. *Considerable* means extensive or large. The author said, "But in other places it ran straight for a considerable distance and he followed it, through smaller lakes and what he thought must be swamps" Let's discuss what that sentence means. I'll read it again. [Reread and discuss, focusing on the word and connecting the sentence to the narrative context.] Other examples would be "The benefits from her current position are considerable" and "He was absent for a considerable period of time." Can you think of other examples using the word *considerable*? What is the word? *Considerable*. Related word: *inconsiderable*.

(cont.)

Chapter	Questions for Discussion
	The second word is **defenseless**. What word? *Defenseless. Defenseless* means without protection. The author said, "He was defenseless." Let's discuss what that sentence means. I'll read it again. [Reread and discuss, focusing on the word and connecting the sentence to the narrative context.] Another example would be "She was left defenseless in the abandoned ship." Can you think of other examples using the word *defenseless*? What is the word? *Defenseless.* Related words: *defense, defending, defended, defensible, defenses, indefensible.*
15	Why did Brian miss his hatchet? Why hadn't Brian taken his hatchet with him? Where did Brian locate the right size of wood?
Vocabulary	The word is **affected**. What word? *Affected. Affected* means influenced in some way. The author said, "Even when he was in danger, even when he had to fight just to live, his decisions only affected him—never another person." Let's discuss what that sentence means. I'll read it again. [Reread and discuss, focusing on the word and connecting the sentence to the narrative context.] Another example would be "The change in the weather affected our plans." Can you think of other examples using the word *affected*? What is the word? *Affected.* Related word: *affect.*
16	How did Brian move Derek on the raft? Why did Brian tie Derek to the raft? Why did Brian leave a note behind?
Vocabulary	The first word is **figured**. What word? *Figured.* To *figure* means to expect. The author said, "He had been soaked since starting to build the raft and figured to remain wet until … " Let's discuss what that sentence means. I'll read it again. [Reread and discuss, focusing on the word and connecting the sentence to the narrative context.] Another example would be "She figured that it would be smart to ignore the problem." Can you think of other examples using the word *figured*? What is the word? *Figured.* Related words: *figure, figures.* The second word is **positioned**. What word? *Positioned. Positioned* means placed. The author said, "Brian positioned him first on his back and then decided he might choke and moved him over onto his side." Let's discuss what that sentence means. I'll read it again. [Reread and discuss, focusing on the word and connecting the sentence to the narrative context.] Another example would be "The coach positioned the shortstop further back because the batter was so strong." Can you think of other examples using the word *positioned*? What is the word? *Positioned.* Related words: *position, positioning, positional.*
17	Why was the raft getting stuck? How did Brian take care of Derek while being on the raft?

(cont.)

Chapter	Questions for Discussion
Vocabulary	The first word is **frantically**. What word? *Frantically. Frantic* means acting with extreme feelings of worry. The author said, "They still did not always stay in the center of the best current, but as the afternoon wore on Brian found that by frantically paddling through each curve . . . " Let's discuss what that sentence means. I'll read it again. [Reread and discuss, focusing on the word and connecting the sentence to the narrative context.] Another example would be "The mother was frantically searching in the laundry room for her daughter's favorite blanket." Can you think of other examples using the word *frantically*? What is the word? *Frantically.* 　　Related words: *frantic, franticness.* The second word is **exposed**. What word? *Exposed. Expose* means to reveal and bring something into view. The author said, "He looked at the unconscious form and saw that the sun had burned his neck where the skin was exposed." Let's discuss what that sentence means. I'll read it again. [Reread and discuss, focusing on the word and connecting the sentence to the narrative context.] Another example would be "The reporter purposely exposed the unfair actions so that people would understand." Can you think of other examples using the word *exposed*? What is the word? *Exposed.* 　　Related words: *expose, exposing, exposable.*
18	Why did Brian feel so strongly about the need to sleep? Why would everything have been easier for Brian with Derek gone?
Vocabulary	The first word is **beckoning**. What word? *Beckoning. Beckon* means to signal someone to come closer. The author said, "He would change into his father who was smiling and beckoning him to paddle faster and faster . . . " Let's discuss what that sentence means. I'll read it again. [Reread and discuss, focusing on the word and connecting the sentence to the narrative context.] Another example would be "The shop owners were beckoning to the visitors to approach their stores." Can you think of other examples using the word *beckoning*? What is the word? *Beckoning.* 　　Related words: *beckon, beckoner, beckoned.* The second word is **instant**. What word? *Instant. Instant* means a brief moment. The author said, "Not even for an instant." Let's discuss what that sentence means. I'll read it again. [Reread and discuss, focusing on the word and connecting the sentence to the narrative context.] Another example would be "It took her only an instant to connect his face with his name and remember him." Can you think of other examples using the word *instant*? What is the word? *Instant.* 　　Related words: *instantly, instantaneous.*
19	How did Brian come to the conclusion that the map was inaccurate? How did Brian provide shade for Derek? Why was it important for Derek to be in the shade?

(cont.)

Chapter	Questions for Discussion
Vocabulary	The first word is **accurate**. What word? *Accurate. Accurate* means correct, without any mistakes. The author said, "There were lakes, some large and small, but he was not moving fast enough to have reached any of them yet and that meant the map was not accurate." Let's discuss what that sentence means. I'll read it again. [Reread and discuss, focusing on the word and connecting the sentence to the narrative context.] Another example would be "She was accurate in her calculations and they proceeded with the experiment." Can you think of other examples using the word *accurate*? What is the word? *Accurate.* Related words: *accurately, accuracy, accurateness, inaccurate, inaccuracy.* The second word is **bothered**. What word? *Bothered. Bother* means to annoy or disturb. The author said, "It bothered him, but it was an old friend/enemy." Another example would be "She was bothered by his remarks about her family." Can you think of other examples using the word *bothered*? What is the word? *Bothered.* Related words: *bother, bothering, bothersome, unbothered.*
20	What stopped Brian from looking at the map?
Vocabulary	The word is **heading**. What word? *Heading. Heading* means moving toward something. The author said, "They were heading for a waterfall." Let's discuss what that sentence means. I'll read it again. [Reread and discuss, focusing on the word and connecting the sentence to the narrative context.] Another example would be "He was heading toward the market." Can you think of other examples using the word *heading*? What is the word? *Heading.* Related words: *head, headed.*
21	Did Brian make it down the waterfall safely? How?
Vocabulary	The word is **urge**. What word? *Urge. Urge* means to encourage someone to do something. It can also mean the feeling of having to do something. The author said, "He willed the urge away, down but it grew worse ... " Let's discuss what that sentence means. I'll read it again. [Reread and discuss, focusing on the word and connecting the sentence to the narrative context.] Other examples would be "At night I have the urge to gobble an entire container of ice cream" and "I urge you not to speak to your friend that way." Can you think of other examples using the word *urge*? What is the word? *Urge.* Related words: *urged, urging.*
22	What was Brian's main worry as soon as he woke up? What was Brian's condition after the fall?
Vocabulary	The word is **apparently**. What word? *Apparently. Apparently* means as far as we know. The author said, "He had taken a little water, but apparently had coughed it out." Let's discuss what that sentence means. I'll read it again. [Reread and discuss, focusing on the word and connecting the sentence to the narrative context.] Another example with the word *apparently* would be "She was apparently a very good writer." Can you think of other examples using the word *apparently*? What is the word? *Apparently.* Related words: *apparent, apparentness, unapparent.*

(cont.)

Chapter	Questions for Discussion
23	How did Brian search for the raft? How did Brian locate the raft? Why did Brian fall across Derek?
Vocabulary	The word is **perversely**. What word? *Perversely*. *Perversely* means behaving unacceptably or improperly. The author said, "Altogether he rounded six shallow bends and still there was no raft, the stupid raft that had hung up on every bend when he was trying to steer it and now perversely held the center of the river somehow." Let's discuss what that sentence means. I'll read it again. [Reread and discuss, focusing on the word and connecting the sentence to the narrative context.] Another example with the word *perversely* would be "Behaving perversely made people dislike him." Can you think of other examples using the word *perversely*? What is the word? *Perversely*. Related words: *perverse, perversity*.
24	How did Brian know he had reached civilization?
Vocabulary	The word is **appeared**. What word? *Appeared*. *Appear* means to arrive or to become visible. *Appear* can also mean seem. The author says, "As Brian watched, the round face of a young boy appeared next to the dog." Let's discuss what that sentence means. I'll read it again. [Reread and discuss, focusing on the word and connecting the sentence to the narrative context.] Another example would be "The magician appeared to be a fake." Can you think of other examples using the word *appeared*? What is the word? *Appeared*. Related words: *appear, appearing, appearance, reappear, reappeared, reappearance*.
Measurements	What was Derek's condition after the rescue? Why did Derek send Brian a canoe named "the raft"?
Vocabulary	The first word is **suffered**. What word? *Suffered*. *Suffer* means to feel pain or discomfort. The author said, "although he would have suffered significantly from dehydration." Let's discuss what that sentence means. I'll read it again. [Reread and discuss, focusing on the word and connecting the sentence to the narrative context.] Another example would be "The dog suffered in the cold and the snow." Can you think of other examples using the word *suffered*? What is the word? *Suffered*. Related words: *suffer, suffering, sufferer*. The second word is **significantly**. What word? *Significantly*. *Significantly* means in a very important way. The author said, "although he would have suffered significantly from dehydration." Let's discuss what that sentence means. I'll read it again. [Reread and discuss, focusing on the word and connecting the sentence to the narrative context.] Another example would be "Her grades improved significantly during the spring when she worked hard." Can you think of other examples using the word *significantly*? What is the word? *Significantly*. Related words: *significant, significance, insignificant, insignificance*.

Sample Lessons for a Fifth-Grade Vocabulary and Comprehension Group

The Usborne Internet-Linked Introduction to Weather and Climate Change, by Laura Howell
Lexile Level: IG980; 95 pages

All lessons take the same format. Remember: We recommend that students in this group do their reading and complete the guide independently, returning to the teacher the following day.

1. What do we already know about these topics? or Let's review what we learned in yesterday's reading.
2. Introduce Tier 3 vocabulary (science words, in this case).
3. Have the students read and complete the reading guide.
4. Use the inferential questions below as a reading guide and then to structure a discussion.

Pages	Questions for Discussion
1–9	*-ology* is a suffix that means the study of something. The word *meteorology* is a Greek derivative (*meteor*: celestial phenomenon). What are some other words that have the suffix *-ology*? *-ology: biology, sociology, archaeology, radiology, pathology, psychology, geology* *-sphere* is the second word part we will find in this book. The word is derived from Greek and means ball or globe. *Hydro* comes from the Greek word for water. *Hydrosphere* literally means ball of water and refers to the water on the earth and in its atmosphere. Since *-sphere* is a root that we will see often, we will record all the instances we find. What determines the nature of life on Earth? What is climate? What is the climate in our area? What is the job of meteorologists? How are weather satellites used? What would happen to the Earth's surface if the global energy system were not in place? Why does the Earth have so many weather changes compared with other planets?
10–17	*Atmosphere* is another word with the root *sphere. Atmos* is a Greek derivative that means vapor or smoke. *Atmosphere* literally means a ball of vapor, and it refers to the air that surrounds the earth. What are some of the places where the climate is extreme? Why? What climate changes have taken place on Earth since the formation of our planet? What do we call the rays that the sun emits? What is one of the causes of skin cancer? What causes the seasons? What happens to the sun's rays as they reach the Earth?

(cont.)

Pages	Questions for Discussion
	There are some additional words containing *-sphere* that we will see in this section. *Troposphere* is the lowest layer of the atmosphere (from the Greek word *tropos*: turn). *Stratosphere* is the second layer (The word is of Latin origin. *Stratum*: a cover). *Mesosphere* is the next layer of the atmosphere. *Meso-* is of Greek origin (*mesos*) and means middle. *Thermosphere* is the next layer. *Thermo* is also a Greek derivative (*thermos*) and means hot. Exosphere is the last layer of the atmosphere. *Exo* is of Greek origin (*exo*) and means outside or outer. How are the layers of the atmosphere determined? Use a pyramid to show students how the layers of the atmosphere are ordered, where the peak represents the farthest layer from the Earth. What causes the division of the atmosphere into layers? In what layer would you expect to find an aircraft? Why? What is ozone? What is the function of ozone?
18–23	What is the greenhouse effect? How is the greenhouse effect helpful to humans and life in general? What is global warming? What are the effects of global warming on water vapor? What lessons do we learn from observing Venus? What is the cause of the greenhouse effect according to many scientists? What evidence exists to support the fears that are raised by global warming? What is the IPCC? What predictions are made regarding the Earth's temperature?

(cont.)

Pages	Questions for Discussion
24–31	What are some of the causes of the destruction of rainforests? What are the climate conditions in rainforests? What are the climate conditions in deserts? Why are the temperatures in the polar regions low even if the areas receive sun for 6 months? What is the mountain climate?
32–35	What do we call the combination of salty and fresh water on the Earth? Use the cycle graph below to illustrate the water cycle for students. Water vapor forms clouds and falls to Earth The sun causes the water to evaporate Water returns to the sea, oceans, lakes, and rivers How does sea water travel around the world? What are the Earth's major currents? How might global warming affect the North Atlantic Conveyor? What are the effects of El Niño and La Niña on the Earth?
36–53	What is the relationship between condensation and evaporation? How do clouds form? What are the four groups of clouds? How would you define precipitation? How are rainbows formed? How is fog formed? How does frost develop? How are the Earth's temperatures controlled by the convection currents? Where and how do the jet streams develop? What are some types of extreme weather? What might cause a drought?

(cont.)

Pages	Questions for Discussion
54–59	*Meter* is a word of Greek origin that means to measure. Some of the instruments used to study the weather contain the root *meter*. One of them is the *anemometer*. *Anemo* is derived from Greek (*anemos*) and means wind. An *anemometer* is an instrument that measures the wind. Additional words with the root *-meter*: *thermometer, hydrometer, chronometer, odometer, radiometer, barometer, speedometer* What are some of the other instruments used to study the weather? What is the difference between a thermometer and a hydrometer? How do weather balloons assist in the study of weather? How do meteorologists create a weather forecast?
60–69	*Paleo* means old, *climat* means climate or weather conditions, and *ologist* means a person who studies. We can put these word elements together to make *paleoclimatologist*, a person who studies the climate in ancient times. What is the work of paleoclimatologists? Why do scientists use proxy data? What information can scientists take from fossils? What information do scientists get about the weather from tree trunks? What are some of the gradual climate changes? How does the Earth's core affect the climate system? Where do natural aerosols come from?
70–end	How are alpine and continental glaciers different? How does the human body adjust to temperature change? How do animals protect themselves in different weather conditions? How can the population growth affect the atmosphere? What is the Kyoto Protocol and why was it created? What are some of the alternative sources of energy that humans can use to support their needs? How can we reduce the amount of energy we use? How can recycling support the Earth? What are the effects of reduced krill in the food chain? How do skeptics respond to the fear of global warming? What is the Beaufort scale?

Glossary of Reading Terms

accent: prominence of a syllable within a word in terms of loudness and emphasis (*see* **primary accent** and **secondary accent**)

accuracy: the successful pronunciation of words encountered in print; sometimes contrasted with speed.

assessment-driven instruction: instruction that is planned on the basis of screening and diagnostic testing designed to reveal a child's specific needs; such assessments are subsequently repeated and modified as instruction proceeds.

basal reader: a textbook designed to improve reading ability; contains selections at roughly the same level of readability (*see* **core instructional materials**).

basal reading series: an organized series of materials, including leveled readers, workbooks, etc.; the rationale is that children should be placed in the series at an appropriate point and then be allowed to move through the remaining levels (*see* **core instructional materials**).

before–during–after lesson format: any of several three-phase lesson plans in which the teacher first prepares students to read a particular text, then provides opportunities for them to read purposely, and finally follows up their reading with discussion and other activities.

benchmark: a score indicating an acceptable level of proficiency, often determined by studies that predict subsequent achievement.

big book: an oversized book used to model the reading process, to teach conventions of print, and to conduct decoding instruction on a teachable-moment basis.

blend: *See* **consonant blend.**

blending: pronouncing a word by pronouncing each phoneme in sequence.

chunk: two or more letters within a word that operate together to represent either sound or meaning.

compound word: a word consisting of two or more root words that have not been altered in forming the compound (examples: *farmhand, gingerbread*); some linguists consider certain physically divided words, like *high school*, to be compounds, but this is not an important distinction in reading instruction since the white space allows each part to be identified separately; in compound words written as a single word, children must learn to recognize the components.

comprehension: "the process of simultaneously extracting and constructing meaning through interaction and involvement with written language" (RAND Reading Study Group, 2002, p. xiii).

comprehension monitoring: continuously checking one's own understanding during reading; a form of metacognition.

comprehension strategy: any of several techniques employed by proficient readers to ensure adequate comprehension; such strategies include activating prior knowledge, setting specific purposes for reading, predicting, summarizing, visualizing, and employing "fix-up" techniques like rereading (*see* **fix-up strategy**).

consonant blend: two or more consonants appearing together in a word and representing the sound of each individual consonant (examples: *bl* in *blend*, and *nd* in *blend*).

consonant cluster: two or more consonants appearing together in a word.

consonant digraph: two consonants appearing together in a word and representing a sound not associated with either consonant individually (examples: *sh, ch, th, ph, ng*).

core instructional materials: the main commercial reading program (usually a basal series) used in an elementary school; the core program may be supplemented by additional programs, trade books, etc.

curriculum-based measurement: an approach to assessment that uses children's performance with curricular materials to make judgments about instructional growth and needs (e.g., a basal passage might be used to assess oral reading fluency).

decodable book: a book consisting solely of words that are regular in terms of letter–sound relationships; exceptions (e.g., *of, who*) are excluded.

decoding: analyzing an unfamiliar word in order to arrive at its pronunciation.

decoding by analogy: determining the pronunciation of a word encountered in print by comparing it with one or more words already familiar to the reader (e.g., to pronounce the nonsense word *zum*, a proficient reader might relate it to the word *gum* rather than attempt to blend the individual phonemes); for multisyllabic words, the process is more complex and may involve two or more known words (e.g., the word *bandiferous* might be likened to *band, different*, and *generous*).

diagnostic assessment: a test that is typically administered to identify specific instructional needs after a screening assessment has indicated a general weakness in a given area (e.g., a phonics screening test might be followed by a phonics inventory to identify specific skill deficits).

diphthong: a combination of two vowels in which the sound of the first glides seamlessly into the second (examples: *oi* in *oil*; *ou* in *our*).

direct explanation: teaching that focuses specifically on a skill or strategy in such a way that it is presented (explained), its use is modeled, and its application by the child is monitored and assisted until it can be applied independently; direct explanation can be contrasted with incidental instruction that is not systematic and the focus of which does not center on the skill or strategy; also called **direct instruction** or **explicit instruction.**

direct instruction: *See* **direct explanation.**

dysfluent: performing well below the benchmark for oral reading fluency.

etymology: the origin of a word and the development of its meaning over time.

explicit instruction: *See* **direct explanation.**

expository text: a form of nonfiction that is not organized chronologically but is structured instead according to subtopics, arguments, etc.

fiction: collectively, any of several prose genres (e.g., novel, short story) representing imaginary events and characters, although real events and characters may be incorporated as well.

fix-up strategy: a comprehension strategy applied when text appears not to make sense or is unclear; such strategies include rereading, reading ahead, reflecting, and referring to outside sources.

fluency: the developmental stage at which word recognition is quick and phrasing is adult-like; this stage is thought to lie between the stage during which a child learns to decode and the stage at which the child can effectively learn from printed sources; note that this term is sometimes extended to any set of skills that a child can apply automatically, such as letter naming or phoneme segmentation.

genre: an established form of writing with agreed-upon conventions (examples: novel, short story, lyric poem, limerick, news story, essay).

graphic organizer: a diagram or chart showing how key terms are related.

high-frequency word: a word that occurs so often in text that readers must be able to pronounce it automatically in order to achieve fluency; examples include function words like prepositions and conjunctions but also many content words, such as colors, animals, days of the week, etc.

inference: a logical conclusion arrived at on the basis of stated facts and/or facts known to the reader prior to reading; inferences can be certain or merely probable, depending on the available facts; "a statement about the unknown made on the basis of the known" (S. I. Hayakawa).

informal assessments: tests that have few specific requirements as to how they are administered and scored, leaving much to the discretion of the teacher; such tests are never interpreted through the use of norms because the conditions under which they are given can vary considerably.

information text: text designed primarily to convey information; this term is often used synonymously with **nonfiction** and is broader in scope than **expository text.**

leveled readers: short trade books sequenced by difficulty level and used in small-group instruction, usually in the primary grades.

long-term memory: that portion of memory in which knowledge and experiences are stored indefinitely for later retrieval.

long vowel: a vowel sound associated with the name of the vowel letter (examples: *a* in *lane*, *e* in *lean*, *i* in *line*, *o* in *lone*, *u* in *lute*); note that long *u* imperfectly expresses the letter name of *u*.

modeling: demonstrating how a skill or strategy is properly applied.

morpheme: the smallest unit of meaning in a language; the term applies to words (e.g., *cat*) and to certain letters (e.g., -*s*) so that *cats* contains two morphemes; a distinction is sometimes made between free morphemes (those, like *cat*, that can stand alone) and bound morphemes (those, like -*s*, that have meaning only when attached to a free morpheme).

nonfiction: collectively, any of several prose genres (e.g., essay, biography, textbook) presenting factual information and involving actual events and persons; nonfiction may have an expository or narrative organization.

phoneme: the smallest recognizable unit of sound in a language; the word *cat* contains three phonemes, the word *the* two, and the word *great* four.

phonemic awareness: cognizance of the phonemes that make up spoken words; this ability is causally related to learning to read (cf. **phonological awareness**).

phonics: instruction in reading and spelling that stresses letter–sound relationships.

phonological awareness: cognizance of any of the component speech sounds that make up spoken words; while not directly connected to written language, this ability is a prerequisite for learning phonics; this term includes an awareness not only of phonemes but of larger units as well, like rimes (cf. **phonemic awareness**).

prefix: a letter or letter combination that, when added to the beginning of a word, changes its meaning.

primary accent: a strong emphasis or stress on a syllable in a multisyllabic word (cf. **secondary accent**).

progress monitoring assessment: a test that is administered periodically after an intervention has begun in order to determine its impact and whether to modify or discontinue its use.

prosody: a component of oral reading fluency that is characterized by appropriate, expressive phrasing and intonation; prosody depends on automatic, accurate word recognition but adds another dimension—think of the difference between an auctioneer and an actor.

***r*-controlled vowel:** a vowel followed by the letter *r*, which causes the vowel to have a sound that is neither long nor short (examples: *a* in *car*, *e* in *her*); sometimes called the "bossy *r*."

rate: speed of reading, typically expressed as either the number of words per minute (WPM) or the number of words correctly read per minute (WCPM).

readability: the estimated difficulty level of a particular selection, generally expressed as a grade level.

Reading First: a large-scale K–3 federal program through which funded schools apply scientifically based reading instruction, employ literacy coaches, and plan instruction based on periodic screening assessments.

reliable assessment: a test that tends to produce similar results under similar circumstances; factors that increase reliability include the clarity of directions, the structure of test items, and the length of the test; reliability is a prerequisite to validity (cf. **valid assessment**).

repeated reading: an instructional method for building fluency in which the same text is read two or more times.

root word: a word that has been altered by the addition of one or more affixes.

schwa sound: the vowel sound heard in most unaccented syllables.

scope and sequence: a reading skills curriculum organized by the order in which the skills are taught and reinforced; the organizing rationale behind a basal reading series.

screening assessment: a test designed to provide a quick indication of whether a problem exists in a broad area; without more, screening assessments can do little to help with instructional planning (cf. **diagnostic assessment**).

secondary accent: a weaker emphasis or stress on the pronunciation of a syllable in a multisyllabic word (cf. **primary accent**).

short vowel: a vowel sound typically heard in consonant–vowel–consonant words (*a* in *pat*, *e* in *pet*, *i* in *pit*, *o* in *pot*, *u* in *pub*).

skills: specific proficiencies that are largely independent of a particular context or purpose for reading; skills, like tools, may be more or less relevant to a particular occasion (comprehension skills might include inferring a cause-and-effect relationship or noting an explicitly stated fact) (cf. **strategies**).

sociocultural context: a setting in which related social and cultural factors might influence literacy learning or the application of literacy skills and strategies; for example, instruction based on interaction among students assumes that learning is optimized through social interplay.

strategies: proficiencies that involve the application of skills to achieve a particular goal, depending on the context of and purpose for reading (comprehension strategies might include predicting an outcome or generating self-questions to guide thinking) (cf. **skills**).

stress: emphasis, in terms of loudness, placed on the pronunciation of syllable within a word.

suffix: a letter or letter combination that, when added to the end of a word, changes its meaning.

syllable: a unit of spoken language that consists of a vowel sound and, typically, one or more adjacent consonant sounds.

syntax: rules governing the ordering of words in a sentence.

systematic instruction: instruction organized in a logical manner to achieve a set of objectives; sequencing may be implied in such an organization but it may depend on a child's progress, so that systematic instruction may not adhere to a rigid sequence.

valid assessment: a test that adequately addresses the purpose for which it is administered; validity may concern how a construct, skill, or standard is conceptualized and reflected in the test, how well a test predicts a future outcome, or how well it correlates with another measure given at nearly the same time; validity requires that the test be reliable, but reliability in itself is not enough to ensure validity (cf. **reliable assessment**).

vocabulary: in general, word knowledge; however, the term *vocabulary* is often preceded by a qualifier that limits its scope by function (e.g., meaning vocabulary, sight vocabulary, listening vocabulary).

vowel team: two or more vowel letters appearing together in a word and representing a single vowel sound (also called a vowel combination).

word recognition: the composite set of abilities by which a reader associates printed words with their spoken equivalents; these abilities include phoneme–grapheme relationships (phonics), sight words, knowledge of affixes, and recognition of compounds and contractions.

References

Allington, R. L. (1983). Fluency: The neglected reading goal. *The Reading Teacher, 36,* 556–561.

Anderson, R., & Pearson, P.D. (1984). A schema-theoretic view of basic processes in reading. In P.D. Pearson, R. Barr, M. Kamil, & P. Mosenthal (Eds.), *Handbook of reading research* (Vol. 1, pp. 255–291). New York: Longman.

Ash, G., Kuhn, M., & Walpole, S. (2009). Analyzing "inconsistencies" in practice: Teachers' continued use of round robin reading. *Reading and Writing Quarterly, 25,* 87–103.

Baumann, J., Ware, D., & Edwards, E. (2007). "Bumping into spicy, tasty words that catch your tongue": A formative experiment on vocabulary instruction. *The Reading Teacher, 61,* 108–122.

Bear, D. R., Invernizzi, M., Templeton, S., & Johnston, F. (2008). *Words their way* (4th ed.). Upper Saddle River, NJ: Prentice Hall.

Beck, I. L., & McKeown, M. G. (1994). Outcomes of history instruction: Paste-up accounts. In M. Carretero & J. F. Voss (Eds.), *Cognitive and instructional processes in history and the social sciences* (pp. 237–256). Hillsdale, NJ: Erlbaum.

Beck, I. L., McKeown, M. G., & Kucan, L. (2002). *Bringing words to life: Robust vocabulary instruction.* New York: Guilford Press.

Biemiller, A. (2004). Teaching vocabulary in the primary grades. In J. F. Baumann & E. J. Kame'enui (Eds.), *Vocabulary instruction: Research to practice* (pp. 28–40). New York: Guilford Press.

Brophy, J. E. (1983). Classroom organization and management. *Elementary School Journal, 83,* 264–285.

Brown-Chidsey, R., Bronaugh, L., & McGraw, K. (Eds.). (2009). *RTI in the classroom: Guidelines and recipes for success.* New York: Guilford Press.

Calhoon, M. B. (2005). Effects of a peer-mediated phonological skill and reading comprehension program on reading skill acquisition for middle school students with reading disabilities. *Journal of Learning Disabilities, 38,* 424–433.

Carlo, M., August, D., & McLaughlin, B. (2004). Closing the gap: Addressing the vocabulary needs of English-language learners in bilingual and mainstream classrooms. *Reading Research Quarterly, 39,* 188–215.

277

Carmichael, S. B., Martino, G., Porter-Magee, K., & Wilson, W.S. (2010, July). *The state of state standards—and the Common Core—in 2010.* Washington, DC: Thomas B. Fordham Institute.

Chall, J. E. (1996). *Stages of reading development* (2nd ed.). New York: McGraw-Hill.

Chall, J. E., Jacobs, V., & Baldwin, L. (1990). *The reading crisis: Why poor children fall behind.* Cambridge, MA: Harvard University Press.

Clark, K. (2009). The nature and influence of comprehension strategy use during peer-led literature discussions: An analysis of intermediate grade students' practice. *Literacy Research and Instruction, 48,* 95–119.

Cramer, E. H. (1994). Connecting in the classroom: Ideas from teachers. In E.H. Cramer & M. Castle (Eds.), *Fostering the love of reading: The affective domain in reading education.* Newark, DE: International Reading Association.

Crosson, A., & Lesaux, N. (2010). Revisiting assumptions about the relationship of fluent reading to comprehension: Spanish-speakers' text-reading fluency in English. *Reading and Writing, 23,* 475–494.

Cunningham, A. E., & Stanovich, K. E. (1997). Early reading acquisition and its relation to experience and ability 10 years later. *Developmental Psychology, 33,* 934–945.

Daniels, H. (2001). *Literature circles: Voice and choice in book clubs and reading groups.* Portland, ME: Stenhouse.

Deeney, T. A. (2010). One-minute fluency measures: Mixed messages in assessment and instruction. *The Reading Teacher, 63,* 440–450.

Deshler, D. D., Ellis, E. S., & Lenz, B. K. (1979). *Teaching adolescents with learning disabilities: Strategies and methods.* Denver, CO: Love Publishing.

Diliberto, J. A., Beattie, J. R., Flowers, C. P., & Algozzine, R. F. (2009). Effects of teaching syllable skills instruction on reading achievement in struggling middle school readers. *Literacy Research and Instruction, 48,* 14–27.

Duffy, G. G. (2009). *Explaining reading: A resource for teaching concepts, skills, and strategies* (2nd ed.). New York: Guilford Press.

Duke, N. K. (2000). 3.6 minutes per day: The scarcity of informational texts in first grade. *Reading Research Quarterly, 35,* 202–224.

Duke, N. K., & Pearson, P. D. (2002). Comprehension instruction in the primary grades. In C.C. Block & M. Pressley (Eds.), *Comprehension instruction: Research-based best practices* (pp. 247–258). New York: Guilford Press.

Eeds, M., & Wells, D. (1989). Great conversations: An exploration of meaning construction in literature study groups. *Research in the Teaching of English, 23*(1), 4–29.

Eldredge, J. L. (2005). *Teaching decoding: Why and how.* Upper Saddle River, NJ: Pearson.

Eldredge, J. L., Reutzel, D. R., & Hollingsworth, P. M. (1996). Comparing the effectiveness of two oral reading practices: Round-robin reading and the shared book experience. *Journal of Reading Behavior, 28,* 201–225.

Florida Center for Reading Research. (2007). *Guidelines for reviewing a reading program.* Tallahassee, FL: Author. Available at *www.fcrr.org.*

Fuchs, D., Fuchs, L. S., Mathes, P. G., & Simmons, D. C. (1997). Peer-assisted learning strategies: Making classrooms more responsive to diversity. *American Educational Research Journal, 34,* 174–206.

Fuchs, L. S., Fuchs, D., Hosp, M. K., & Jenkins, J. R. (2001). Oral reading fluency as an indicator of reading competence: A theoretical, empirical, and historical analysis. *Scientific Studies of Reading, 5,* 239–256.

Guthrie, J. T., & McCann, A. D. (1996). Idea circles: Peer collaborations for conceptual learning. In L. B. Gambrell & J. F. Almasi (Eds.), *Lively discussions! Fostering engaged reading* (pp. 87–105). Newark, DE: International Reading Association.

Guthrie, J. T., McRae, A., Coddington, C., Klauda, S., Wigfield, A., & Barbosa, P. (2009). Impacts of comprehensive reading instruction on diverse outcomes of low- and high-achieving readers. *Journal of Learning Disabilities, 42,* 195–214.

Hare, V. C., & Borchardt, K. M. (1984). Direct instruction of summarization skills. *Reading Research Quarterly, 20,* 62–78.

Hart, B., & Risley, T. R. (1995). *Meaningful differences in the everyday experience of young American children.* Baltimore, MD: Brookes.

Henk, W. A., & Melnick, S. A. (1995). The Reader Self-Perception Scale (RSPS): A new tool for measuring how children feel about themselves as readers. *The Reading Teacher, 48,* 470–482.

Hosp, M. K., Hosp, J. L., & Howell, K. W. (2006). *The ABCs of CBM: A practical guide to curriculum-based measurement.* New York: Guilford Press.

Jacobs, V. A., Baldwin, L. E., & Chall, J. S. (1990). *The reading crisis: Why poor children fall behind.* Cambridge, MA: Harvard University Press.

Jeong, J., Gaffney, J., & Choi, J. (2010). Availability and use of informational texts in second-, third-, and fourth-grade classrooms. *Research in the Teaching of English, 44,* 435–456.

Johnson, A. W., & Johnson, R. T. (1998). *Learning together and alone: Cognitive, competitive, and individualistic learning* (5th ed.). Boston: Allyn & Bacon.

Kamil, M. L., Borman, G. D., Dole, J., Kral, C. C., Salinger, T., & Torgesen, J. (2008). *Improving adolescent literacy: Effective classroom and intervention practices: A practice guide* (NCEE Report No. 2008-4027). Washington, DC: National Center for Education Evaluation and Regional Assistance, Institute of Education Sciences, U.S. Department of Education.

Kieffer, M., & Lesaux, N. (2007). Breaking down words to build meaning: Morphology, vocabulary, and reading comprehension in the urban classroom. *The Reading Teacher, 61,* 134–144.

Kim, J. (2006). Effects of a voluntary summer reading intervention on reading achievement: Results from a randomized field trial. *Educational Evaluation & Policy Analysis, 28,* 335–355.

Kintsch, W. (1994). The role of knowledge in discourse comprehension: A construction-integration model. In R. Ruddell, M. R. Ruddell, & H. Singer (Eds.), *Theoretical models and processes in reading* (4th ed., pp. 951–995). Newark, DE: International Reading Association.

Kovaleski, J. F., & Black, L. (2010). Multi-tier service delivery: Current status and future directions. In T. A. Glover & S. Vaughn (Eds.), *The promise of response to intervention: Evaluating current science and practice* (pp. 23–56). New York: Guilford Press.

LaBerge, D., & Samuels, S. J. (1974). Toward a theory of automatic information processing in reading. *Cognitive Psychology, 6,* 293–323.

Leal, D. J. (1993). The power of literary peer group discussions: How children collaboratively negotiate meaning. *The Reading Teacher, 47,* 114–120.

Lipka, O., Lesaux, N., & Siegel, L. (2006). Retrospective analyses of the reading development of grade 4 students with reading disabilities: Risk status and profiles over 5 years. *Journal of Learning Disabilities, 39,* 364–378.

Lou, Y., Abrami, P. C., Spence, J. C., Poulsen, C., Chambers, B., & d'Apollonia, S. (1996). Within-class grouping: A meta-analysis. *Review of Educational Research, 66,* 423–458.

Lubliner, S., & Smetana, L. (2005). The effects of comprehensive vocabulary instruction on Title I students' metacognitive word-learning skills and reading comprehension. *Journal of Literacy Research, 37,* 163–200.

Manzo, A. V., & Casale, U. P. (1985). Listen–Read–Discuss: A content reading heuristic. *Journal of Reading, 28,* 732–734.

Martínez, R., Aricak, O., & Jewell, J. (2008). Influence of reading attitude on reading achievement: A test of the temporal-interaction model. *Psychology in the Schools, 45*(10), 1010–1022.

Marzano, R.J. (2004). The developing vision of vocabulary instruction. In J.F. Baumann & E.J. Kame'enui (Eds.), *Vocabulary instruction: Research to practice* (pp. 100–117). New York: Guilford Press.

McCardle, P., Chhabra, V., & Kapinus, B. (2008). *Reading research in action: A teacher's guide for student success.* Baltimore, MD: Brookes.

McKenna, M. C., Franks, S., Conradi, K., & Lovette, G. (2011). Using reading guides with struggling readers in grades 3 and above. In R. L. McCormick & J. R. Paratore (Eds.), *After early intervention, then what?: Teaching struggling readers in grades 3 and beyond* (2nd ed.). Newark, DE: International Reading Association.

McKenna, M. C., & Kear, D. J. (1990). Measuring attitude towards reading: A new tool for teachers. *The Reading Teacher, 43,* 626–639.

McKenna, M. C., Kear, D. J., & Ellsworth, R. A. (1995). Children's attitudes toward reading: A national survey. *Reading Research Quarterly, 30,* 934–956.

McKenna, M. C., & Picard, M. (2006/2007). Does miscue analysis have a role in effective practice? *The Reading Teacher, 60,* 378–380.

McKenna, M. C., & Robinson, R. D. (1990). Content literacy: A definition and implications. *Journal of Reading, 34,* 184–186.

McKenna, M. C., & Robinson, R. D. (2011). *Teaching through text: Reading and writing in the content areas* (2nd ed.). New York: Guilford Press.

McKenna, M. C., & Stahl, K. A. D. (2009). *Assessment for reading instruction* (2nd ed.). New York: Guilford Press.

McKeown, M., Beck, I., & Blake, R. (2009). Rethinking reading comprehension instruction: A comparison of instruction for strategies and content approaches. *Reading Research Quarterly, 44,* 218–253.

McMaster, K., Fuchs, D., & Fuchs, L. (2006). Research on peer-assisted learning strategies: The promise and limitations of peer-mediated instruction. *Reading and Writing Quarterly, 22,* 5–25.

Miller, S. D. (2003). How high- and low-challenge tasks affect motivation and learning: Implications for struggling learners. *Reading and Writing Quarterly, 19,* 39–57.

Moody, S. W., Vaughn, S., & Schumm, J. S. (1997). Instructional grouping for reading: Teachers' views. *Remedial and Special Education, 18,* 347–355.

National Institute of Child Health and Human Development. (2000). *Report of the National Reading Panel. Teaching children to read: An evidence-based assessment of the scientific research literature on reading and its implications for reading instruction* (NIH Publication No. 00-4769). Washington, DC: U.S. Government Printing Office.

Palinscar, A.S., & Brown, A. L. (1984). Reciprocal teaching of comprehension-fostering and monitoring activities. *Cognition and Instruction, 1,* 117–175.

Perie, M., Baker, D. P., & Bobbitt, S. (2007). *Time spent teaching core academic subjects in elementary schools: Comparisons across community, school, teacher, and school characteristics.* Washington, DC: National Center for Education Statistics, USDOE.

RAND Reading Study Group. (2002). *Reading for understanding: Toward an R&D program in reading comprehension.* Santa Monica, CA: RAND. Available at *www.rand.org/pubs/monograph_reports/MR1465.*

Raphael, T. E. (1984). Teaching learners about sources of information for answering comprehension questions. *Journal of Reading, 27,* 303–311.

Raphael, T. E., Highfield, K., & Au, K. H. (2006). *QAR now: Question answer relationships: A powerful and practical framework that develops comprehension and higher-level thinking in all students.* New York: Scholastic.

Rasinski, T. V. (2003). *The fluent reader: Oral reading strategies for building word recognition, fluency, and comprehension.* New York: Scholastic Professional Books.

Rasinski, T., Rikli, A., & Johnston, S. (2009). Reading fluency: More than automaticity? More than a concern for the primary grades? *Literacy Research and Instruction, 48,* 350–361.

Roberts, G., Torgesen, J. K., Boardman, A., & Scammacca, N. (2008). Evidence-based strategies for reading instruction of older students with reading disabilities. *Learning Disabilities Research and Practice, 23,* 63–69.

Sanacore, J., & Palumbo, A. (2009). Understanding the fourth-grade slump: Our point of view. *The Educational Forum, 73*(1), 67–74.

Scammacca, N., Roberts, G., Vaughn, S., Edmonds, M., Wexler, J., Reutebuch, C. K., et al. (2007). *Interventions for adolescent struggling readers: A meta-analysis with implications for practice.* Portsmouth, NH: RMC Research Corporation, Center on Instruction.

Schlick Noe, K. L., & Johnson, N. J. (1999). *Getting started with literature circles.* Norwood, MA: Christopher-Gordon.

Schumm, J. S., Moody, S. W., & Vaughn, S. (2000). Grouping for reading instruction: Does one size fit all? *Journal of Learning Disabilities, 33,* 477–488.

Schwartz, R. M., & Raphael, T. E. (1985). Concept of definition: A key to improving students' vocabulary. *The Reading Teacher, 39,* 198–205.

Simmons, D. C., Fuchs, D., Fuchs, L. S., Hodge, J. P., & Mathes, P. G. (1994). Importance of instructional complexity and role reciprocity to classwide peer tutoring. *Learning Disabilities Research and Practice, 9,* 203–212.

Slavin, R. E. (1987). Ability grouping and student achievement in elementary schools: A best-evidence synthesis. *Review of Educational Research, 57,* 293–336.

Sonnenschein, S., Stapleton, L., & Benson, A. (2010). The relation between the type and amount of instruction and growth in children's reading competencies. *American Educational Research Journal, 47,* 358–389.

Stahl, K. A. D. (2008). The effects of three instructional methods on the reading comprehension and content acquisition of novice readers. *Journal of Literacy Research, 40,* 359–393.

Stahl, S. A., & Nagy, W. E. (2005). *Teaching word meanings.* Mahwah, NJ: Erlbaum.

Stanovich, K. E. (1986). Matthew effects in reading: Some consequences of individual differences in the acquisition of literacy. *Reading Research Quarterly, 21,* 360–407.

Stauffer, R. G. (1969). *Teaching reading as a thinking process.* New York: Harper & Row.

Swan, E. A. (2002). *Concept-Oriented Reading Instruction: Engaging classrooms, lifelong learners.* New York: Guilford Press.

Swanborn, M. S. L., & de Glopper, K. (1999). Incidental word learning while reading: A meta-analysis. *Review of Educational Research, 69,* 261–285.

Taylor, S. E. (1989). *EDL core vocabularies in reading, mathematics, science, and social studies.* Orlando, FL: Steck-Vaughn.

Tierney, R. J., & Readence, J. E. (2004). *Reading strategies and practices: A compendium* (6th ed.). Boston: Allyn & Bacon.

Torgesen, J. K., & Miller, D. H. (2009). *Assessments to guide adolescent literacy instruction.* Portsmouth, NH: RMC Research Corporation, Center on Instruction.

Vadasy, P., & Sanders, E. (2008). Benefits of repeated reading intervention for low-achieving fourth- and fifth-grade students. *Remedial and Special Education, 29,* 235–249.

Valencia, S., & Buly, M. (2004). Behind test scores: What struggling readers really need. *The Reading Teacher, 57,* 520–531.

Walpole, S., & McKenna, M. C. (2006). The role of informal reading inventories in assessing word recognition. *The Reading Teacher, 59,* 592–594.

Walpole, S., & McKenna, M. C. (2007). *Differentiated reading instruction: Strategies for the primary grades.* New York: Guilford Press.

Walpole, S., & McKenna, M. C. (2009). *How to plan differentiated reading instruction: Resources for grades K–3.* New York: Guilford Press.

Wanzek, J., Vaughn, S., Wexler, J., Swanson, E. A., Edmonds, & Kim, A. H. (2006). A synthesis of spelling and reading interventions and their effects on the spelling outcomes of students with LD. *Journal of Learning Disabilities, 39,* 528–543.

Wigfield, A., Guthrie, J., Perencevich, K., Taboada, A., Klauda, S., McRae, A., et al. (2008). Role of reading engagement in mediating effects of reading comprehension instruction on reading outcomes. *Psychology in the Schools, 45,* 432–445.

Wilfong, L. G. (2009). Textmasters: Bringing literature circles to textbook reading across the curriculum. *Journal of Adolescent and Adult Literacy, 53,* 164–171.

Zutell, J., & Rasinski, T. V. (1991). Training teachers to attend to their students' oral reading fluency. *Theory into Practice, 30,* 211–217.

Index

f following a page number indicates a figure. Numbers in bold represent entries in the glossary.